Modern Computer Architecture

Modern Computer Architecture

Stephanie Collins

MURPHY & MOORE
www.murphy-moorepublishing.com

Murphy & Moore Publishing,
1 Rockefeller Plaza,
New York City, NY 10020, USA

ISBN: 978-1-63987-367-8

Cataloging-in-Publication Data

Modern computer architecture / Stephanie Collins.
    p. cm.
Includes bibliographical references and index.
ISBN 978-1-63987-367-8
1. Computer architecture. 2. Computer engineering. 3. Computer network architectures.
4. Computer organization. I. Collins, Stephanie.
QA76.9.A73 M63 2022
004.22--dc23

For information on all Murphy & Moore Publications
visit our website at www.murphy-moorepublishing.com

MURPHY & MOORE

Contents

Preface

The set of rules and methods which govern the organization, functionality and implementation of computer systems is termed as computer architecture. It focuses on the ways in which various hardware components are connected together to form a computer system. Computer architecture deals with the high-level design issues and acts as an interface between the hardware and the software. The various sub-fields of this discipline are microarchitecture, instruction set architecture and systems design. The instruction set architecture is responsible for defining items in a computer which are accessed by a program such as registers, data types and addressing modes. The major design goals of computer architecture are to achieve maximum performance and power efficiency. This book presents the complex subject of computer architecture in the most comprehensible and easy to understand language. The various sub-fields of computer architecture along with technological progress that have future implications are glanced at herein. This book will serve as a valuable source of reference for those interested in this field.

To facilitate a deeper understanding of the contents of this book a short introduction of every chapter is written below:

Chapter 1- Computer architecture is the collection of the rules and methods that are necessary for the functionality, organization and implementation of computer systems. Instruction set architecture is concerned with the basic operations a computer must support. This is an introductory chapter which will introduce briefly all the significant aspects of computer architecture.

Chapter 2- The process of cumulating instructions from the processor through a pipeline is known as pipelining or pipeline processing. There are various hazards associated with pipelining of computers like data hazards, structural hazards and control hazards. The aim of this chapter is to explore the various processes and hazards associated with the pipelining of computers.

Chapter 3- All the different types of data storage technologies used by a computer, fall under computer memory including RAM, ROM and Flash memory. Memory hierarchy separates the computer storage on the basis of speed as well as use. This chapter discusses in detail the theories and methodologies related to computer memory.

Chapter 4- Central Processing Unit is the main electronic circuitry within the computer that executes instructions that make up a computer program. The arithmetic and bitwise operations on integer binary numbers are performed by Arithmetic Logic Unit. All the diverse principles related to the central processing unit are carefully analyzed in this chapter.

Chapter 5- Synchronization refers to the orderly sharing of system resources by processes. Synchronization involves two concepts: synchronization of processes and synchronization of data. Barrier is a type of synchronization. In a group of threads; a thread must stop at this point and is unable to proceed until all threads reach this barrier. Synchronization is a vast subject that branches out into significant processes which have been thoroughly discussed in this chapter.

Chapter 6- The process of breaking down larger problems into smaller parts that can be executed simultaneously by multiple processors and the results of which are combined upon completion is known as parallel computing. There are four types of parallelism; Bit-level parallelism, Instruction-level parallelism, Task parallelism and Superword level parallelism. This chapter has been carefully written to provide an easy understanding of the varied facets of parallel computing.

I owe the completion of this book to the never-ending support of my family, who supported me throughout the project.

Stephanie Collins

An Introduction to Computer Architecture

Computer architecture is the collection of the rules and methods that are necessary for the functionality, organization and implementation of computer systems. Instruction set architecture is concerned with the basic operations a computer must support. This is an introductory chapter which will introduce briefly all the significant aspects of computer architecture.

Computer architecture is a specification describing how hardware and software technologies interact to create a computer platform or system. When we think of the word architecture, we think of building a house or a building. Keeping that same principle in mind, computer architecture involves building a computer and all that goes into a computer system.

Types of Computer Architecture

Von-neumann Architecture

This architecture is proposed by john von-neumann. Now a day's computer we are using are based on von-neumann architecture. It is based on some concepts. The memory we have a single read/write memory available for read and write instructions and data. When we talk about memory, it is nothing but the single location which is used for reading and writing instructions for the data and instructions are also present in it. Data and instructions are stored in a single read/write memory within the computer system.

Each memory has multiple locations and each location has a unique address. We can address the contents of memory by its location irrespective of what type of data and instructions are present in the memory, because of which we can read or write any data and instructions. Execution always occurs in a sequential manner unless the change is required. For example, suppose we are executing an instruction from line 1 to line 10 but now we required to execute line 50 instead of line 11 then we jump to instruction 50 and execute it.

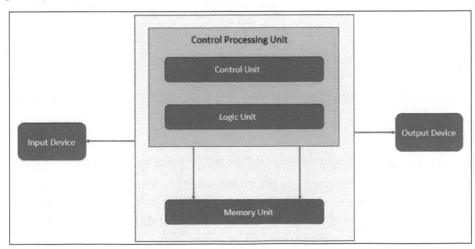

There is a bus (address bus/data bus/control bus) used for the instruction and data code execution. Input device takes data or instruction and the Central processing unit (CPU) performs one operation at a time, either fetching data or instruction in/out of the memory. Once the operation is done it is sent to the output device. Control and logic units for processing operations are within the central processing unit.

Harvard Architecture

Harvard architecture is used when data and code is present in different memory blocks. A separate memory block is needed for data and instruction. Data can be accessed by one memory location and instruction can be accessed by a different location. It has data storage entirely contained within the central processing unit (CPU). A single set of clock cycles is required. The pipeline is possible. It is complex to design. CPU can read and write instructions and process data access. Harvard architecture has different access codes and data address spaces that is, the instruction address zero is not the same as data address zero. Instruction address zero identifies 24-byte value and data address zero identifies 8-byte value which is not the part of the 24-byte value.

Modified harvard architecture is like a harvard architecture machine and it has a common address space for the separate data and instruction cache. It has digital signal processors that will execute small or highly audio or video algorithms and it is reproducible. Microcontrollers have a small number of programs and data memory and it speeds up the processing by executing parallel instructions and data access.

We can observe in the below image, there are separate data and instruction memory that is a bus available to perform operations. It is contained entirely within the Central processing unit. It can perform Input/output operation simultaneously and it has a separate arithmetic and logic unit.

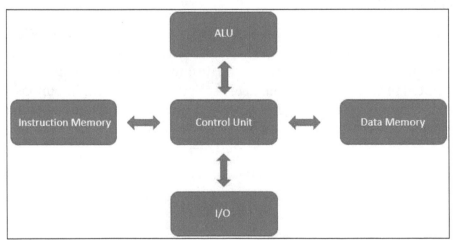

Microarchitecture

Microarchitecture is known as computer organizations and it is the way when instruction set architecture is a built-in processor. Instruction set architecture is implemented with various microarchitecture and it varies because of changing technology. Microarchitecture performs in a certain way. It reads the instruction and decodes it, will find parallel data to process the instruction and then will process the instruction and output will be generated.

It is used in microprocessors, microcontrollers. Some architectures overlap multiple instructions while executing but this does not happen in microarchitecture. Execution units like arithmetic logic units, floating-point units, load units, etc are needed and it performs the operation of the processor. There are microarchitecture decisions within the system such as size, latency, and connectivity of the memories.

System Design

The name defines itself, the design will satisfy user requirements such as architecture, module, interfaces and data for a system and it is connected to product development. It is the process of taking marketing information and creating product design to be manufacture. Modular systems are made by standardizing hardware and software.

Instruction Set Architecture

An instruction set architecture (ISA) defines a set of native instructions to be executed directly by hardware. It specifies native data types, instructions, registers, addressing modes, memory architecture, interrupts, and external I/O. An ISA may be implemented in different microarchitectures, e.g., Intel Pentium and AMD Athlon implement the x86 instruction set, but their microarchitectures may be essentially different. A native instruction is executed directly by a CPU and is composed of an operator (opcode) and operands. A collection of instructions is called machine code to fulfill some function. Based on the design strategy, basically there are two models: complex instruction set computer (CISC) and reduced instruction set computer (RISC). In CISC, the length of the instruction is variable and thus the instruction encoding is quite complex, whereas in RISC, the length of the instruction is fixed, and therefore, the instruction encoding is simple. Generally, there are more instructions in CISC than in RISC. Companies making CISC processors include Intel and AMD, whereas those making RISC processors contain IBM, Apple, and Sun microsystems.

Designing the Instruction Set Architecture

The different features that need to be considered when designing the instruction set architecture. They are:

- Types of instructions (Operations in the instruction set).
- Types and sizes of operands.
- Addressing modes.
- Addressing memory.
- Encoding and instruction formats.
- Compiler related issues.

First of all, you have to decide on the types of instructions, i.e. what are the various instructions that you want to support in the ISA. The tasks carried out by a computer program consist of a sequence of small steps, such as multiplying two numbers, moving a data from a register to a memory location, testing for a particular condition like zero, reading a character from the input device or sending a character to be displayed to the output device, etc. A computer must have the following types of instructions:

- Data transfer instructions.

- Data manipulation instructions.

- Program sequencing and control instructions.

- Input and output instructions.

Data transfer instructions perform data transfer between the various storage places in the computer system, viz. registers, memory and I/O. Since, both the instructions as well as data are stored in memory, the processor needs to read the instructions and data from memory. After processing, the results must be stored in memory. Therefore, two basic operations involving the memory are needed, namely, Load (or Read or Fetch) and Store (or Write). The Load operation transfers a copy of the data from the memory to the processor and the Store operation moves the data from the processor to memory. Other data transfer instructions are needed to transfer data from one register to another or from/to I/O devices and the processor. Data manipulation instructions perform operations on data and indicate the computational capabilities for the processor. These operations can be arithmetic operations, logical operations or shift operations. Arithmetic operations include addition (with and without carry), subtraction (with and without borrow), multiplication, division, increment, decrement and finding the complement of a number. The logical and bit manipulation instructions include AND, OR, XOR, Clear carry, set carry, etc. Similarly, you can perform different types of shift and rotate operations.

We generally assume a sequential flow of instructions. That is, instructions that are stored in consequent locations are executed one after the other. However, you have program sequencing and control instructions that help you change the flow of the program. This is best explained with an example. Consider the task of adding a list of n numbers. A possible sequence is given below:

```
Move DATA1, R0
 Add DATA2, R0
 Add DATA3, R0
 Add DATAn, R0
 Move R0, SUM
```

The addresses of the memory locations containing the n numbers are symbolically given as DATA1, DATA2, . . , DATAn, and a separate Add instruction is used to add each Databer to the contents of register R0. After all the numbers have been added, the result is placed in memory location SUM. Instead of using a long list of Add instructions, it is possible to place a single Add instruction in a program loop, as shown below:

```
Move N, R1
 Clear R0
```

```
LOOP        Determine address of "Next" number

            and add "Next" number to R0

  Decrement R1

Branch > 0, LOOP

Move R0, SUM
```

The loop is a straight-line sequence of instructions executed as many times as needed. It starts at location LOOP and ends at the instruction Branch>0. During each pass through this loop, the address of the next list entry is determined, and that entry is fetched and added to R0. For now, you need to know how to create and control a program loop. Assume that the number of entries in the list, n, is stored in memory location N. Register R1 is used as a counter to determine the number of times the loop is executed. Hence, the contents of location N are loaded into register R1 at the beginning of the program. Then, within the body of the loop, the instruction, Decrement R1 reduces the contents of R1 by 1 each time through the loop. The execution of the loop is repeated as long as the result of the decrement operation is greater than zero.

You should now be able to understand branch instructions. This type of instruction loads a new value into the program counter. As a result, the processor fetches and executes the instruction at this new address, called the branch target, instead of the instruction at the location that follows the branch instruction in sequential address order. The branch instruction can be conditional or unconditional. An unconditional branch instruction does a branch to the specified address irrespective of any condition. A conditional branch instruction causes a branch only if a specified condition is satisfied. If the condition is not satisfied, the PC is incremented in the normal way, and the next instruction in sequential address order is fetched and executed. In the example above, the instruction Branch>0 LOOP (branch if greater than 0) is a conditional branch instruction that causes a branch to location LOOP if the result of the immediately preceding instruction, which is the decremented value in register R1, is greater than zero. This means that the loop is repeated as long as there are entries in the list that are yet to be added to R0.

At the end of the nth pass through the loop, the Decrement instruction produces a value of zero, and, hence, branching does not occur. Instead, the Move instruction is fetched and executed. It moves the final result from R0 into memory location SUM. Some ISAs refer to such instructions as Jumps. The processor keeps track of information about the results of various operations for use by subsequent conditional branch instructions. This is accomplished by recording the required information in individual bits, often called condition code flags. These flags are usually grouped together in a special processor register called the condition code register or status register. Individual condition code flags are set to 1 or cleared to 0, depending on the outcome of the operation performed. Some of the commonly used flags are: Sign, Zero, Overflow and Carry.

The call and return instructions are used in conjunction with subroutines. A subroutine is a self-contained sequence of instructions that performs a given computational task. During the execution of a program, a subroutine may be called to perform its function many times at various points in the main program. Each time a subroutine is called, a branch is executed to the beginning of the subroutine to start executing its set of instructions. After the subroutine has been executed, a branch is made back to the main program, through the return instruction. Interrupts can also change the flow of a program. A program interrupt refers to the transfer of program control from a currently running program to another service program as a result of an external or internally generated request. Control returns to the original program after the service program is executed.

The interrupt procedure is, in principle, quite similar to a subroutine call except for three variations: (1) The interrupt is usually initiated by an internal or external signal apart from the execution of an instruction (2) the address of the interrupt service program is determined by the hardware or from some information from the interrupt signal or the instruction causing the interrupt; and (3) an interrupt procedure usually stores all the information necessary to define the state of the CPU rather than storing only the program counter. Therefore, when the processor is interrupted, it saves the current status of the processor, including the return address, the register contents and the status information called the Processor Status Word (PSW), and then jumps to the interrupt handler or the interrupt service routine. Upon completing this, it returns to the main program.

Input and Output instructions are used for transferring information between the registers, memory and the input / output devices. It is possible to use special instructions that exclusively perform I/O transfers, or use memory – related instructions itself to do I/O transfers.

Suppose you are designing an embedded processor which is meant to be performing a particular application, then definitely you will have to bring instructions which are specific to that particular application. When you're designing a general-purpose processor, you only look at including all general types of instructions. Examples of specialized instructions may be media and signal processing related instructions, say vector type of instructions which try to exploit the data level parallelism, where the same operation of addition or subtraction is going to be done on different data and then you 6 may have to look at saturating arithmetic operations, multiply and accumulator instructions.

The data types and sizes indicate the various data types supported by the processor and their lengths. Common operand types - Character (8 bits), Half word (16 bits), Word (32 bits), Single Precision Floating Point (1 Word), Double Precision Floating Point (2 Words), Integers - two's complement binary numbers, Characters usually in ASCII, Floating point numbers following the IEEE Standard 754 and Packed and unpacked decimal numbers.

Addressing Modes

The operation field of an instruction specifies the operation to be performed. This operation must be executed on some data that is given straight away or stored in computer registers or memory words. The way the operands are chosen during program execution is dependent on the addressing mode of the instruction. The addressing mode specifies a rule for interpreting or modifying the address field of the instruction before the operand is actually referenced. Computers use addressing mode techniques for the purpose of accommodating one or both of the following:

- To give programming versatility to the user by providing such facilities as pointers to memory, counters for loop control, indexing of data, and program relocation.

- To reduce the number of bits in the addressing field of the instruction.

When you write programs in a high-level language, you use constants, local and global variables, pointers, and arrays. When translating a high-level language program into assembly language, the compiler must be able to implement these constructs using the facilities provided in the instruction set of the computer in which the program will be run. The different ways in which the location of an operand is specified in an instruction are referred to as addressing modes. Variables and constants are the simplest data types and are found in almost every computer program. In assembly language, a variable is represented by allocating a register or a memory location to hold its value.

- Register mode: The operand is the contents of a processor register; the name (address) of the register is given in the instruction.

- Absolute mode: The operand is in a memory location; the address of this location is given explicitly in the instruction. This is also called Direct. Address and data constants can be represented in assembly language using the immediate mode.

- Immediate mode: The operand is given explicitly in the instruction. For example, the instruction Move 200immediate, R0 places the value 200 in register R0. Clearly, the immediate mode is only used to specify the value of a source operand. A common convention is to use the sharp sign (#) in front of the value to indicate that this value is to be used as an immediate operand. Hence, we write the instruction above in the form Move #200, R0. Constant values are used frequently in high-level language programs. For example, the statement A = B + 6 contains the constant 6. Assuming that A and B have been declared earlier as variables and may be accessed using the Absolute mode, this statement may be compiled as follows:

```
Move B, R1

Add #6, R1

Move R1, A
```

Constants are also used in assembly language to increment a counter, test for some bit pattern, and so on.

Indirect Mode

In the addressing modes that follow, the instruction does not give the operand or its address explicitly. Instead, it provides information from which the memory address of the operand can be determined. We refer to this address as the effective address (EA) of the operand. In this mode, the effective address of the operand is the contents of a register or memory location whose address appears in the instruction. We denote indirection by placing the name of the register or the memory address given in the instruction in parentheses. For example, consider the instruction, Add (R1), R0.

To execute the Add instruction, the processor uses the value in register R1 as the effective address of the operand. It requests a read operation from the memory to read the contents of this location. The value read is the desired operand, which the processor adds to the contents of register R0. Indirect addressing through a memory location is also possible as indicated in the instruction Add (A), R0. In this case, the processor first reads the contents of memory location A, then requests a second read operation using this value as an address to obtain the operand. The register or memory location that contains the address of an operand is called a pointer. Indirection and the use of pointers are important and powerful concepts in programming. Changing the contents of location A in the example fetches different operands to add to register Ro.

Index Mode

The next addressing mode you learn provides a different kind of flexibility for accessing operands. It is useful in dealing with lists and arrays. In this mode, the effective address of the operand is generated by adding a constant value (displacement) to the contents of a register. The register used may be either a special register provided for this purpose, or may be any one of the general-purpose registers in the processor. In either case, it is referred to as an index register. We indicate the Index mode symbolically as $X(Ri)$, where X denotes the constant value contained in the instruction and Ri is the name of the register involved. The effective address of the operand is given by $EA = X + [Ri]$.

The contents of the index register are not changed in the process of generating the effective address. In an assembly language program, the constant X may be given either as an explicit number or as a symbolic name representing a numerical value. When the instruction is translated into machine code, the constant X is given as a part of the instruction and is usually represented by fewer bits than the word length of the computer. Since X is a signed integer, it must be sign-extended to the register length before being added to the contents of the register.

Relative Mode

The Index mode using general-purpose processor registers. A useful version of this mode is obtained if the program counter, PC, is used instead of a general purpose register. Then, $X(PC)$ can be used to address a memory location that is X bytes away from the location presently pointed to by the program counter. Since the addressed location is identified "relative" to the program counter, which always identifies the current execution point in a program, the name Relative mode is associated with this type of addressing. In this case, the effective address is determined by the Index mode using the program counter in place of the general-purpose register Ri. This addressing mode is generally used with control flow instructions.

Though this mode can be used to access data operands. But, its most common use is to specify the target address in branch instructions. An instruction such as Branch > 0 LOOP, which we discussed earlier, causes program execution to go to the branch target location identified by the name LOOP if the branch condition is satisfied. This location can be computed by specifying it as an offset from the current value of the program counter. Since the branch target may be either before or after the branch instruction, the offset is given as a signed number. Recall that during the execution of an instruction, the processor increments the PC to point to the next instruction. Most computers use this updated value in computing the effective address in the Relative mode. The two modes described next are useful for accessing data items in successive locations in the memory.

Auto-increment Mode

The effective address of the operand is the contents of a register specified in the instruction. After accessing the operand, the contents of this register are automatically incremented to point to the next item in a list. We denote the Auto-increment mode by putting the specified register in parentheses, to show that the contents of the register are used as the effective address, followed by a plus sign to indicate that these contents are to be incremented after the operand is accessed. Thus, the Auto-increment mode is written as (Ri)⁺.

Auto-decrement Mode

As a companion for the Auto-increment mode, another useful mode accesses the items of a list in the reverse order. In the auto-decrement mode, the contents of a register specified in the instruction are first automatically decremented and are then used as the effective address of the operand. We denote the Auto-decrement mode by putting the specified register in parentheses, preceded by a minus sign to indicate that the contents of the register are to be decremented before being used as the effective address. Thus, we write - (Ri). In this mode, operands are accessed in descending address order. You may wonder why the address is decremented before it is used in the Auto-decrement mode and incremented after it is used in the Auto-increment mode. The main reason for this is that these two modes can be used together to implement a stack.

Instruction Formats

The processor can execute different types of instructions and there are different ways of specifying the operands. Once all this is decided, this information has to be presented to the processor in the form of an instruction format. The number of bits in the instruction is divided into groups called fields. The most common fields found in instruction formats are:

- An operation code field that specifies the operation to be performed. The number of bits will indicate the number of operations that can be performed.

- An address field that designates a memory address or a processor register. The number of bits depends on the size of memory or the number of registers.

- A mode field that specifies the way the operand or the effective address is determined. This depends on the number of addressing modes supported by the processor.

The number of address fields may be three, two or one depending on the type of ISA used. Also, observe that, based on the number of operands that are supported and the size of the various fields, the length of the instructions will vary. Some processors fit all the instructions into a single sized format, whereas others make use of formats of varying sizes. Accordingly, you have a fixed format or a variable format.

Interpreting memory addresses - You basically have two types of interpretation of the memory addresses – Big endian arrangement and the little endian arrangement. Memories are normally arranged as bytes and a unique address of a memory location is capable of storing 8 bits of information. But when you look at the word length of the processor, the word length of the processor may be more than one byte. Suppose you look at a 32-bit processor, it is made up of four bytes. These four bytes span over four memory locations. When you specify the address of a word how you would specify the address of the word - are you going to specify the address of the most significant byte as the address of the word (big end) or specify the address of the least significant byte (little end) as the address of the word. That distinguishes between a big endian arrangement and a little endian arrangement. IBM, Motorola, HP follow the big endian arrangement and Intel follows the little endian arrangement. Also, when a data spans over different memory locations, and if you try to access a word which is aligned with the word boundary, we say there is an alignment. If you try to access the words not starting at a word boundary, you can still access, but they are not aligned. Whether there is support to access data that is misaligned is a design issue. Even if you're allowed to access data that is misaligned, it normally takes more number of memory cycles to access the data.

Finally, looking at the role of compilers the compiler has a lot of role to play when you're defining the instruction set architecture. Gone are the days where people thought that compilers and architectures are going to be independent of each other. Only when the compiler knows the internal architecture of the processor it'll be able to produce optimised code. So the architecture will have to expose itself to the compiler and the compiler will have to make use of whatever hardware is exposed. The ISA should be compiler friendly. The basic ways in which the ISA can help the compiler are regularity, orthogonality and the ability to weigh different options.

- Class of ISA: Nearly all ISAs today are classified as general-purpose register architectures, where the operands are either registers or memory locations. The 80x86 has 16 general-purpose registers and 16 that can hold floating point data, while MIPS has 32 general-purpose and 32 floating-point registers. The two popular versions of this class are register-memory ISAs such as the 80x86, which can access memory as part of many instructions, and load-store ISAs such as MIPS, which can access memory only with load or store instructions. All recent ISAs are load-store.

- Memory addressing: Virtually all desktop and server computers, including the 80x86 and MIPS, use byte addressing to access memory operands. Some architectures, like MIPS, require that objects must be aligned. An access to an object of size s bytes at byte address A is aligned if A mod s = 0. The 80x86 does not require alignment, but accesses are generally faster if operands are aligned.

- Addressing modes: In addition to specifying registers and constant operands, addressing modes specify the address of a memory object. MIPS addressing modes are Register, Immediate (for constants), and Displacement, where a constant offset is added to a register to form the memory address. The 80x86 supports those three plus three variations of displacement: no register (absolute), two registers (based indexed with displacement), two registers where one register is multiplied by the size of the operand in bytes (based with scaled index and displacement). It has more like the last three, minus the displacement field: register indirect, indexed, and based with scaled index.

- Types and sizes of operands: Like most ISAs, MIPS and 80x86 support operand sizes of 8-bit (ASCII character), 16-bit (Unicode character or half word), 32-bit (integer or word), 64-bit (double word or long integer), and IEEE 754 floating point in 32-bit (single precision) and 64-bit (double precision). The 80x86 also supports 80-bit floating point (extended double precision).

- Operations: The general categories of operations are data transfer, arithmetic logical, control, and floating point. MIPS is a simple and easy-to-pipeline instruction set architecture, and it is representative of the RISC architectures being used in 2006. The 80x86 has a much richer and larger set of operations.

- Control flow instructions: Virtually all ISAs, including 80x86 and MIPS, support conditional branches, unconditional jumps, procedure calls, and returns. Both use PC-relative addressing, where the branch address is specified by an address field that is added to the PC. There are some small differences. MIPS conditional branches (BE, BNE, etc.) test the contents of registers, while the 80x86 branches (JE, JNE, etc.) test condition code bits set as side effects of arithmetic/logic operations. MIPS procedure call (JAL) places the return address in a register, while the 80x86 call (CALLF) places the return address on a stack in memory.

- Encoding an ISA: There are two basic choices on encoding: fixed length and variable length. All MIPS instructions are 32 bits long, which simplifies instruction decoding (shown below). The 80x86 encoding is variable length, ranging from 1 to 18 bytes. Variable length instructions can take less space than fixed-length instructions, so a program compiled for the 80x86 is usually smaller than the same program compiled for MIPS. For example, the number of registers and the number of addressing modes both have a significant impact on the size of instructions, as the register field and addressing mode field can appear many times in a single instruction.

I-type instruction

6	5	5	16
Opcode	Rs	Rt	immediate

R-type instruction

6	5	5	5	5	6
Opcode	Rs	Rt	Rd	shamt	funct

J-type instruction

6	
Opcode	Offset

Execution of Complete Instruction

An instruction cycle consists of an instruction fetch, followed by zero or more operand fetches, followed by zero or more operand stores, followed by an interrupt check (if interrupts are enabled) The major computer system components (processor, main memory, I/O modules) need to be interconnected in order to exchange data and control signals. The most popular means on interconnection is the use of a shared system bus consisting on multiple lines.

Instruction Cycle

The basic function performed by a computer is execution of a program, which consists of a set of instructions stored in memory. The processor does the actual work by executing instructions specified in the program. In the simplest form, instruction processing consists of two steps: the processor reads (fetches) instructions from memory one at a time and executes each instruction.

The processing required for a single instruction is called an instruction cycle. An instruction cycle is shown below:

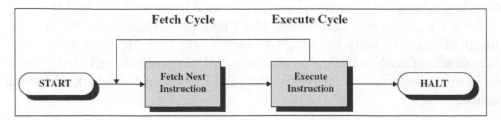

Program execution halts only if the machine is turned off, some sort of unrecoverable error occurs, or a program instruction that halts the computer is encountered. Instruction Fetch and Execute:

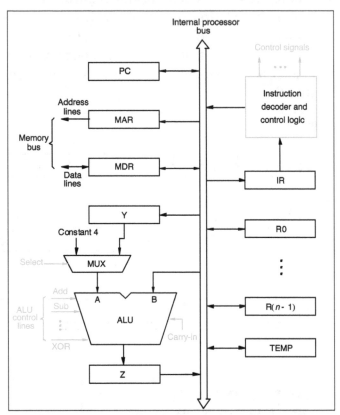

Single-bus organization of the datapath inside a processor.

- The processor fetches an instruction from memory – program counter (PC) register holds the address of the instruction to be fetched next.

- The processor increments the PC after each instruction fetch so that it will fetch the next instruction in the sequence – unless told otherwise.

- The fetched instruction is loaded into the instruction register (IR) in the processor – the instruction contains bits that specify the action the processor will take.

- The processor interprets the instruction and performs the required action In general, these actions fall into four categories:

  ◦ Processor-memory: Data transferred to or from the processor to memory.

- ○ Processor-I/O: Data transferred to or from a peripheral device by transferring between the processor and an I/O module.

- ○ Data processing: The processor performs some arithmetic or logic operation on data.

- ○ Control: An instruction may specify that the sequence of execution be altered an instruction execution may involve a combination of these actions.

Data Implementation

The data path comprises of the elements that process data and addresses in the CPU - Registers, ALUs, mux's, memories, etc. We will build a MIPS data path incrementally. We shall construct the basic model and keep refining it. The portion of the CPU that carries out the instruction fetch operation is given in Figure below.

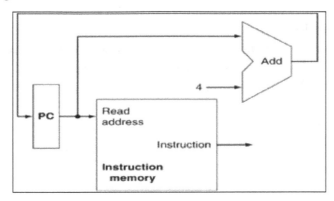

The PC is used to address the instruction memory to fetch the instruction. At the same time, the PC value is also fed to the adder unit and added with 4, so that PC+4, which is the address of the next instruction in MIPS is written into the PC, thus making it ready for the next instruction fetch.

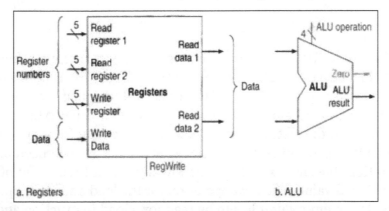

The next step is instruction decoding and operand fetch. In the case of MIPS, decoding is done and at the same time, the register file is read. The processor's 32 general purpose registers are stored in a structure called a register file. A register file is a collection of registers in which any register can be read or written by specifying the number of the register in the file.

The R-format instructions have three register operands and we will need to read two data words from the register file and write one data word into the register file for each instruction. For each data word to be read from the registers, we need an input to the register file that specifies the register number to be read and an output from the register file that will carry the value that has been read from the registers. To write a data word, we will need two inputs- one to specify the register number to be written and one to supply the data to be written into the register. The 5-bit register specifiers indicate one of the 32 registers to be used. The register file always outputs the contents of whatever register numbers are on the Read register inputs. Writes, however, are controlled by the write control signal, which must be asserted for a write to occur at the clock edge. Thus, we need a total of four inputs (three for register numbers and one for data) and two outputs (both for data), as shown in Figure above. The register number inputs are 5 bits wide to specify one of 32 registers, whereas the data input and two data output buses are each 32 bits wide.

After the two register contents are read, the next step is to pass on these two data to the ALU and perform the required operation, as decided by the control unit and the control signals. It might be and add, subtract or any other type of operation, depending on the opcode. Thus the ALU takes two 32-bit inputs and produces a 32-bit result, as well as a 1-bit signal if the result is 0. The same arithmetic or logical operation with an immediate operand and a register operand, uses the I-type of instruction format. Here, Rs forms one of the source operands and the immediate component forms the second operand. These two will have to be fed to the ALU. Before that, the 16-bit immediate operand is sign extended to form a 32-bit operand. This sign extension is done by the sign extension unit.

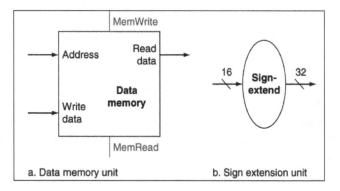

a. Data memory unit   b. Sign extension unit

We shall next consider the MIPS load word and store word instructions, which have the general form lw $t1,offset_value($t2) or sw $t1,offset_value ($t2). These instructions compute a memory address by adding the base register, which is $t2, to the 16-bit signed offset field contained in the instruction. If the instruction is a store, the value to be stored must also be read from the register file where it resides in $t1. If the instruction is a load, the value read from memory must be written into the register file in the specified register, which is $t1. Thus, we will need both the register file and the ALU. In addition, the sign extension unit will sign extend the 16-bit offset field in the instruction to a 32-bit signed value. The next operation for the load and store operations is the data memory access. The data memory unit has to be read for a load instruction and the data memory must be written for store instructions; hence, it has both read and write control signals, an address input, as well as an input for the data to be written into memory.

The branch on equal instruction has three operands, two registers that are compared for equality, and a 16-bit offset used to compute the branch target address, relative to the branch instruction address. Its form is beq $t1, $t2, offset. To implement this instruction, we must compute the branch target address by adding the sign-extended offset field of the instruction to the PC. The instruction set architecture specifies that the base for the branch address calculation is the address of the instruction following the branch. Since we have already computed PC + 4, the address of the next instruction, in the instruction fetch data path, it is easy to use this value as the base for computing the branch target address. Also, since the word boundaries have the 2 LSBs as zeros and branch target addresses must start at word boundaries, the offset field is shifted left 2 bits. In addition to computing the branch target address, we must also determine whether the next instruction is the instruction that follows sequentially or the instruction at the branch target address. This depends on the condition being evaluated. When the condition is true (i.e., the operands are equal), the branch target address becomes the new PC, and we say that the branch is taken. If the operands are not equal, the incremented PC should replace the current PC (just as for any other normal instruction); in this case, we say that the branch is not taken.

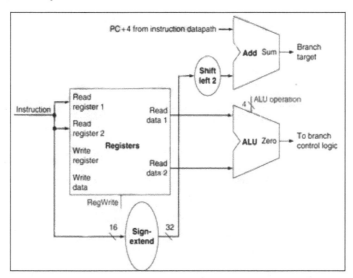

Thus, the branch data path must do two operations: compute the branch target address and compare the register contents. This is illustrated in Figure above. To compute the branch target address, the branch data path includes a sign extension unit and an adder. To perform the compare, we need to use the register file to supply the two register operands. Since the ALU provides an output signal that indicates whether the result was 0, we can send the two register operands to the ALU with the control set to do a subtract. If the Zero signals out of the ALU unit is asserted, we know that the two values are equal. Although the Zero output always signals if the result is 0, we will be using it only to implement the equal test of branches. Later, we will show exactly how to connect the control signals of the ALU for use in the data path.

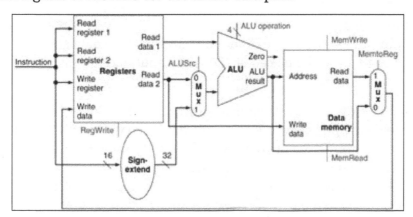

Now, that we have examined the data path components needed for the individual instruction classes, we can combine them into a single data path and add the control to complete the implementation. The combined data path is shown figure.

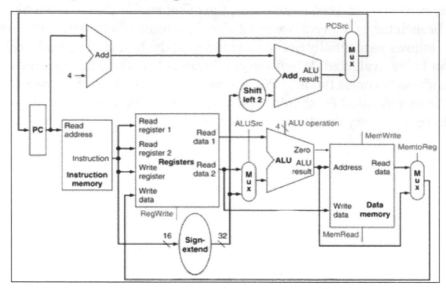

The simplest data path might attempt to execute all instructions in one clock cycle. This means that no data path resource can be used more than once per instruction, so any element needed more than once must be duplicated. We therefore need a memory for instructions separate from one for data. Although some of the functional units will need to be duplicated, many of the elements can be shared by different instruction flows. To share a data path element between two different instruction classes, we may need to allow multiple connections to the input of an element, using a multiplexor and control signal to select among the multiple inputs. While adding multiplexors, we should note that though the operations of arithmetic/logical (R-type) instructions and the memory related instructions data path are quite similar, there are certain key differences:

- The R-type instructions use two register operands coming from the register file. The memory instructions also use the ALU to do the address calculation, but the second input is the sign-extended 16-bit offset field from the instruction.

- The value stored into a destination register comes from the ALU for an R-type instruction, whereas, the data comes from memory for a load.

To create a data path with a common register file and ALU, we must support two different sources for the second ALU input, as well as two different sources for the data stored into the register file. Thus, one multiplexor needs to be placed at the ALU input and another at the data input to the register file, as shown in figure.

We have discussed the individual instructions - arithmetic/logical, memory related and branch. Now we can combine all the pieces to make a simple data path for the MIPS architecture by adding the data path for instruction fetch, the data path from R-type and memory instructions and the data path for branches. Figure below shows the data path we obtain by combining the separate pieces. The branch instruction uses the main ALU for comparison of the register operands, so we must keep the adder shown earlier for computing the branch target address. An additional multiplexor is required to select either the sequentially following instruction address, PC + 4, or the branch target address to be written into the PC.

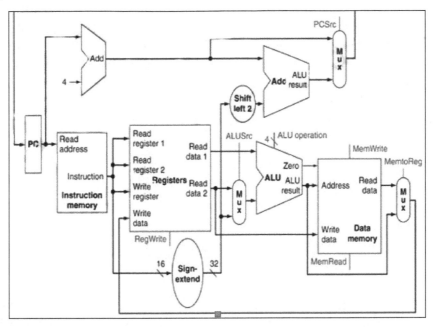

Control Flow

The control unit must be capable of taking inputs about the instruction and generate all the control signals necessary for executing that instruction, for e.g. the write signal for each state element, the selector control signal for each multiplexor, the ALU control signals, etc. Figure below shows the complete data path implementation for the MIPS architecture along with an indication of the various control signals required.

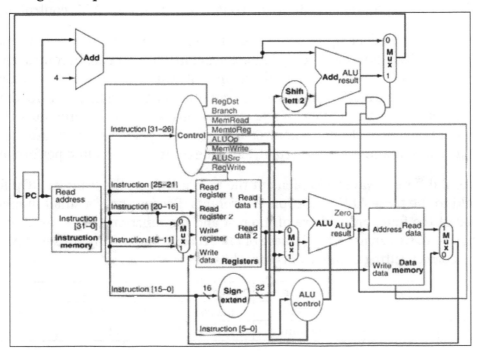

We shall first of all look at the ALU control. The implementation discussed here is specifically for the MIPS architecture and for the subset of instructions pointed out earlier. The ALU uses 4 bits for control. Out of the 16 possible combinations, only 6 are used for the subset under consideration. Depending on the type of instruction class, the ALU will need to perform one of the first five functions. For the load word and store word instructions, we use the ALU to compute the memory address. This is done by addition. For the R-type instructions, the ALU needs to perform one of the five actions (AND, OR, subtract, add, or set on less than), depending on the value of the 6-bit function (or function) field in the low-order bits of the instruction. For a branch on equal instruction, the ALU must perform a subtraction, for comparison.

ALU Control	Function
0000	AND
0001	OR
0010	add
0110	subtract
0111	set-on-less-than
1100	NOR

We can generate the 4-bit ALU control input using a small control unit that takes as inputs the function field of the instruction and a 2-bit control field, which we call ALUOp. ALUOp indicates whether the operation to be performed should be add (00) for loads and stores, subtract (01) for beq, or determined by the operation encoded in the funct field (10). The output of the ALU control unit is a 4-bit signal that directly controls the ALU by generating one of the 4-bit combinations shown previously. In Figure, we show how to set the ALU control inputs based on the 2-bit ALUOp control and the 6-bit function code. The opcode, listed in the first column, determines the setting of the ALUOp bits. When the ALUOp code is 00 or 01, the desired ALU action does not depend on the function code field and this is indicated as don't cares, and the function field is shown as XXXXXX. When the ALUOp value is 10, then the function code is used to set the ALU control input.

For completeness, the relationship between the ALUOp bits and the instruction opcode is also shown. Later on we will see how the ALUOp bits are generated from the main control unit. This style of using multiple levels of decoding—that is, the main control unit generates the ALUOp bits, which then are used as input to the ALU control that generates the actual signals to control the ALU unit— is a common implementation technique. Using multiple levels of control can reduce the size of the main control unit. Using several smaller control units may also potentially increase the speed of the control unit. Such optimizations are important, since the control unit is often performance-critical.

There are several different ways to implement the mapping from the 2-bit ALUOp field and the 6-bit funct field to the three ALU operation control bits. Because only a small number of the 64 possible values of the function field are of interest and the function field is used only when the ALUOp bits equal 10, we can use a small piece of logic that recognizes the subset of possible values and causes the correct setting of the ALU control bits.

opcde	ALUop	Operation	funct	ALU function	ALU control
lw	00	load word	xxxxxx	add	0010
sw	00	store word	xxxxxx	add	0010

beq	01	branch equal	xxxxxx	subtract	0110
R-type	10	add	100000	add	0010
		subtract	100010	subtract	0110
		AND	100100	AND	0000
		OR	10010	OR	0001
		set-on-less-then	101010	set-on-less-then	0111

Now, we shall consider the design of the main control unit. For this, we need to remember the following details about the instruction formats of the MIPS ISA:

- For all the formats, the opcode field is always contained in bits 31:26 – Op[5:0].

- The two registers to be read are always specified by the Rs and Rt fields, at positions 25:21. and 20:16. This is true for the R-type instructions, branch on equal, and for store.

- The base register for the load and store instructions is always in bit positions 25:21 (Rs).

- The destination register is in one of two places. For a load it is in bit positions 20:16 (Rt), while for an R-type instruction it is in bit positions 15:11 (Rd). To select one of these two registers, a multiplexor is needed.

- The 16-bit offset for branch equal, load, and store is always in positions 15:0.

To the simple data path already shown, we shall add all the required control signals. Figure below shows these additions plus the ALU control block, the write signals for state elements, the read signal for the data memory, and the control signals for the multiplexors. Since all the multiplexors have two inputs, they each require a single control line. There are seven single-bit control lines plus the 2-bit ALUOp control signal. The seven control signals are listed below:

- RegDst: The control signal to decide the destination register for the register write operation – The register in the Rt field or Rd field.

- RegWrite: The control signal for writing into the register file.

- ALUSrc: The control signal to decide the ALU source – Register operand or sign extended operand.

- PCSrc: The control signal that decides whether PC+4 or the target address is to written into the PC.

- MemWrite: The control signal which enables a write into the data memory.

- MemRead: The control signal which enables a read from the data memory.

- MemtoReg: The control signal which decides what is written into the register file, the result of the ALU operation or the data memory contents.

The data path along with the control signals included is shown in Figure below. Note that the control unit takes in the opcode information from the fetched instruction and generates all the control signals, depending on the operation to be performed.

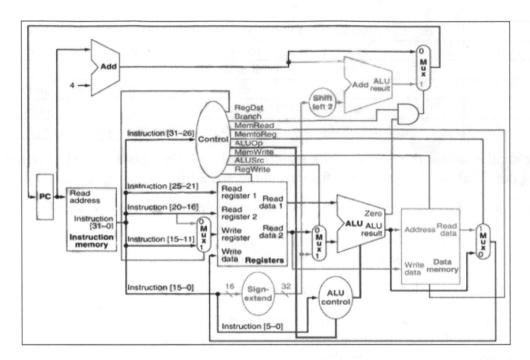

Now, we shall trace the execution flow for different types of instructions and see what control signals have to be activated. Let us consider the execution of an R type instruction first. For all these instructions, the source register fields are Rs and Rt, and the destination register field is Rd. The various operations that take place for an arithmetic / logical operation with register operands are:

- The instruction is fetched from the code memory.

- Since the Branch control signal is set to 0, the PC is unconditionally replaced with PC + 4.

- The two registers specified in the instruction are read from the register file.

- The ALU operates on the data read from the register file, using the function code (bits 5:0, which is the funct field, of the instruction) to generate the ALU function.

- The ALUSrc control signal is deserted, indicating that the second operand comes from a register.

- The ALUOp field for R-type instructions is set to 10 to indicate that the ALU control should be generated from the funct field.

- The result from the ALU is written into the register file using bits 15:11 of the instruction to select the destination register.

- The RegWrite control signal is asserted and the RegDst control signal is made 1, indicating that Rd is the destination register.

- The MemtoReg control signal is made 0, indicating that the value fed to the register write data input comes from the ALU.

Furthermore, an R-type instruction writes a register (RegWrite = 1), but neither reads nor writes data memory. So, the MemRead and MemWrite control signals are set to 0. These operations along with the required control signals are indicated in figure.

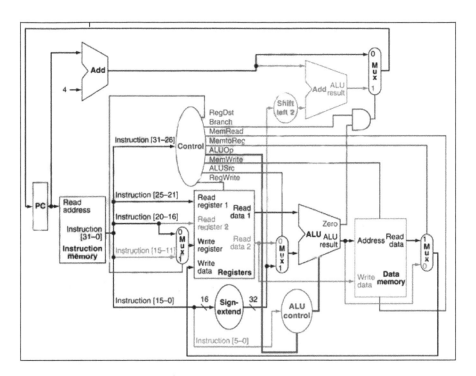

Similarly, we can illustrate the execution of a load word, such as lw $t1, offset ($t2). Figure below shows the active functional units and asserted control lines for a load. We can think of a load instruction as operating in five steps:

- The instruction is fetched from the code memory.

- Since the Branch control signal is set to 0, the PC is unconditionally replaced with PC + 4.

- A register ($t2) value is read from the register file.

- The ALU computes the sum of the value read from the register file and the sign-extended, lower 16 bits of the instruction (offset).

- The ALUSrc control signal is asserted, indicating that the second operand comes from the sign extended operand.

- The ALUOp field for R-type instructions is set to 00 to indicate that the ALU should perform addition for the address calculation.

- The sum from the ALU is used as the address for the data memory and a data memory read is performed.

- The MemRead is asserted and the MemWrite control signals are set to 0.

- The result from the ALU is written into the register file using bits 20:16 of the instruction to select the destination register.

- The RegWrite control signal is asserted and the RegDst control signal is made 0, indicating that Rt is the destination register.

- The MemtoReg control signal is made 1, indicating that the value fed to the register write data input comes from the data memory.

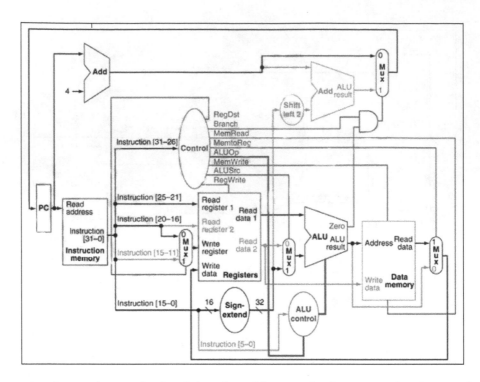

A store instruction is similar to the load for the address calculation. It finishes in four steps The control signals that are different from load are:

- MemWrite is 1 and MemRead is 0.

- RegWrite is 0.

- MemtoReg and RegDst are X's (don't cares).

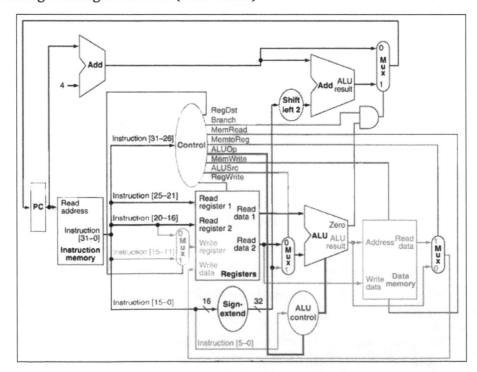

The branch instruction is similar to an R-format operation, since it sends the Rs and Rt registers to the ALU. The ALUOp field for branch is set for a subtract (ALU control = 01), which is used to test for equality. The MemtoReg field is irrelevant when the RegWrite signal is 0. Since the register is not being written, the value of the data on the register data write port is not used. The Branch control signal is set to 1. The ALU performs a subtract on the data values read from the register file. The value of PC + 4 is added to the sign-extended, lower 16 bits of the instruction (offset) shifted left by two; the result is the branch target address. The Zero result from the ALU is used to decide which adder result to store into the PC. The control signals and the data flow for the Branch instruction is shown in figure.

We shall add a jump instruction. The jump instruction looks somewhat similar to a branch instruction but computes the target PC differently and is not conditional. Like a branch, the low order 2 bits of a jump address are always 00. The next lower 26 bits of this 32-bit address come from the 26-bit immediate field in the instruction, as shown in Figure. The upper 4 bits of the address that should replace the PC come from the PC of the jump instruction plus 4. Thus, we can implement a jump by storing into the PC the concatenation of the upper 4 bits of the current PC + 4 (these are bits 31:28 of the sequentially following instruction address), the 26-bit immediate field of the jump instruction and the bits 00.

2	address
31:26	25:0

Figure below shows the addition of the control for jump added to the previously discussed control. An additional multiplexor is used to select the source for the new PC value, which is either the incremented PC (PC + 4), the branch target PC, or the jump target PC. One additional control signal is needed for the additional multiplexor. This control signal, called Jump, is asserted only when the instruction is a jump—that is, when the opcode is 2.

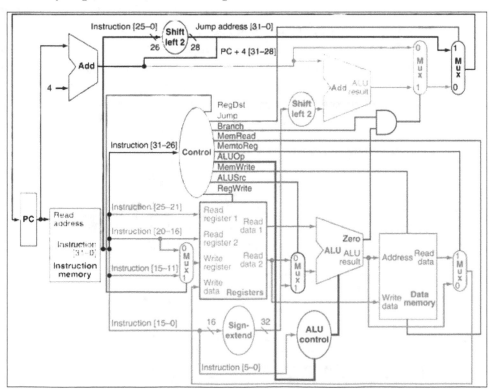

Since we have assumed that all the instructions get executed in one clock cycle, the longest instruction determines the clock period. For the subset of instructions considered, the critical path is that of the load, which takes the following path Instruction memory, register file, ALU, data memory, register file.

The single cycle implementation may be acceptable for this simple instruction set, but it is not feasible to vary the period for different instructions, for e.g. floating point operations. Also, since the clock cycle is equal to the worst case delay, there is no point in improving the common case, which violates the design principle of making the common case fast. In addition, in this single-cycle implementation, each functional unit can be used only once per clock. Therefore, some functional units must be duplicated, raising the cost of the implementation. A single-cycle design is inefficient both in its performance and in its hardware cost. These shortcomings can be avoided by using implementation techniques that have a shorter clock cycle—derived from the basic functional unit delays—and that require multiple clock cycles for each instruction.

There is an alternative approach by which the control signals required inside the CPU can be generated. This alternative approach is known as micro-programmed control unit. In micro-programmed control unit, the logic of the control unit is specified by a micro-program. A micro-program consists of a sequence of instructions in a microprogramming language. These are instructions that specify micro-operations. A micro-programmed control unit is a relatively simple logic circuit that is capable of (1) sequencing through microinstructions and (2) generating control signals to execute each microinstruction.

The concept of micro-program is similar to computer program. In computer program the complete instructions of the program is stored in main memory and during execution it fetches the instructions from main memory one after another. The sequence of instruction fetch is controlled by the program counter (PC). Micro-programs are stored in micro-program memory and the execution is controlled by the micro-program counter (PC). Micro-programs consist of microinstructions which are nothing but strings of 0's and 1's. In a particular instance, we read the contents of one location of micro-program memory, which is nothing but a microinstruction. Each output line (data line) of micro-program memory corresponds to one control signal. If the content of the memory cell is 0, it indicates that the signal is not generated and if the contents of memory cell are 1, it indicates the generation of the control signal at that instant of time.

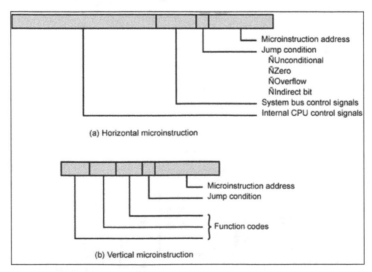

(a) Horizontal microinstruction

(b) Vertical microinstruction

There are basically two types of micro-programmed control – horizontal organization and vertical organization. In the case of horizontal organization, you can assume that every bit in the control word corresponds to a control signal. In the case of a vertical organization, the signals are grouped and encoded in order to reduce the size of the control word. Normally some minimal level of encoding will be done even in the case of horizontal control. The fields will remain encoded in the control memory and they must be decoded to get the individual control signals. Horizontal organization has more control over the potential parallelism of operations in the data path; however, it uses up lots of control store. Vertical organization, on the other hand, is easier to program, not very different from programming a RISC machine in assembly language, but needs extra level of decoding and may slow the machine down. Figure shows the two formats. The different terminologies related to micro-programmed control unit are:

Control Word (CW): Control word is defined as a word whose individual bits represent the various control signals. Therefore each of the control steps in the control sequence of an instruction defines a unique combination of 0s and 1s in the CW. A sequence of control words (CWs) corresponding to the control sequence of a machine instruction constitute the micro-program for that instruction. The individual control words in this micro-program are referred to as microinstructions. The micro-programs corresponding to the instruction set of a computer are stored in a special memory that will be referred to as the micro-program memory or control store. The control words related to all instructions are stored in the micro-program memory.

The control unit can generate the control signals for any instruction by sequentially reading the CWs of the corresponding micro-program from the micro-program memory. To read the control word sequentially from the micro-program memory a micro-program counter (PC) is needed. The basic organization of a micro-programmed control unit is shown in the Figure. The starting address generator block is responsible for loading the starting address of the micro-program into the PC everytime a new instruction is loaded in the IR. The PC is then automatically incremented by the clock, and it reads the successive microinstruction from memory. Each microinstruction basically provides the required control signal at that time step. The micro-program counter ensures that the control signal will be delivered to the various parts of the CPU in correct sequence.

We have some instructions whose execution depends on the status of condition codes and status flag, as for example, the branch instruction. During branch instruction execution, it is required to take the decision between alternative actions. To handle such type of instructions with micro-programmed control, the design of the control unit is based on the concept of conditional branching in the micro-program. In order to do that, it is required to include some conditional branch microinstructions. In conditional microinstructions, it is required to specify the address of the micro-program memory to which the control must be directed to. It is known as the branch address. Apart from the branch address, these microinstructions can specify which of the state's flags, condition codes, or possibly, bits of the instruction register should be checked as a condition for branching to take place.

In a computer program we have seen that execution of every instruction consists of two parts – fetch phase and execution phase of the instruction. It is also observed that the fetch phase of all instruction is the same. In a micro-programmed control unit, a common micro-program is used to fetch the instruction. This microprogram is stored in a specific location and execution of each instruction starts from that memory location. At the end of the fetch micro-program, the starting address generator unit calculates the appropriate starting address of the micro-program for the instruction which is currently present in IR. After that the PC controls the execution of micro-program which generates the appropriate control signals in the proper sequence. During the execution of a micro-program, the PC is incremented everytime a new microinstruction is fetched from the micro-program memory, except in the following situations:

- When an End instruction is encountered, the PC is loaded with the address of the first CW in the micro-program for the next instruction fetch cycle.

- When a new instruction is loaded into the IR, the PC is loaded with the starting address of the micro-program for that instruction.

- When a branch microinstruction is encountered, and the branch condition is satisfied, the PC is loaded with the branch address.

The organization of a micro-programmed control unit is given in Figure below.

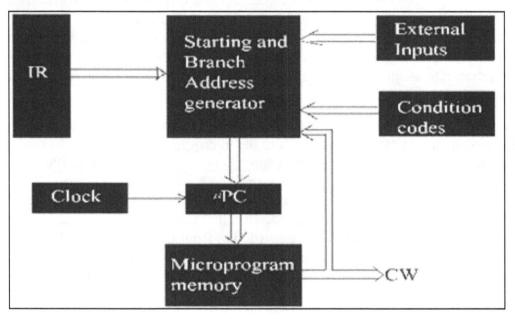

Micro-programmed control pros and cons:
- Ease of design.
- Flexibility.
- Easy to adapt to changes in organization, timing, technology.
- Can make changes late in design cycle, or even in the field.
- Can implement very powerful instruction sets (just more control memory).
- Generality.
- Can implement multiple instruction sets on same machine.
- Can tailor instruction set to application.

- Compatibility.
- Many organizations, same instruction set.
- Costly to implement.
- Slow.

References

- What-is-computer-architecture: computersciencedegreehub.com, Retrieved 02, January 2020
- Types-of-computer-architecture: educba.com, Retrieved 13, May 2020
- Execution-of-a-complete-instruction-control-flow: cs.umd.edu, Retrieved 26, August 2020

Pipelining in Computer Architecture

The process of cumulating instructions from the processor through a pipeline is known as pipelining or pipeline processing. There are various hazards associated with pipelining of computers like data hazards, structural hazards and control hazards. The aim of this chapter is to explore the various processes and hazards associated with the pipelining of computers.

Pipelining is the process of accumulating instruction from the processor through a pipeline. It allows storing and executing instructions in an orderly process. It is also known as pipeline processing. Pipelining is a technique where multiple instructions are overlapped during execution. Pipeline is divided into stages and these stages are connected with one another to form a pipe like structure. Instructions enter from one end and exit from another end. Pipelining increases the overall instruction throughput.

In pipeline system, each segment consists of an input register followed by a combinational circuit. The register is used to hold data and combinational circuit performs operations on it. The output of combinational circuit is applied to the input register of the next segment.

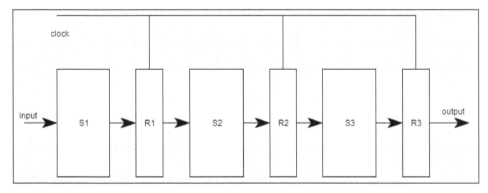

Pipeline system is like the modern day assembly line setup in factories. For example in a car manufacturing industry, huge assembly lines are setup and at each point, there are robotic arms to perform a certain task, and then the car moves on ahead to the next arm.

Types of Pipeline

Arithmetic Pipeline

Arithmetic pipelines are usually found in most of the computers. They are used for floating point operations, multiplication of fixed point numbers etc. For example: The input to the Floating Point Adder pipeline is:

$X = A*2^a$

$Y = B*2^b$

Here A and B are mantissas (significant digit of floating point numbers), while a and b are exponents. The floating point addition and subtraction is done in 4 parts:

- Compare the exponents.

- Align the mantissas.

- Add or subtract mantissas

- Produce the result.

Registers are used for storing the intermediate results between the above operations.

Instruction Pipeline

In this a stream of instructions can be executed by overlapping fetch, decode and execute phases of an instruction cycle. This type of technique is used to increase the throughput of the computer system. An instruction pipeline reads instruction from the memory while previous instructions are being executed in other segments of the pipeline. Thus we can execute multiple instructions simultaneously. The pipeline will be more efficient if the instruction cycle is divided into segments of equal duration.

Pipeline Conflicts

There are some factors that cause the pipeline to deviate its normal performance. Some of these factors are given below:

- Timing Variations: All stages cannot take same amount of time. This problem generally occurs in instruction processing where different instructions have different operand requirements and thus different processing time.

- Data Hazards: When several instructions are in partial execution, and if they reference same data then the problem arises. We must ensure that next instruction does not attempt to access data before the current instruction, because this will lead to incorrect results.

- Branching: In order to fetch and execute the next instruction, we must know what that instruction is. If the present instruction is a conditional branch, and its result will lead us to the next instruction, then the next instruction may not be known until the current one is processed.

- Interrupts: Interrupts set unwanted instruction into the instruction stream. Interrupts effect the execution of instruction.

- Data Dependency: It arises when an instruction depends upon the result of a previous instruction but this result is not yet available.

Advantages of Pipelining

- The cycle time of the processor is reduced.

- It increases the throughput of the system.

- It makes the system reliable.

Disadvantages of Pipelining

- The design of pipelined processor is complex and costly to manufacture.

- The instruction latency is more.

To apply the concept of instruction execution in pipeline, it is required to break the instruction execution into different tasks. Each task will be executed in different processing elements of the CPU. As we know that there are two distinct phases of instruction execution: one is instruction fetch and the other one is instruction execution. Therefore, the processor executes a program by fetching and executing instructions, one after another. The cycle time τ of an instruction pipeline is the time needed to advance a set of instructions one stage through the pipeline. The cycle time can be determined as,

$$\tau = \max[\tau_i] + d = \tau_m + d \quad 1 \le i \le k$$

where τm = maximum stage delay (delay through the stage which experiences the largest delay), k = number of stages in the instruction pipeline, d = the time delay of a latch needed to advance signals and data from one stage to the next. Now suppose that n instructions are processed and these instructions are executed one after another. The total time required T_k to execute all n instructions is,

$$T_k = \left[k + (n-1)\right]\tau$$

In general, let the instruction execution be divided into five stages as fetch, decode, execute, memory access and write back, denoted by F_i, D_i, E_i, M_i and W_i. Execution of a program consists of a sequence of these steps. When the first instruction's decode happens, the second instruction's fetch is done. When the pipeline is filled, you see that there are five different activities taking place in parallel. All these activities are overlapped. Five instructions are in progress at any given time. This means that five distinct hardware units are needed. These units must be capable of performing their tasks simultaneously and without interfering with one another. Information is passed from one unit to the next through a storage buffer. As an instruction progresses through the pipeline, all the information needed by the stages downstream must be passed along. If all stages are balanced, i.e., all take the same time,

$$\text{Time between instructions}_{\text{pipelined}} = \frac{\text{Time between instructions}_{\text{nonpipelined}}}{\text{Number of stages}}$$

If the stages are not balanced, speedup will be less. Observe that the speedup is due to increased throughput and the latency (time for each instruction) does not decrease. The basic features of pipelining are:

- Pipelining does not help latency of single task, it only helps throughput of entire workload.

- Pipeline rate is limited by the slowest pipeline stage.

- Multiple tasks operate simultaneously.

- It exploits parallelism among instructions in a sequential instruction stream.

- Unbalanced lengths of pipe stages reduce speedup.

- Time to "fill" pipeline and time to "drain" it reduces speedup.

- Ideally the speedup is equal to the number of stages and the CPI is 1.

Let us consider the MIPS pipeline with five stages, with one step per stage:

- IF: Instruction fetch from memory.

- ID: Instruction decode and register read.

- EX: Execute operation or calculate address.

- MEM: Access memory operand.

- WB: Write result back to register.

Consider the details given below. Assume that it takes 100ps for a register read or write and 200ps for all other stages. Let us calculate the speedup obtained by pipelining.

Instr	Instr fetch	Register read	ALU op	Memory access	Register write	Total time
lw	200ps	100ps	200ps	200ps	100ps	800ps
sw	200ps	100ps	200ps	200ps		700ps
R-format	200ps	100ps	200ps		100ps	600ps
beq	200ps	100ps	200ps			500ps

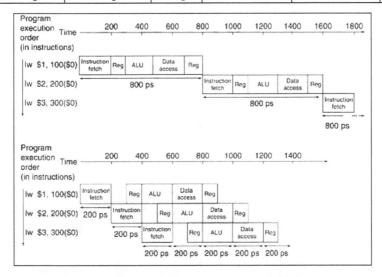

For a non-pipelined implementation it takes 800ps for each instruction and for a pipelined implementation it takes only 200ps. Observe that the MIPS ISA is designed in such a way that it is suitable for pipelining. Figure below shows the MIPS pipeline implementation.

- All instructions are 32-bits:

  ○ Easier to fetch and decode in one cycle.

  ○ Comparatively, the x86 ISA: 1- to 17-byte instructions.

- Few and regular instruction formats:
  - Can decode and read registers in one step.
- Load/store addressing:
  - Can calculate address in 3rd stage, access memory in 4th stage.
- Alignment of memory operands:
  - Memory access takes only one cycle.

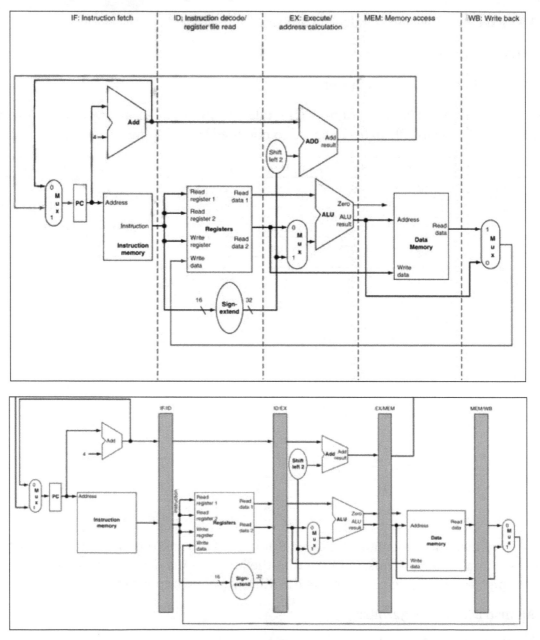

Figure above shows how buffers are introduced between the stages. This is mandatory. Each stage takes in data from that buffer, processes it and write into the next buffer. Also note that as an instruction moves down the pipeline from one buffer to the next, its relevant information also moves along with it. For example, during clock cycle 4, the information in the buffers is as follows:

- Buffer IF/ID holds instruction I4, which was fetched in cycle 4.

- Buffer ID/EX holds the decoded instruction and both the source operands for instruction I3. This is the information produced by the decoding hardware in cycle 3.

- Buffer EX/MEM holds the executed result of I2. The buffer also holds the information needed for the write step of instruction I2. Even though it is not needed by the execution stage, this information must be passed on to the next stage and further down to the Write back stage in the following clock cycle to enable that stage to perform the required Write operation.

- Buffer MEM/WB holds the data fetched from memory (for a load) for I1, and for the arithmetic and logical operations, the results produced by the execution unit and the destination information for instruction I1 are just passed.

We shall look at the single-clock-cycle diagrams for the load & store instructions of the MIPS ISA. Figure below shows the instruction fetch for a load / store instruction. Observe that the PC is used to fetch the instruction, it is written into the IF/ID buffer and the PC is incremented by 4. The instruction is decoded, the register file is read and the operands are written into the ID/EX buffer. Note that the entire information of the instruction including the destination register is written into the ID/EX buffer. The highlights in the figure show the resources involved. Figure shows the execution stage. The base register's contents and the sign extended displacement are fed to the ALU, the addition operation is initiated and the ALU calculates the memory address. This effective address is stored in the EX/MEM buffer. Also the destination register's information is passed from the ID/EX buffer to the EX/MEM buffer. Next, the memory access happens and the read data is written into the MEM/WB buffer. The destination register's information is passed from the EX/MEM buffer to the MEM/WB buffer. The write back happens in the last stage. The data read from the data memory is written into the destination register specified in the instruction. The destination register information is passed on from the MEM/WB memory backwards to the register file, along with the data to be written.

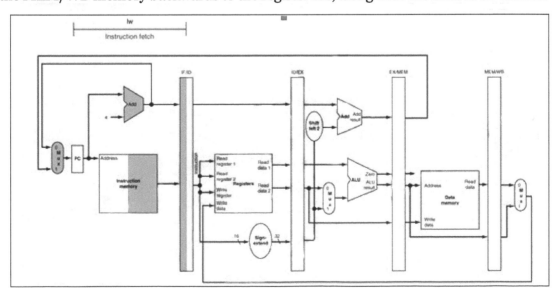

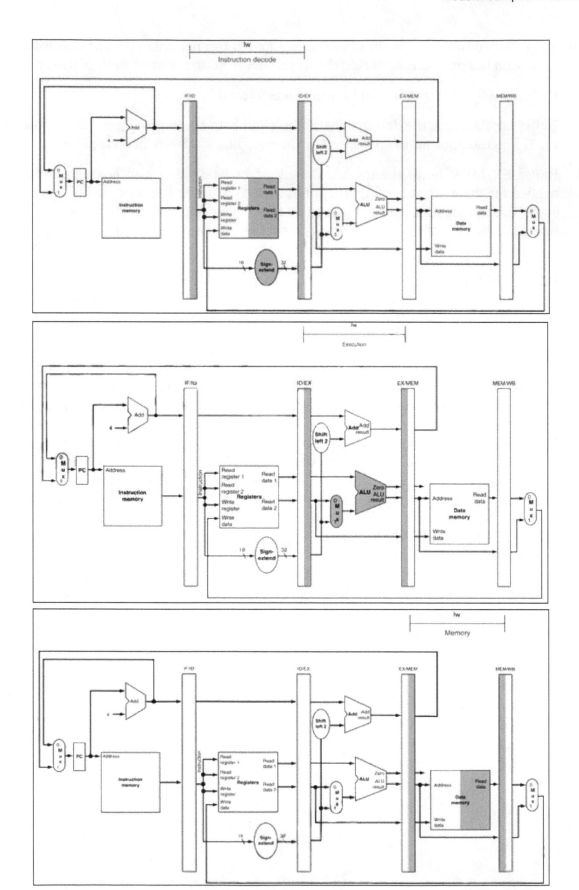

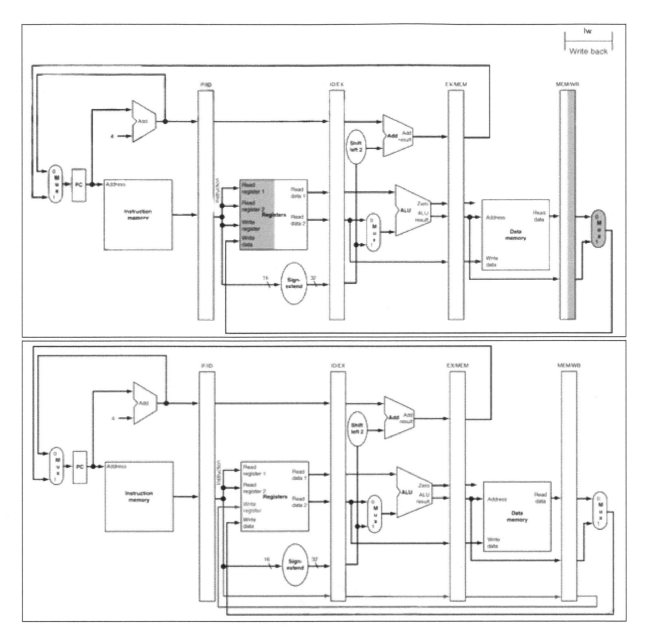

For a store instruction, the effective address calculation is the same as that of load. But when it comes to the memory access stage, store performs a memory write. The effective address is passed on from the execution stage to the memory stage; the data read from the register file is passed from the ID/EX buffer to the EX/MEM buffer and taken from there. The store instruction completes with this memory stage. There is no write back for the store instruction.

While discussing the cycle-by-cycle flow of instructions through the pipelined data path, we can look at the following options:

- "Single-clock-cycle" pipeline diagram:
  - Shows pipeline usage in a single cycle.
  - Highlight resources used.

- • "Multi-clock-cycle" diagram:

  ○ Graph of operation over time.

The multi-clock-cycle pipeline diagram showing the resource utilization is given in Figure below. It can be seen that the Instruction memory is used in eth first stage. The register file is used in the second stage, the ALU in the third stage, the data memory in the fourth stage and the register file in the fifth stage again.

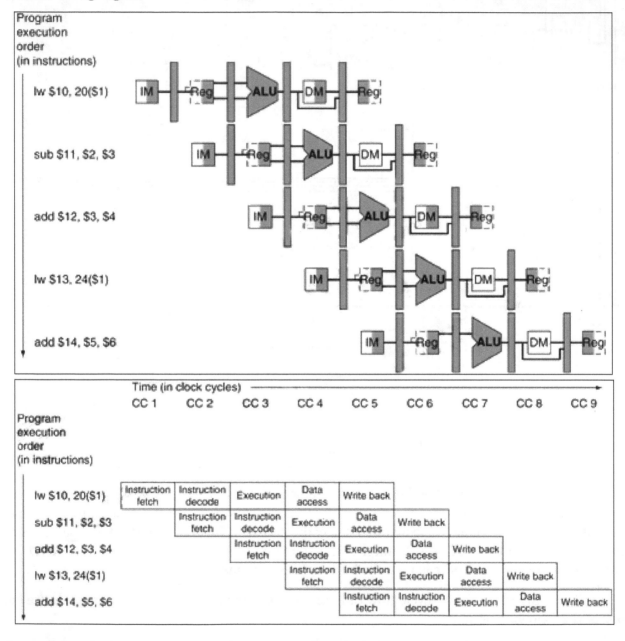

The multi-cycle diagram showing the activities happening in each clock cycle is given in Figure above. Now, having discussed the pipelined implementation of the MIPS architecture, we need to discuss the generation of control signals. The pipelined implementation of MIPS, along with the control signals is given in figure.

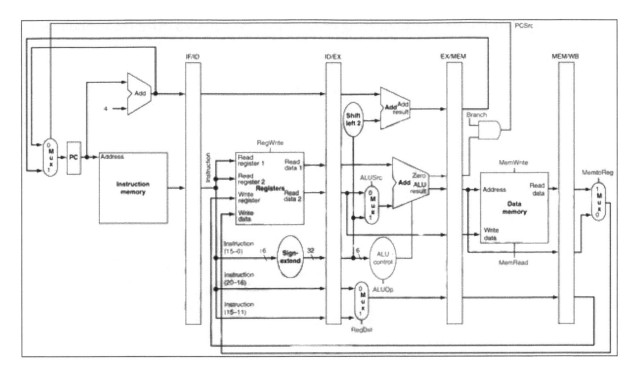

All the control signals indicated are not required at the same time. Different control signals are required at different stages of the pipeline. But the decision about the generation of the various control signals is done at the second stage, when the instruction is decoded. Therefore, just as the data flows from one stage to another as the instruction moves from one stage to another, the control signals also pass on from one buffer to another and are utilized at the appropriate instants. This is shown in Figure above. The control signals for the execution stage are used in that stage. The control signals needed for the memory stage and the write back stage move along with that instruction to the next stage. The memory related control signals are used in the next stage, whereas, the write back related control signals move from there to the next stage and used when the instruction performs the write back operation.

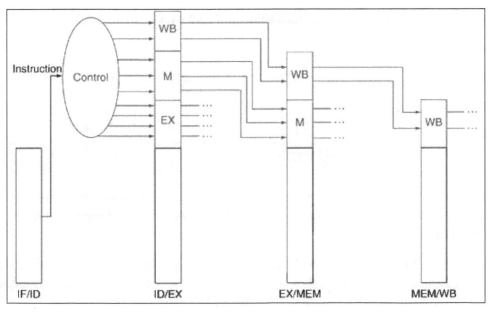

The complete pipeline implementation, along with the control signals used at the various stages is given in Figure below.

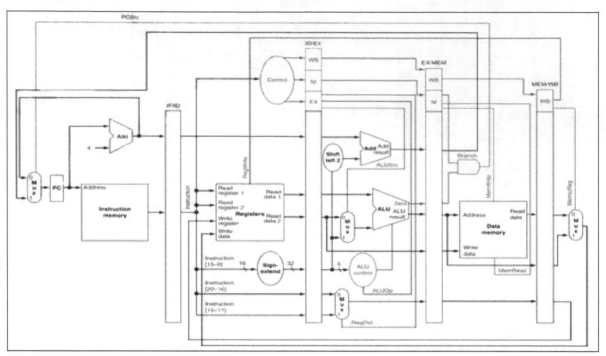

Pipeline Hazards

Whenever a pipeline has to stall due to some reason it is called pipeline hazards.

Data Dependency

Consider the following two instructions and their pipeline execution:

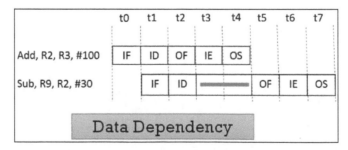

In the figure above, you can see that result of the Add instruction is stored in the register R2 and we know that the final result is stored at the end of the execution of the instruction which will happen at the clock cycle t4.

But the Sub instruction needs the value of the register R2 at the cycle t3. So the Sub instruction has to stall two clock cycles. If it doesn't stall it will generate an incorrect result. Thus depending of one instruction on other instruction for data is data dependency.

Memory Delay

When an instruction or data is required, it is first searched in the cache memory if not found then it is a cache miss. The data is further searched in the memory which may take ten or more cycles. So, for that number of cycle the pipeline has to stall and this is a memory delay hazard. The cache miss, also results in the delay of all the subsequent instructions.

Branch Delay

Suppose the four instructions are pipelined I_1, I_2, I_3, I_4 in a sequence. The instruction I_1 is a branch instruction and its target instruction is Ik. Now, processing starts and instruction I_1 is fetched, decoded and the target address is computed at the 4th stage in cycle t3.

But till then the instructions I2, I3, I4 are fetched in cycle 1, 2 & 3 before the target branch address is computed. As I1 is found to be a branch instruction, the instructions I2, I3, I4 has to be discarded because the instruction I_k has to be processed next to I_1. So, this delay of three cycles 1, 2, 3 is a branch delay.

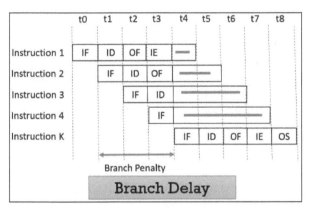

Prefetching the target branch address will reduce the branch delay. Like if the target branch is identified at the decode stage then the branch delay will reduce to 1 clock cycle.

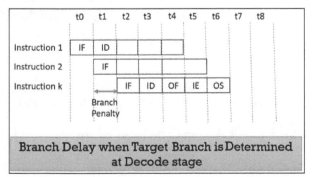

Branch delay when target branch is determined at decode stage.

Resource Limitation

If the two instructions request for accessing the same resource in the same clock cycle, then one of the instruction has to stall and let the other instruction to use the resource. This stalling is due to resource limitation. However, it can be prevented by adding more hardware.

Classes of Hazards

- Structural hazards: Hardware cannot support certain combinations of instructions (two instructions in the pipeline require the same resource).

- Data hazards: Instruction depends on result of prior instruction still in the pipeline.

- Control hazards: Caused by delay between the fetching of instructions and decisions about changes in control flow (branches and jumps).

Structural hazards arise because there is not enough duplication of resources. Resolving structural hazards:

- Solution 1: Wait-

    ◦ Must detect the hazard.

    ◦ Must have mechanism to stall.

    ◦ Low cost and simple.

    ◦ Increases CPI.

    ◦ Used for rare cases.

- Solution 2: Throw more hardware at the problem-

    ◦ Pipeline hardware resource is a useful for multi-cycle resources, good performance, sometimes complex e.g., RAM.

    ◦ Replicate resource is a good performance, increases cost (+ maybe interconnect delay), useful for cheap or divisible resource.

One possibility of a structural hazard in the MIPS pipeline. Instruction 3 is accessing memory for an instruction fetch and instruction 1 is accessing memory for a data access (load/store). These two are conflicting requirements and gives rise to a hazard. We should either stall one of the operations, or have two separate memories for code and data. Structural hazards will have to handled at the design time itself.

There are two types of data dependence - true data dependences and name dependences. An instruction j is data dependent on instruction i if either of the following holds:

- Instruction i produces a result that may be used by instruction j.

- Instruction j is data dependent on instruction k, and instruction k is data dependent on instruction i.

A name dependence occurs when two instructions use the same register or memory location, called a name, but there is no flow of data between the instructions associated with that name. Two types of name dependences between an instruction i that precedes instruction j in program order:

- An anti-dependence between instruction i and instruction j occurs when instruction j writes a register or memory location that instruction i reads. The original ordering must be preserved.

- An output dependence occurs when instruction i and instruction j write the same register or memory location. The ordering between the instructions must be preserved.

- Since this is not a true dependence, renaming can be more easily done for register operands, where it is called register renaming.

- Register renaming can be done either statically by a compiler or dynamically by the hardware.

Control dependences determine the ordering of an instruction with respect to a branch instruction so that an instruction i is executed in correct program order. There are two general constraints imposed by control dependences:

- An instruction that is control dependent on its branch cannot be moved before the branch so that its execution is no longer controlled by the branch.

- An instruction that is not control dependent on its branch cannot be moved after the branch so that its execution is controlled by the branch.

Having introduced the various types of data dependences and control dependence, let us discuss how these dependences cause problems in the pipeline. Dependences are properties of programs and whether the dependences turn out to be hazards and cause stalls in the pipeline are properties of the pipeline organization. Data hazards may be classified as one of three types, depending on the order of read and write accesses in the instructions:

- RAW (Read After Write):

  - Corresponds to a true data dependence.

  - Program order must be preserved.

  - This hazard results from an actual need for communication.

  - Considering two instructions i and j, instruction j reads the data before i writes it:

    ```
    i: ADD R1, R2, R3

    j: SUB R4, R1, R3
    ```

Add modifies R1 and then Sub should read it. If this order is changed, there is a RAW hazard.

- WAW (Write After Write):

  - Corresponds to output dependence.

  - Occurs when there are multiple writes or a short integer pipeline and a longer floating-point pipeline or when an instruction proceeds when a previous instruction is stalled WAW (write after write).

- ○ This is caused by name dependence. There is no actual data transfer. It is the same name that causes the problem.

- ○ Considering two instructions i and j, instruction j should write after instruction i has written the data:

  ```
  i: SUB R1, R4, R3

  j: ADD R1, R2, R3
  ```

- ○ Instruction i has to modify register R1 first, and then j has to modify it. Otherwise, there is a WAW hazard. There is a problem because of R1. If some other register had been used, there will not be a problem.

- ○ Solution is register renaming, that is, use some other register. The hardware can do the renaming or the compiler can do the renaming.

- WAR (Write After Read):

  - ○ Arises from an anti-dependence.

  - ○ Cannot occur in most static issue pipelines.

  - ○ Occurs either when there are early writes and late reads, or when instructions are re-ordered.

  - ○ There is no actual data transfer. It is the same name that causes the problem.

  - ○ Considering two instructions i and j, instruction j should write after instruction i has read the data.

    ```
    i: SUB R4, R1, R3

    j: ADD R1, R2, R3
    ```

Instruction i has to read register R1 first, and then j has to modify it. Otherwise, there is a WAR hazard. There is a problem because of R1. If some other register had been used, there will not be a problem.

- Solution is register renaming, that is, use some other register. The hardware can do the renaming or the compiler can do the renaming.

The use of the result of the ADD instruction in the next three instructions causes a hazard, since the register is not written until after those instructions read it. The write back for the ADD instruction happens only in the fifth clock cycle, whereas the next three instructions read the register values before that, and hence will read the wrong data. This gives rise to RAW hazards.

A control hazard is when we need to find the destination of a branch, and can't fetch any new instructions until we know that destination. The first instruction is a branch and it gets resolved only in the fourth clock cycle. So, the next three instructions fetched may be correct, or wrong, depending on the outcome of the branch. This is an example of a control hazard.

Now, having discussed the various dependences and the hazards that they might lead to, we shall see what are the hazards that can happen in our simple MIPS pipeline.

- Structural hazard:

  - Conflict for use of a resource.

- In MIPS pipeline with a single memory:

  - Load/store requires data access.

  - Instruction fetch would have to stall for that cycle.

- Would cause a pipeline "bubble".

- Hence, pipelined data paths require separate instruction/data memories or separate instruction/data caches.

- RAW hazards - Can happen in any architecture.

- WAR hazards - Can't happen in MIPS 5 stage pipeline because all instructions take 5 stages, and reads are always in stage 2, and writes are always in stage 5.

- WAW hazards - Can't happen in MIPS 5 stage pipeline because all instructions take 5 stages, and writes are always in stage 5.

- Control hazards:

  - Can happen.

  - The penalty depends on when the branch is resolved – in the second clock cycle or the third clock cycle.

  - More aggressive implementations resolve the branch in the second clock cycle itself, leading to one clock cycle penalty.

Let us look at the speedup equation with stalls and look at an example problem:

$$CPI_{pipelined} = Ideal\ CPI + Average\ Stall\ cycles\ per\ Inst$$

$$Speedup = \frac{Ideal\ CPI \times Pipeline\ depth}{Ideal\ CPI + Pipeline\ stall\ CPI} \times \frac{Cycle\ Time_{unpipelined}}{Cycle\ Time_{pipelined}}$$

For simple RISC pipeline, CPI = 1. Therefore,

$$Speedup = \frac{Pipeline\ depth}{1 + Pipeline\ stall\ CPI} \times \frac{Cycle\ Time_{unpipelined}}{Cycle\ Time_{pipelined}}$$

Let us assume we want to compare the performance of two machines. Which machine is faster?

- Machine A: Dual ported memory - so there are no memory stalls.

- Machine B: Single ported memory, but its pipelined implementation has a 1.05 times faster clock rate.

Assume:

- Ideal CPI = 1 for both.

- Loads are 40% of instructions executed.

$Speedup_A$ = Pipeline Depth/(1+0) × ($clock_{unpipe}$/$clock_{pipe}$)

$\qquad$ = Pipeline Depth

$Speedup_B$ = Pipeline Depth/(1 + 0.4 × 1) × ($clock_{unpipe}$/($clock_{unpipe}$/1.05)

$\qquad$ = (Pipeline Depth/1.4) × 1.05

$\qquad$ = 0.75 × Pipeline Depth

$Speedup_A$ / $Speedup_B$ = Pipeline Depth / (0.75 × Pipeline Depth) = 1.33

Machine A is 1.33 times faster.

Handling Data Hazards

True data dependences give rise to RAW hazards and name dependences (anti-dependence and output dependence) give rise to WAR hazards and WAW hazards, respectively. The use of the result of the ADD instruction in the next three instructions causes a hazard, since the register is not written until after those instructions read it. The write back for the ADD instruction happens only in the fifth clock cycle, whereas the next three instructions read the register values before that, and hence will read the wrong data. This gives rise to RAW hazards.

One effective solution to handle true data dependences is forwarding. Forwarding is the concept of making data available to the input of the ALU for subsequent instructions, even though the generating instruction hasn't gotten to WB in order to write the memory or registers. This is also called short circuiting or by passing.

The first instruction has finished execution and the result has been written into the EX/MEM buffer. So, during the fourth clock cycle, when the second instruction, SUB needs data, this can be forwarded from the EX/MEM buffer to the input of the ALU. Similarly, for the next AND instruction, the result of the first instruction is now available in the MEM/WB buffer and can be forwarded from there. For the OR instruction, the result is written into the register file during the first half of the clock cycle and the data from there is read during the second half. So, this instruction has no problem. In short, data will have to be forwarded from either the EX/MEM buffer or the MEM/WB buffer.

The hardware changes required to support forwarding. The inputs to the ALU have increased. The multiplexors will have to be expanded, in order to accommodate the additional inputs from the two buffers.

The first instruction is a load and the data becomes available only after the fourth clock cycle. So, forwarding will not help and the second instruction will anyway have a stall of one cycle. For the next instruction, AND, data is forwarded from the MEM/WB buffer. There are thus instances where stalls may occur even with forwarding. However, forwarding is helpful in minimizing hazards and sometimes in totally eliminating them.

The other method of avoiding / minimizing stalls due to true data dependences is to reorder the code – separate the dependent instructions. The snippet shown calculates A = B + E; C = B + F; The dependent instruction after the load can be reordered to avoid use of load result in the next instruction. This reordering has helped in reducing the number of clock cycles for execution from 13 to 11. Two stalls have been avoided.

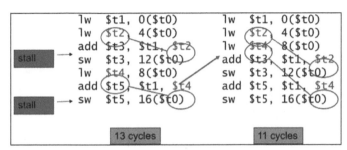

Based on the discussion given earlier, we can identify the two pairs of hazard conditions as:

`1a. EX/MEM.RegisterRd = ID/EX.RegisterRs`

`1b. EX/MEM.RegisterRd = ID/EX.RegisterRt`

`2a. MEM/WB.RegisterRd = ID/EX.RegisterRs`

`2b. MEM/WB.RegisterRd = ID/EX.RegisterRt`

The notation used here is as follows: The first part of the name, to the left of the period, is the name of the pipeline register and the second part is the name of the field in that register. For example, "`ID/EX.RegisterRs`" refers to the number of one register whose value is found in the pipeline register ID/EX; that is, the one from the first read port of the register file. We shall discuss the various hazards based on the following sequence of instructions.

```
sub    $2, $1, $3    # Register $2 set by sub
and    $12, $2, $5   # 1st operand($2) set by sub
or     $13, $6, $2   # 2nd operand($2) set by sub
add    $14, $2, $2   # 1st($2) & 2nd($2) set by sub
sw     $15, 100($2)  # Index($2) set by sub
```

The first hazard in the sequence is on register $2, between the result of sub $2,$1,$3 and the first read operand of and $12,$2,$5. This hazard can be detected when the and instruction is in the EX stage and the prior instruction is in the MEM stage, so this is hazard `1a:EX/MEM.RegisterRd = ID/EX.RegisterRs = $2`.

The sub-or is a type 2b hazard:

`MEM/WB.RegisterRd = ID/EX.RegisterRt = $2`

The two dependences on sub-add are not hazards because the register file supplies the proper data during the ID stage of add. There is no data hazard between sub and sw because sw reads $2 the clock cycle *after* sub writes $2. However, as some instructions do not write into the register file, this rule has to be modified. Otherwise, sometimes it would forward when it was unnecessary. One solution is simply to check to see if the `RegWrite` signal will be active. Examining the WB control field of the pipeline registers during the EX and MEM stages determine if `RegWrite` is asserted or not. Also, MIPS require that every use of $0 as an operand must yield an operand value of zero. In the event that an instruction in the pipeline has $0 as its destination (for example, sll $0, $1, 2), we want to avoid forwarding its possibly nonzero result value. The conditions above thus work properly as long as we add `EX/MEM`. `RegisterRd` $\neq$ 0 to the first hazard condition and `MEM/WB`. `RegisterRd` $\neq$ 0 to the second.

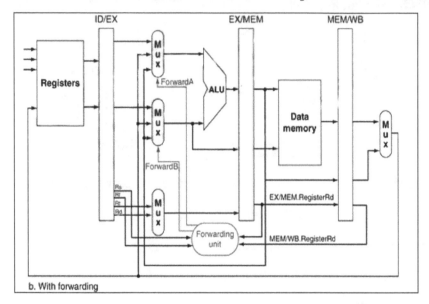

b. With forwarding

Figure above shows the forwarding paths added to the MIPS pipeline. The Forward A and Forward B are the additional control signals added. These control signals take on a value of 00, 10 or 01, depending on whether the multiplexor will pass on the data from the ID/EX, EX/MEM or MEM/WB buffers, respectively. The conditions for detecting hazards and the control signals to resolve them are as follows:

EX hazard:

```
if (EX/MEM.RegWrite

and (EX/MEM.RegisterRd _ 0)

and (EX/MEM.RegisterRd = ID/EX.RegisterRs)) ForwardA = 10

if (EX/MEM.RegWrite

and (EX/MEM.RegisterRd _ 0)

and (EX/MEM.RegisterRd = ID/EX.RegisterRt)) ForwardB = 10
```

This case forwards the result from the previous instruction to either input of the ALU. If the previous instruction is going to write to the register file and the write register number matches the read register number of ALU inputs A or B, provided it is not register 0, then direct the multiplexor to pick the value instead from the pipeline register EX/MEM.

MEM hazard:

```
if (MEM/WB.RegWrite

and (MEM/WB.RegisterRd _ 0)

and (MEM/WB.RegisterRd = ID/EX.RegisterRs)) ForwardA = 01

if (MEM/WB.RegWrite

and (MEM/WB.RegisterRd _ 0)

and (MEM/WB.RegisterRd = ID/EX.RegisterRt)) ForwardB = 01
```

There is no hazard in the WB stage because we assume that the register file supplies the correct result if the instruction in the ID stage reads the same register written by the instruction in the WB stage. Such a register file performs another form of forwarding, but it occurs within the register file.

 Another complication is the potential data hazards between the result of the instruction in the WB stage, the result of the instruction in the MEM stage, and the source operand of the instruction in the ALU stage. For example, when summing a vector of numbers in a single register, a sequence of instructions will all read and write to the same register as indicated below:

```
add $1,$1,$2

add $1,$1,$3

add $1,$1,$4
```

. . .

In this case, the result is forwarded from the MEM stage because the result in the MEM stage is the more recent result. Thus the control for the MEM hazard would be (with the additions highlighted).

```
if (MEM/WB.RegWrite

and (MEM/WB.RegisterRd _ 0)

and (EX/MEM.RegisterRd _ ID/EX.RegisterRs)

and (MEM/WB.RegisterRd = ID/EX.RegisterRs)) ForwardA = 01

if (MEM/WB.RegWrite

and (MEM/WB.RegisterRd _ 0)

and (EX/MEM.RegisterRd _ ID/EX.RegisterRt)

and (MEM/WB.RegisterRd = ID/EX.RegisterRt)) ForwardB = 01
```

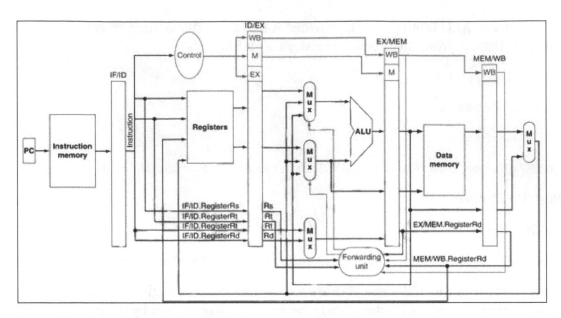

Figure above shows the data path modified to resolve hazards via forwarding. Compared with the data path already shown, the additions are the multiplexors to the inputs to the ALU.

One case where forwarding cannot help eliminate hazards is when an instruction tries to read a register following a load instruction that writes the same register. The data is still being read from memory in clock cycle 4 while the ALU is performing the operation for the following instruction. Something must stall the pipeline for the combination of load followed by an instruction that reads its result. Hence, in addition to a forwarding unit, we need a hazard detection unit. It operates during the ID stage so that it can insert the stall between the load and its use. Checking for load instructions, the control for the hazard detection unit is this single condition:

```
if (ID/EX.MemRead and

((ID/EX.RegisterRt = IF/ID.RegisterRs) or

(ID/EX.RegisterRt = IF/ID.RegisterRt)))

stall the pipeline
```

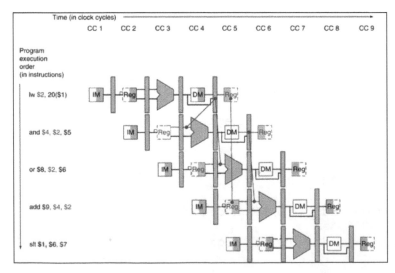

The first line tests to see if the instruction is a load. The only instruction that reads data memory is a load. The next two lines check to see if the destination register field of the load in the EX stage matches either source register of the instruction in the ID stage. If the condition holds, the instruction stalls 1 clock cycle. After this 1-cycle stall, the forwarding logic can handle the dependence and execution proceeds. If there were no forwarding, then the instructions would need another stall cycle.

If the instruction in the ID stage is stalled, then the instruction in the IF stage must also be stalled; otherwise, we would lose the fetched instruction. Preventing these two instructions from making progress is accomplished simply by preventing the PC register and the IF/ID pipeline register from changing. Provided these registers are preserved, the instruction in the IF stage will continue to be read using the same PC, and the registers in the ID stage will continue to be read using the same instruction fields in the IF/ID pipeline register. The back half of the pipeline starting with the EX stage must be executing instructions that have no effect. This is done by executing *nops*. Disserting all the nine control signals (setting them to 0) in the EX, MEM, and WB stages will create a "do nothing" or nop instruction. By identifying the hazard in the ID stage, we can insert a bubble into the pipeline by changing the EX, MEM, and WB control fields of the ID/EX pipeline register to 0. These control values are percolated forward at each clock cycle with the proper effect – no registers or memories are written if the control values are all 0.

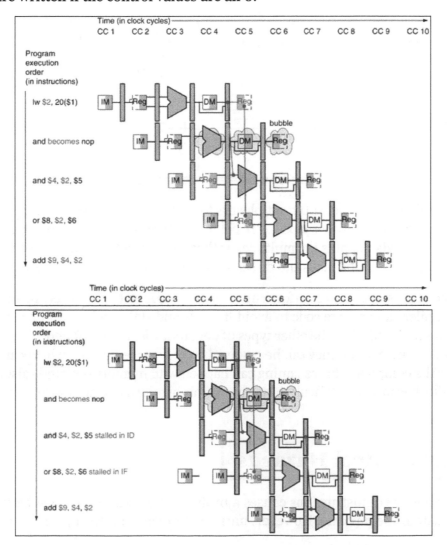

Both the above figures show what really happens in the hardware: the pipeline execution slot associated with the AND instruction is turned into a NOP and all instructions beginning with the AND instructions are delayed one cycle. The hazard forces the AND and OR instructions to repeat in clock cycle 4 what they did in clock cycle 3: and reads registers and decodes, and OR is refetch from instruction memory. Such repeated work is what a stall looks like, but its effect is to stretch the time of the AND and OR instructions and delay the fetch of the ADD instruction. Like an air bubble in a water pipe, a stall bubble delays everything behind it and proceeds down the instruction pipe one stage each cycle until it exits at the end.

Figure below highlights the pipeline connections for both the hazard detection unit and the forwarding unit.

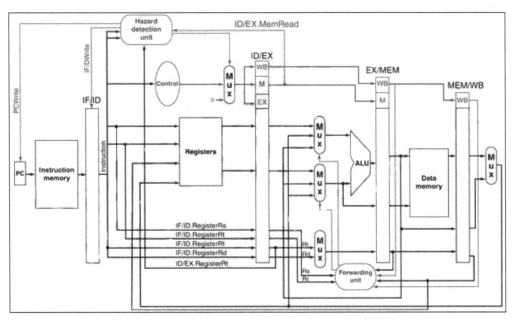

The forwarding unit controls the ALU multiplexors to replace the value from a general-purpose register with the value from the proper pipeline register. The hazard detection unit controls the writing of the PC and IF/ID registers plus the multiplexor that chooses between the real control values and all 0s. The hazard detection unit stalls and disserts the control fields if the load-use hazard test is true.

It should be noted that stalls reduce performance, but are required to get correct results. Also remember that the compiler can arrange code to avoid hazards and stalls and it requires knowledge of the pipeline structure to do this. For the other types of data hazards, viz. WAR and WAW hazards where there is no true sharing of data, they can be resolved by register renaming, which can be handled by the hardware or the compiler. This renaming can happen with memory operands also, which is more difficult to handle, because it is difficult to resolve the ambiguity associated with memory operands.

Handling Control Hazards

A branch in a sequence of instructions causes a problem. An instruction must be fetched at every clock cycle to sustain the pipeline. However, until the branch is resolved, we will not know where to fetch the next instruction from and this causes a problem. This delay in determining the proper instruction to fetch is called a control hazard or branch hazard, in contrast to the data hazards. Control hazards are caused by control dependences. An instruction that is control dependent on a branch cannot be moved in front of the branch, so that the branch no longer controls it and an instruction that is not control dependent on a branch cannot be moved after the branch so that the branch controls it. This will give rise to control hazards.

The two major issues related to control dependences are exception behavior and handling and preservation of data flow. Preserving exception behavior requires that any changes in instruction execution order must not change how exceptions are raised in program. That is, no new exceptions should be generated. Example:

ADD R2,R3,R4

BEQZ R2,L1

LD R1,0(R2)

L1:

What will happen with moving LD before BEQZ? This may lead to memory protection violation. The branch instruction is a guarding branch that checks for an address zero and jumps to L1. If this is moved ahead, then an additional exception will be raised. Data flow is the actual flow of data values among instructions that produce results and those that consume them. Branches make flow dynamic and determine which instruction is the supplier of data. Example:

DADDU R1,R2,R3

BEQZ R4,L

DSUBU R1,R5,R6

L: ...

OR R7,R1,R8

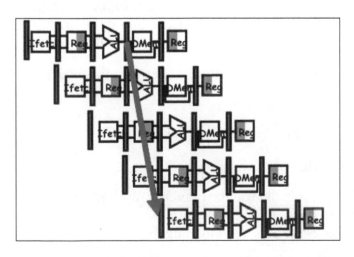

The instruction OR depends on DADDU or DSUBU? We must ensure that we preserve data flow on execution. The general rule to reduce branch penalties is to resolve branches as early as possible.

In the MIPS pipeline, the comparison of registers and target address calculation is normally done at the execution stage. This gives rise to three clock cycles penalty. This is indicated in Figure above. If we do a more aggressive implementation by adding hardware to resolve the branch in the ID stage, the penalty can be reduced.

Resolving the branch earlier requires two actions to occur – computing the branch target address and evaluating the branch decision early. The easy part of this change is to move up the branch address calculation. We already have the PC value and the immediate field in the IF/ID pipeline register, so we just move the branch adder from the EX stage to the ID stage; of course, the branch target address calculation will be performed for all instructions, but only used when needed. The harder part is the branch decision itself. For branch equal, we would compare the two registers read during the ID stage to see if they are equal. Equality can be tested by first exclusive ORing their respective bits and then ORing all the results. Moving the branch test to the ID stage also implies additional forwarding and hazard detection hardware, since a branch dependent on a result still in the pipeline must still work properly with this optimization. For example, to implement branch-on-equal (and its inverse), we will need to forward results to the equality test logic that operates during ID. There are two complicating factors:

- During ID, we must decode the instruction, decide whether a bypass to the equality unit is needed, and complete the equality comparison so that if the instruction is a branch, we can set the PC to the branch target address. Forwarding for the operands of branches was formerly handled by the ALU forwarding logic, but the introduction of the equality test unit in ID will require new forwarding logic. Note that the bypassed source operands of a branch can come from either the ALU/MEM or MEM/WB pipeline latches.

- Because the values in a branch comparison are needed during ID but may be produced later in time, it is possible that a data hazard can occur and a stall will be needed. For example, if an ALU instruction immediately preceding a branch produces one of the operands for the comparison in the branch, a stall will be required, since the EX stage for the ALU instruction will occur after the ID cycle of the branch.

Despite these difficulties, moving the branch execution to the ID stage is an improvement since it reduces the penalty of a branch to only one instruction if the branch is taken, namely, the one currently being fetched. There are basically two ways of handling control hazards:

- Stall until the branch outcome is known or perform the fetch again.

- Predict the behavior of branches:

  ◦ Static prediction by the compiler.

  ◦ Dynamic prediction by the hardware.

The first option of stalling the pipeline till the branch is resolved, or fetching again from the resolved address leads to too much of penalty. Branches are very frequent and not handling them effectively brings down the performance. We are also violating the principle of "Make common cases fast".

The second option is predicting about the behavior of branches. Branch Prediction is the ability to make an educated guess about which way a branch will go - will the branch be taken or not. First of all, we shall discuss about static prediction done by the compiler. This is based on typical branch behavior. For example, for loop and if statement branches, we can predict that backward branches will be taken and forward branches will not be taken. So, there are primarily three methods adopted. They are:

- Predict not taken approach:
  - Assume that the branch is not taken, i.e. the condition will not evaluate to be true.
- Predict taken approach:
  - Assume that the branch is taken, i.e. the condition will evaluate to be true.
- Delayed branching:
  - A more effective solution.

In the predict not taken approach, treat every branch as "not taken". Remember that the registers are read during ID, and we also perform an equality test to decide whether to branch or not. We simply load in the next instruction (PC+4) and continue. The complexity arises when the branch evaluates to be true and we end up needing to actually take the branch. In such a case, the pipeline is cleared of any code loaded from the "not-taken" path, and the execution continues.

In the predict-taken approach, we assume that the branch is always taken. This method will work for processors that have the target address computed in time for the IF stage of the next instruction so there is no delay, and the condition alone may not be evaluated. This will not work for the MIPS architecture with a 5-stage pipeline. Here, the branch target is computed during the ID cycle or later and the condition is also evaluated in the same clock cycle.

The third approach is the delayed branching approach. In this case, an instruction that is useful and not dependent on whether the branch is taken or not is inserted into the pipeline. It is the job of the compiler to determine the delayed branch instructions. The slots filled up by instructions which may or may not get executed, depending on the outcome of the branch, are called the branch delay slots. The compiler has to fill these slots with useful/independent instructions. It is easier for the compiler if there are less number of delay slots. There are three different ways of introducing instructions in the delay slots:

- Before branch instruction.
- From the target address: Only valuable when branch taken.
- From fall through: Only valuable when branch is not taken.
- Cancelling branches allow more slots to be filled.

Figure shows the three different ways of filling in instructions in the branch delay slots. When the first choice is taken, the branch must not depend on the rescheduled instructions and there will always be performance improvement, irrespective of which way the branch goes. When instructions are picked from the target path, the compiler predicts that the branch is going to take. It must be alright to execute rescheduled instructions even if the branch is not taken. That is, the work may be wasted, but the program will still execute correctly. This may need duplication of instructions. There will be improvement in performance only when the branch is taken. When the branch is not taken, the extra instructions may increase the code size. When instructions are picked from the fall through path, the compiler predicts that the branch is not going to take. It must be alright to execute rescheduled instructions even if the branch is taken. This may lead to improvement in performance only if the branch is not taken. The extra instructions added as compensatory code may be an overhead.

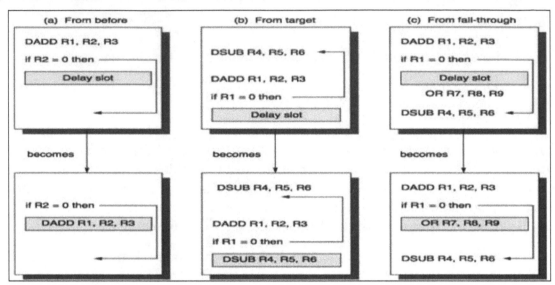

The limitations on delayed-branch scheduling arise from (1) the restrictions on the instructions that are scheduled into the delay slots and (2) our ability to predict at compile time whether a branch is likely to be taken or not. If the compiler is not able to find useful instructions, it may fill up the slots with nops, which is not a good option.

To improve the ability of the compiler to fill branch delay slots, most processors with conditional branches have introduced a cancelling or nullifying branch. In a cancelling branch, the instruction includes the direction that the branch was predicted. When the branch behaves as predicted, the instruction in the branch delay slot is simply executed as it would normally be with a delayed branch. When the branch is incorrectly predicted, the instruction in the branch delay slot is simply turned into a no-op. Examples of such branches are Cancel-if-taken or Cancel-if-not-taken branches. In such cases, the compiler need not be too conservative in filling the branch delay slots, because it knows that the hardware will cancel the instruction if the branch behavior goes against the prediction. The pipeline speedup is given by,

$$\text{Pipeline speedup} = \frac{\text{Pipeline depth}}{1 + \text{Pipeline stall CPI}}$$

$$= \frac{\text{Pipeline depth}}{1 + \text{Branch frequency} \times \text{Branch penalty}}$$

Let us look at an example to calculate the speedup, given the following: 14% Conditional & Unconditional, 65% Taken; 52% Delay slots not usefully filled. The details for the various schemes are provided in the table.

Scheduling Scheme	Branch Penalty	CPI	Pipeline Speedup	Speedup vs Stall
Stall Pipeline	3.00	1.42	3.52	1.00
Predict taken	1.00	1.14	4.39	1.25
Predict not taken	1.00	1.09	4.58	1.30
Delayed branch	0.52	1.07	4.66	1.32

- Stall: 1+.14(branches)*3(cycle stall).

- Taken: 1+.14(branches)*(.65(taken)*1(delay to find address)+.35(not taken)*1(penalty)).

- Not taken: 1+.14*(.65(taken)*1+[.35(not taken)*0]).

- Delayed: 1+.14*(.52(not usefully filled)*1).

Given an application where 20% of the instructions executed are conditional branches and 59% of those are taken. For the MIPS 5-stage pipeline, what speedup will be achieved using a scheme where all branches are predicted as taken over a scheme with no branch prediction (i.e. branches will always incur a 1 cycle penalty)? Ignore all other stalls.

- CPI with no branch prediction:

  $0.8 \times 1 + 0.2 \times 2 = 1.2$

- CPI with branch prediction:

  $0.8 \times 1 + 0.2 \times 0.59 \times 1 + 0.2 \times 0.41 \times 2 = 1.082$

- Speed up = 1.2 / 1.082 = 1.109.

We want to compare the performance of two machines. Which machine is faster?

- Machine A: Dual ported memory - so there are no memory stalls.

- Machine B: Single ported memory, but its pipelined implementation has a 1.05 times faster clock rate.

Assume:

- Ideal CPI = 1 for both,

- Loads are 40% of instructions executed.

SpeedUp_A = Pipeline Depth/(1 + 0) × $(\text{clock}_{unpipe}/\text{clock}_{pipe})$

   = Pipeline Depth

SpeedUp_B = Pipeline Depth/(1 + 0.4 × 1) × $(\text{clock}_{unpipe}/(\text{clock}_{unpipe} / 1.05))$

   = (Pipeline Depth/1.4) x 1.05

   = 0.75 × Pipeline Depth

SpeedUp_A / SpeedUp_B = Pipeline Depth / (0.75 x Pipeline Depth) = 1.33

Machine A is 1.33 times faster.

Branch Prediction

Branch prediction is used to overcome the fetch limitation imposed by control hazards in order to expose instruction-level parallelism (ILP), the key ingredient to pipelined and superscalar architectures that mask instruction execution latencies by exploiting (ILP). Branch prediction can be thought of as a sophisticated form of prefetching or a limited form of data prediction that attempts to predict the result of branch instructions so that a processor can speculatively fetch across basic-block boundaries. Once a prediction is made, the processor can speculatively execute instructions depending on the predicted outcome of the branch. If branch prediction rates are high enough to offset mis-prediction penalties, the processor will likely have a better overall performance. Without branch prediction, such a processor must stall whenever there are unresolved branch instructions. Since on average 20 percent of instructions are branches, this imposes a substantial penalty on the performance of such processors. Many branch prediction schemes have been proposed. This work uses selected benchmark programs from the SPEC95 to compare several well-known branch prediction schemes.

The branch prediction schemes chosen for this comparison are statically taken/not-taken, bimodal, branch history table (BHT), combination, correlation, two-level adaptive (TLA), skewed, and gshare branch prediction schemes. Metrics for the various schemes were generated with the sim-inorder simulator from the SimpleScalar tool suite. Implementation of these schemes included various modifications to the bpred.c, bpred.h and sim-inorder.c files.

In order to explain Dynamic Branch Prediction, one has to differentiate it from Static Branch Prediction. Static Branch Prediction in general is a prediction that uses information that was gathered before the execution of the program. The simplest predictors are to predict that the branch is always taken (MIPS-X, Stanford) or to predict that the branch is always not taken (Motorola MC88000). Another way is to run the program with a profiler and some training input data predict the branch direction which was most frequently taken according to profiling. This prediction can be indicated by a hint bit in the branch opcode.

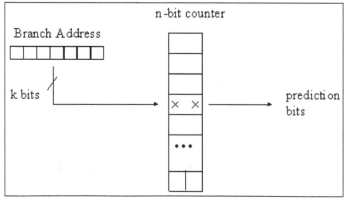

One-Level Branch Predictor.

Dynamic Branch Prediction on the other hand uses information about taken or not taken branches gathered at run-time to predict the outcome of a branch. There are several dynamic branch predictor in use or being researched nowadays. Those include One-Level Branch Predictors, Two-Level Branch Predictors and Multiple Component Branch Predictors.

For One-Level Branch Prediction, in the simple case of direct mapping and just the branch address as information source, one takes k least significant bits of the branch instruction address in order to map it to an entry of a single column table with 2^k entries. Each entry consists in general of a n-bit counter, which is designed as a saturated counter in most cases. A saturated counter works like this: each time the branch is taken the counter is incremented; if the maximum value is already reached, nothing is done. Each time the branch is not taken the counter is decremented; if the minimum value = 0 is reached it stays the same.

The prediction works now after this principle: If the value of the counter is below 2^{n-1}, the branch is predicted as not taken, otherwise the branch is predicted as taken.

Various Features

Mapping

Direct mapping, as explained above, uses the least significant k bits of branch instruction's address. This is the simplest and fastest mapping method and requires the least hardware cost. The table size, however, has to be chosen carefully. If it is too large, only a small part of the buffer will be used. If it is too small, many mappings to the same location will occur.

Fully associative mapping uses tags associated with each table entry such that with the help of the k least significant bits and this tag each entry can be uniquely associated with the same branch instruction. The search gets more complicated on the other hand, especially the comparisons of the tags take a lot of time and hardware, but the table can be used more efficiently as the entries do not have to be ordered in any way. Various replacement strategies in the case of a full table are possible, like "least recently used" or "first in first out". If the outcome of a branch is to be predicted and no table entry matches the branch instruction address, a default predictor has to be used.

Set associative mapping is a combination of the two mappings above. The branch address is directly mapped to sets of multiple table entries, and within those sets the entries are searched fully associative. This is a good compromise of the positive aspects of the different mappings.

Apart from that, the branch instruction address can also be mapped by using Hashing, i.e. a so called "hash function" is used to do the mapping. This function can be chosen pretty arbitrarily using i least significant bits of the branch address. The goal is to distribute the mappings as equally and efficiently over the whole table, avoiding overlapping as much as possible.

N-bit Counter

- 1-bit counter: A 1-bit counter records the last outcome of the branch. This is the simplest version possible, though not very effective.

- 2-bit counter: This is the most commonly used counter. It combines affordable costs with good predictions. It can, for example, predict the outcome of loop branches effectively: During the loop, the loop branch is always predicted as taken, of course. At the last iteration of the loop, it predicts wrongly, but the 2-bit saturated counter is only set back from strongly taken to weakly taken, meaning that at the next entry of the loop the loop branch will again be predicted to be taken, which is then correct, and so on. So only one false prediction occurs.

Buffersize

The Buffersize varies according to the number of bits taken from the branch address for the mapping. Typical are buffersizes from 256 to 4K entries.

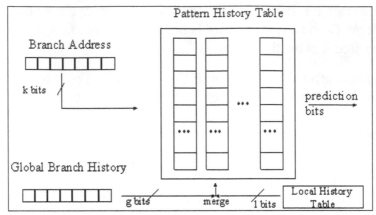

Two-Level Branch Predictor.

The Two-Level Branch Predictor, also referred to as Correlation-Based Branch Predictor, uses a two-dimensional table of counters, also called "Pattern History Table". It was introduced by Yeh and Patt who because of the fact that the outcome of the branch depends not only on the branch address but also on the outcome of other recent branches (inter branch correlation) and a longer history of the same branch itself (intra branch correlation). The table entries are two-bit counters. So in order to predict the branch outcome and choose a table entry, we have:

Three Information Sources

The Branch Address was mentioned before. It uses k least significant bits of branch instruction address. A Global Branch History is a shift register in which the outcome of any branch is stored. A "one" is stored for a taken branch and a "zero" for a non-taken one. The register is shifted through while storing the newest value. In order to address the table, the n last branch outcomes are considered.

The Local History Table is a table of shift registers of the sort of a global branch history. Each shift register, however, refers to the last outcomes of one single branch. Since this local history table is accessed as a one-level branch prediction table, it is not guaranteed that no overlapping of the branches occurs, and in one shift register may be stored the information of different branches.

Since the table has only two dimensions, two of the three information sources have to be selected to access rows and columns. Another method is to merge two sources to one, which will be covered later.

Alternatively to the two-dimensional table as shown in figure, it is also possible to employ a local history table and map the last k entries of the respective shift register to a one-dimensional Global Pattern History Table, that means that each same pattern of the last branch outcomes is mapped onto the same table entry, regardless of the actual branch address. As a matter-of-fact, this is the original correlation-based branch predictor suggested by Yeh and Patt, is also referred to as Yeh's Algorithm and has been proven to be very successful.

In general it can be stated that a two-level branch predictor is more accurate than a one-level branch predictor, but this advantage is also associated with the disadvantage of a more costly implementation and the fact that the so called Warm Up Phase, i.e. the time the table entries contain usable values, is much longer.

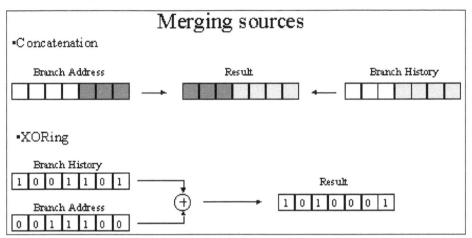

The merging of sources.

The merging of sources can happen in many ways, but two are most common: Concatenation and XORing. Considering figure, both are pretty self-explanatory. In the case of concatenation, simply some k bits of one register are taken and another m-k from the second one, assuming that the result is supposed to have m bits. Both are then concatenated into one.

For XORing, the bits of the two source registers are bitwise XORed with another to form the result. Experimental results have shown that XORing yields the better results, which means that it reduces aliasing in respect to concatenation.

Problems

Aliasing

What was until now referred to as overlapping of the mappings of different branch addresses to the same branch history table entry is actually called Aliasing. Aliasing is due to a limited table size, such that there are more branch instruction addresses than table entries. Due to their nature, aliasing occurs only with direct mapping and hashing, but not with fully associative mapping. A trade-off has to be made between aliasing and affordable table size.

In general, aliasing does not necessarily mean that the number of correct branch predictions is reduced. It is even possible that aliasing improves the correct prediction rate. In this case this is called Constructive Aliasing. If it actually reduces the correct prediction rate one speaks of Destructive Aliasing, and if aliasing does not affect branch prediction at all, it is referred to as Harmless Aliasing.

Context Switches

When several processes are using one processor, then the act of storing the variables of the currently running process, suspending it and switching over to the next process is called a Context

Switch. The reason this effects branch prediction lies in the fact that all Pattern History Tables, Branch History Tables or whatever was used are likely to be flushed. This means that the next time the process is running again all this information has to be collected again in order to allow a reliable branch prediction. During this Warm Up Phase the performance of such history-based predictors is decreased significantly, and a simpler branch predictor that uses a smaller history or none at all (like Always Taken) usually yield better results.

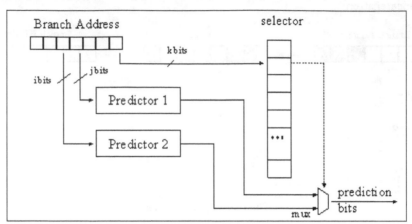

Hybrid Branch Predictor.

A Hybrid Branch Predictor as proposed by McFarling is built by taking two branch predictors that work independently from each other and a selector that chooses which branch prediction to take. The selector consists of a table of 2-bit counters and is mapped to by the k least significant bits of the branch instruction address.

The updating of all the Branch History tables involved with the predictors and the selector works as follows. As both predictors operate independently they are also updated independently. The selector however is updated according to the table shown below:

Predictor 1	Predictor 2	Update to Selector
correct	correct	no change
correct	incorrect	increment
incorrect	correct	decrement
incorrect	incorrect	no change

The idea is to store the success of the predictors. An evaluation can only be done if the predictors suggest different branch directions, though. If they predict the same, no change is made. The selection is made by choosing predictor 1 if the selector entry has a value of 2 or 3, and predictor 2 is taken of values 0 or 1.

The reason for coming up with such a hybrid branch predictor comes from the observation that some branch predictors perform well with one sort of programs, i.e. floating-point programs containing a lot of loops, but bad with others where different branch predictors are more successful. To avoid the negative effect of context switches it is also a good idea to combine a branch predictor with a large history table with another predictor with a small or no history table. Thus with the help of a hybrid branch predictor it is possible to exploit the different properties of the single-scheme components for a better overall performance.

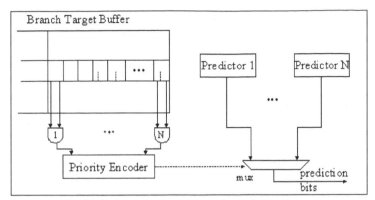

Multiple Component Hybrid Branch Predictor.

The multiple component hybrid branch predictor is a generalization of the hybrid branch predictor and was suggested by Patt. Here N independent branch predictors are combined, thus allowing to combine general predictors that yield acceptable success rates for all programs with specialized predictors designed for special applications. The result is a branch predictor that performs well on most kinds of programs without having to change anything.

The tricky thing lies in the selection of one of the N predictors. One table with 2-bit counters is obviously not sufficient any more. So to perform the selection, adds N 2-bit counters to each entry in the Branch Target Buffer which are then called Predictor Selection Counters. For each new entry in the Branch Target Buffer, all Predictor Selection Counters are initialized to 3.

The predictor to be selected is the one with value 3 in its respective Predictor Selection Counter. If there are more than one predictor with value 3, as in the beginning, a Priority Encoder decides statically which of the predictors to take.

The Predictor Selection Counters are updated by decrementing the counters for all predictors that made an incorrect prediction if one of the predictors with value 3 made a correct prediction. Otherwise all predictors that predicted correctly are incremented. This system guarantees that always one Predictor Selection Counter will be 3. It is also more accurate than a saturated counter: A predictor which was correct for the last 5 times can be differentiated from one that was correct for the last 4 times.

• 2bC
→ 2K entry array of 2-bit counters
• GAs
→ m global history bits, n pattern history tables
• PSg
→ 2K m-bit branch history table, single pattern history table (static)
• gshare
→ m global history bits, XOR with BA, single pattern history table
• pshare
→ 2K m-bit branch hist. table, XOR with BA, single pattern history table
• loop
→ AVG predictor, counts # of iterations of previous loops
• Always Taken and Always Not Taken

Component Predictors involved.

If the time needed for the selection seems to be a bottleneck of the system, it is also possible to compute the predictor to be chosen before the branch instruction is fetched and store it in the Branch Target Buffer, reducing the necessary selection time to the multiplexer operation time.

Figure shows a brief overview of the component predictors. As one can see there is a great variety involved. The loop predictor for example counts the number of iterations a loop takes and with the help of this predicts the number of iterations the loop will take the next time, while Always Taken is the most simple branch predictor but quite effective after a context switch.

In order to choose the priorities of the predictors thorough test runs are necessary: All predictors have to be tested with a variety of test programs, and the parameters for the predictors have to be varied, too. This Multiple Component Hybrid Branch Predictor has yielded better results as all other known branch predictors, with the overall size of it being equal to that of the competitive branch predictors.

Branch Classification

Another approach to improve branch prediction rate is to classify branches statically. This means that the program is run with a profiler and some input data to determine the probability of a branch to be taken or not taken. The branches are basically divided in two classes:

- Uni-Direction Branches are branches with a probability to be taken between 0% and 10%, that means the branch is likely not to be taken, or between 90% and 100% which indicates a branch that is mostly taken.

- Mixed-Direction Branches are the branches in between with a probability to be taken between 10% and 90%.

Within those two classes subdivision are can be made to differentiate the branches further. The idea is then to find suitable branch predictors for each class of branches. It turned out that the most successful approach is to apply a static profiler-guided branch predictor with the uni-direction branches and a dynamic hybrid branch predictor for the remaining mixed-direction branches.

Implementations

Finally an overview over the branch prediction schemes implemented in some current machines is provided:

- The PowerPC604 has a 64 entry fully associative Branch Target Buffer for predicting the Branch Target Address and a decoupled direct mapped 512 entry Pattern History Table.

- The PowerPC620 has a 256 entry two-way set associative Branch Target Buffer for predicting the Branch Target Address and a decoupled direct mapped branch prediction buffer.

- The UltraSPARC is reported to have a 2-bit branch prediction scheme.

- The Intel Pentium contains a 256 entry 4-way set associative Branch Target Buffer. Coupled with each Branch Target Buffer entry is a 2-bit branch predictor that is responsible for the branch prediction. This is a simple One-Level Branch Predictor.

- The Intel Pentium Pro works with a 512 entry 4-way set associative Branch Target Buffer. Coupled with each Branch Target Buffer entry is in this case a 4-bit local branch history.

Implemented Branch Prediction Methods

The Environment

We implemented a number of branch prediction methods, benchmarked them, and analyzed the results. The environment included ECE instructional machines running under Linux OS. In order to implement branch prediction schemes, we used SimpleScalar simulator. SimpleScalar simulator uses its own abstract instruction set (RISC ISA, similar to MIPS) to simulate programs in the superscalar environment. This simulator allows in-order and out-of-order instruction execution. It allows multiple instructions to be fetched, decoded, issued, executed, and committed in one clock cycle. In other words, SimpleScalar simulator simulates truly superscalar execution model, similar to many common superscalar microprocessors. It is also able to incorporate a branch prediction. Its package includes C compiler (gcc) which allows compiling C programs into SimpleScalar ISA to be run on this simulator. Important observation is that each branch misprediction costs 2 cycles of penalty. However, we didn't consider the influence of prediction rates on running time (# cycles to execute n instructions, or IPC). We just looked on prediction rates of different schemes. But, because of high average percentage of branch instructions (about 22% on average), mis-prediction costs can tremendously decrease IPC.

Implemented Methods

Always Untaken and Always Taken

Always untaken scheme just constantly returns the address of the next instruction. Always taken scheme uses branch target address buffer (BTA buffer) to store and re-use target addresses. Each time the branch is resolved, the corresponding target address is stored in the BTA cache. The next time, "always taken" scheme always predicts the branch outcome as taken, retrieves the corresponding branch target address from this cache, and uses this address to fetch the next instruction.

Decode History Table (DHT)

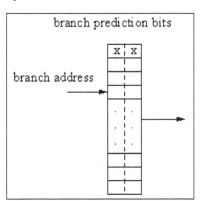

Direct history table (DHT), also called bimodal predictor, is the simplest branch prediction method which uses the address of the branch instruction to index the global table of prediction bits. Usually, low bits of the address are used to index directly into the table entry. Then branch prediction bits are used to predict branch outcome. When the branch outcome is actually known, the corresponding entry in this table is updated. This method is the cheapest in terms of hardware.

Number of bits(order) = $2 \times 2^{(order)}$

Branch History Table (BHT)

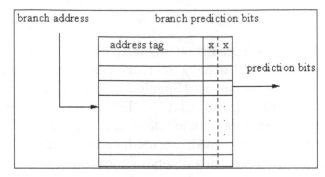

Branch history table method (BHT) is similar to DHT, except that it uses the tagged structure. Each entry in the table, in addition to prediction bits, contains the address of the branch instruction. It introduces the concept of hit and miss. In this scheme, after an entry is referenced (indexed by the address of the branch instruction), its tag is compared against the address of the branch instruction. If it matches, hit occurs and the predictions bits from this entry are used to predict the branch outcome. Otherwise, miss happens, and the branch is predicted as not taken. This method effectively removes all aliasing, so any branch prediction bits, associated with one branch instruction, cannot be affected by another branch instruction (except that a branch instruction can force an entry associated with another branch instruction to be removed). In addition, we have implemented the fully associative array which allows searching the whole table for the matching tag. Least frequently used replacement algorithm has been used here. However, this implementation didn't create any performance advantage over the directly mapped tagged table; as a result, it was abandoned.

Number of bits (order) = $(2 + 32)\ ' \ 2^{(order)}$

Combination of DHT-BHT

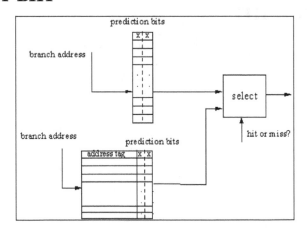

This scheme is a combination of the previous two schemes. This scheme accesses BHT, and, if there is a hit, it uses prediction bits from BHT to predict the branch outcome. Otherwise, DHT is indexed and prediction bits are retrieved from the corresponding entry of DHT. If hit occurs, DHT is not updated after the branch outcome is known. The main advantage of this scheme is that we can make DHT much larger than BHT because of its low hardware requirements.

Number of bits (order1, order2) = $2\ ' \ 2^{(order1)} + (2 + 32)\ ' \ 2^{(order2)}$

Correlation-based Prediction

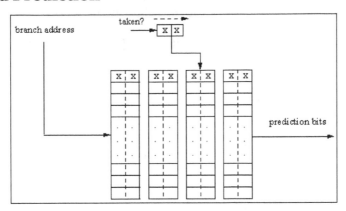

Correlation-based prediction scheme differs from previously described ones in the way that the branch outcome is thought to depend not only on this branch's previous behavior, but also on the behavior of previously executed branches in the instruction stream. The behavior of branches in the instruction stream is recorded in the global shift register. If a branch is taken, 1 is inserted into the shift register and the shift register is shifted; if untaken - 0 is inserted into the shift register and the shift register is shifted. The table of prediction bits is two-dimensional. The row is selected by the low bits of the address of the branch instruction, and the column is selected by the value in the shift register. The underlining idea behind this scheme is that the behavior of a branch can correlate with the behavior of other branches. This scheme has large hardware requirements in comparison to one-level predictors.

Number of bits (order, history bits) = (2) $'$ $2^{(order + history bits)}$

Two-level Adaptive Prediction

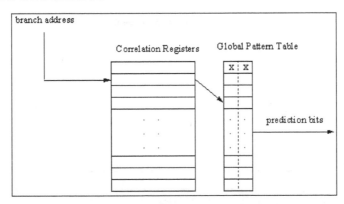

Two-level adaptive prediction scheme (also referred as the Yeh algorithm), like the previously described method, also contains history information of the previous branch outcomes. But this information is local and kept in correlation registers. For each branch, there is an associated correlation register, and the pattern of the branch history is stored there. Based on this pattern, a particular entry in the global pattern table (GPT) is accessed. The corresponding correlation register and the corresponding entry in GPT are updated each time a branch is resolved. Any entry in GPT can be shared by several branches. In order to lookup, we index the table by the low bits of the address of the branch instruction to find the corresponding correlation register, and use its value to index GPT to get the appropriate prediction bits. This scheme has reasonable hardware requirements which are much lower that of the correlation-based predictor.

Number of bits (order, correlation bits) = (correlation bits) $'$ $2^{(order)}$ + (2) $'$ $2^{(correlation\ bits)}$

Skewed Branch Predictor

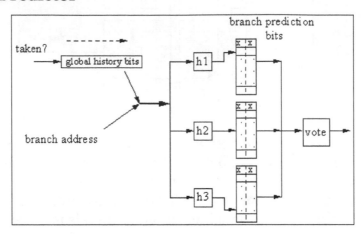

Skewed branch predictor uses the global history, like correlation-based scheme. It takes global history bits and the address of the branch instruction, and uses this information to index three separate arrays of branch prediction bits. Three different hash functions are used to index these tables (each hash function indexes its own table). Then, these three sets of prediction bits are obtained and three branch outcomes are computed based on each set. Voting by majority is used to make the final prediction. During the update, this method updates all three tables. By Michard, at al., good choice of hash functions can eliminate almost all aliasing. The hardware requirements are small, just three times the hardware requirements for the bimodal predictor.

Number of bits (order, history bits) = 3 $'$ (2) $'$ $2^{(order\ after\ hashing)}$

Gshare Scheme

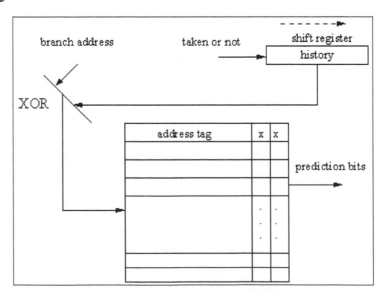

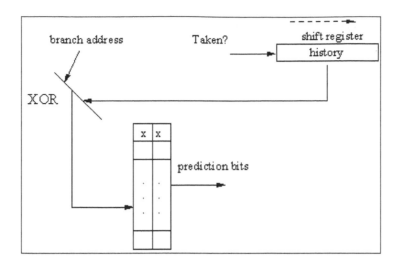

Gshare scheme is similar to bimodal predictor or branch history table. However, like correlation-based prediction, this method records history of branches into the shift register. Then, it uses the address of the branch instruction and branch history (shift register) to XOR's them together. The result is used to index the table of prediction bits. Implementation can use either tagged or tagless tables. In the tagged table, we compare the indexed entry with a tag and, if they don't match, we just predict as not taken. If they match, we use the corresponding prediction bits to predict the branch outcome. In the tagless implementation, the table is just directly indexed and the corresponding prediction bits are used to predict the branch outcome. We have tried both these methods, and found that tagless table performs better. We just index an entry and use its contents (prediction bits) to predict the branch outcome. The hardware requirements with tagless table are the same as for the bimodal predictor.

Number of bits(order, history) = (2) $'$ $2^{\text{(order after hashing)}}$

Original Implementation

After we implemented all these methods, we tried to look on some new approaches and improvements. We didn't reinvent the wheel and we just slightly modified the best scheme. The best scheme happened to be the two-level adaptive predictor. We modified it to shift both taken? bit and correct? bit (whether the prediction was correct) into the correlation register.

Number of bits(order, correlation bits) = (correlation bits) $'$ $2^{\text{(order)}}$ + (2) $\times$ $2^{\text{(correlation bits)}}$

Storing the Branch Target Addresses: BTA Buffer

We were concerned with the correct prediction of the branch outcome. If we predict the branch as untaken, we just fetch the next instruction. However, if we predict the branch as taken, we need somehow to figure out the branch target address before it is actually calculated. In order to solve this problem, we use the cache for branch target addresses (BTA). Each time the branch outcome and BTA are calculated, while updating predictor's data (prediction bits and, sometimes, history bits), we can also store BTA in a cache, called BTA buffer. We will call it BTA instead of BTB (as some implementations call it) because some implementations even store the target instruction (used for branch folding).

Direct-mapped Cache Implementation

The first implementation of BTA was straightforward: use the table of pairs - tag (the address of branch instruction) and branch target address, and index these pairs by using low bits of the address of the branch instruction. If tag matches the address of the branch instruction, it is a hit, and we use the corresponding BTA. Otherwise, it is a miss, and we use zero for BTA.

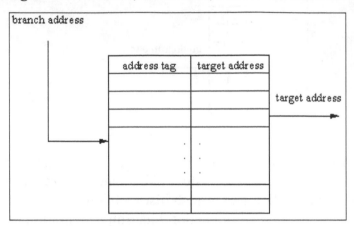

N-ways Set-associative Cache Implementation

However this direct mapped cache is not very efficient. It requires too large size to produce "reasonable" good hit rates. As a result, we have implemented n-ways set-associative cache for BTA buffer.

The address of the branch instruction is used to index the table (low bits). Each entry contains a list of <tag, BTA> pairs. The cache simultaneously searches for the matching tag. If it finds it, it returns the corresponding BTA (hit). If not, it returns 0 (miss). Cyclic (LIFO) replacement policy was used to implement the replacement of the BTA. Counters are associated with each entry to implement the replacement strategy.

BTA with associativity > 1 proved to be very effective, comparing to the direct mapped cache with the same number of entries (1-way cache uses k entries, and n-ways set-associative cache uses k/n entries for comparison).

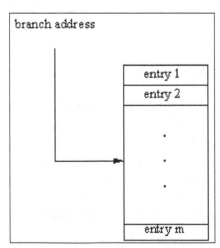

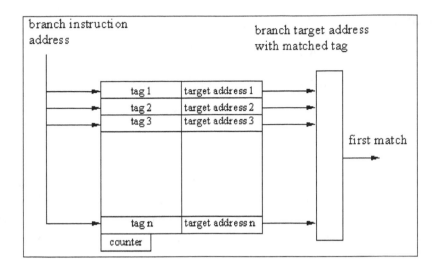

Implementation Issues

After implementation, we could see several implementation issues which are important to consider:

- Branch prediction bits table size.
- Number of prediction bits in each entry.
- BTA cache size.
- Non-associative vs. associative cache for BTA.
- Associativity of BTA.
- Fully associative array of branch prediction bits vs. direct mapped array (in BHT).
- Branch prediction bits update policy.
- BTA buffer update policy (always update or only when the branch is taken).
- Number of history bits in the shift register.
- DFA's for changing the prediction bits states.
- Hash function choice: take low bits of branch instruction address or use more complicated operations.
- How to combine history bits and PC:
  - Concatenate.
  - XOR.

DFA's for Prediction Bits

In addition several different DFA's have been implemented to update prediction bits. There are:

- 1-bit scheme.

- 2-bit saturating counter.

- 2-bit saturating counter with taken shortcut.

- 2-bit saturating counter with taken and not taken shortcuts.

- 2-bit taken bias where three of the states represent taken.

Simulation Platform

The simulation platform was a Pentium Pro 200 running Linux. This platform is acceptable for generating branch prediction statistics. The simulation can execute one million branch instructions between one and five minutes simulation time depending on the processor load and the percentage of branch instructions in a program relative to non-branch instructions.

The branch prediction software has been implemented for the sim-inorder executable. Sim-inorder was used because of our ability to modify the program without compromising program functionality or stability. Shown below are the command line options for the simulator:

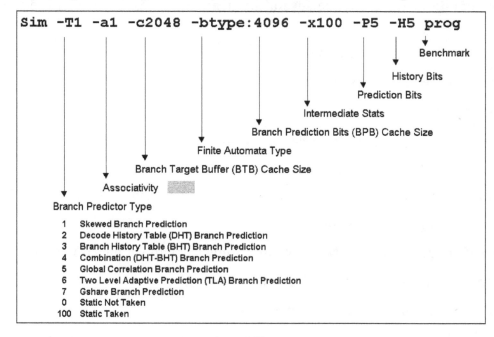

As you can see, the simulator has a number of command line options. The command line options are as follows:

Option	Option
-T*n*	Predictor Type. This option lets the user select the branch predictor type for the simulation. There are currently nine branch predictor types implemented within this software:
	1 Skewed Branch Prediction,
	2 Decode History Table (DHT) Branch Prediction,
	3 Branch History Table (BHT) Branch Prediction,
	4 Combination (DHT-BHT) Branch Prediction,
	5 Global Correlation Branch Prediction,

	6 Two Level Adaptive Prediction (TLA) Branch Prediction, 7 Gshare Branch Prediction, 0 Static Not Taken, 100 Static Taken.
-an	Associativity. This option allows the user to adjust the BTB associativity. Setting n to a value of one will make the BTB non-associative. Making the n value greater than one will make the cache n-way set associative. Keep in mind that making the cache associative can make the cache consume large amounts of memory during simulation. Increasing n beyond reasonable limits will cause the software to run out of memory during the simulation.
-cn	BTB Cache Size. This option sets the size of the Branch Table buffer. This number must be a power of 2. If this number is not a power of 2 the simulation will not execute.
-bn:m	BPB Cache Size and Automata Type. The variable n sets the automata type for the prediction bits. There are four automata type implemented on the simulator: 2B2SC, 2BTS, 2BTB, 2B. These are a follows: • 2B2SC - 2 Bit with Dual Short Cut. • 2BTS - 2 Bit with Taken Short Cut. • 2BTB - 2 Bit with Taken Bias. • 2B - 2 Bit Saturating Counter. The m variable sets the size of the Branch Prediction Bits buffer size. This number must be a power of 2. If this number is not a power of 2 the simulation will not execute.
-xn	Intermediate Statistics. This option will force the simulator to output intermediate prediction rates every 100 branch instructions when n is non-zero. If this option is not input to the simulator or n is set to zero there will be no intermediate output.
-Pn	Prediction Bits. This option allows the user to set the number of prediction bits used per cache entry. If this option is used and n is set to any number other than 2 bits, an n-bit saturating counter will be used as the automata type.
-Hn	History Bits. This option allows the user to set the number of history bits (Global or Local depending on the predictor type). Keep in mind that large values of n will have large memory requirements for the simulation. If the simulator runs low on memory, it will terminate.

Additional things that should be considered when using this executable are as follows:

- When using the command line options for branch prediction, use the -b option last in the series of options, because it initializes the branch predictor. If other branch prediction options are set after the -b option, they will not be updated and the variables will use their default values.

- You must use the -b option in order to initialize the software correctly. If the -b option is not used, the simulation will not initialize correctly and as a result, the prediction statistics will be incorrect.

- Keep in mind of the approximate memory requirements for the options set. It is easy to create simulations that require more memory than is available to the simulator.

Once these points are kept in mind it is easy to generate scripts that will execute multiple simulations and generate output files. The following script will run a number of Spec95 benchmarks for a given predictor type and generate a Matlab compatible output file that can used to view initial results:

```
sim-inorder -T$1 -a4 -c16 -b16 gcc1 spec/test.c

sim-inorder -T$1 -a4 -c16 -b16 ijpeg -image_data specmun.ppm

sim-inorder -T$1 -a4 -c16 -b16 swim < swim.in

sim-inorder -T$1 -a4 -c16 -b16 spec/hydro2d < hydro2d.in

sim-inorder -T$1 -a4 -c16 -b16 spec/wave5 < wave5.in

sim-inorder -T$1 -a4 -c16 -b16 spec/turb3d < turb3d.in

sim-inorder -T$1 -a4 -c16 -b16 tomcatv < tomcatv.in

sim-inorder -T$1 -a4 -c16 -b16 compress95 < gcc1

sim-inorder -T$1 -a4 -c16 -b16 anagram words < input.txt
```

Statistics

The branch instruction outcome prediction accuracy is affected by many different variables. This paper attempts to focus on those main components individually. The components that will be focused on here are as follows:

- Cache Size.
- Cache Initialization Time.
- Hashing Technique.
- Prediction Bits.
- Deterministic Finite Automata.
- Associativity.
- History Bits.
- Prediction Scheme.
- Software.

Here we will focus on each of these components individually in an attempt to increase the overall prediction accuracy.

Cache Size

The overall cache size has a large effect on the overall prediction rates. When the cache is small, there is a large amount of aliasing into the cache. As a result, there is a lower overall cache hit rate when the cache size is small because many cache entries need to be victimized before they can contribute toward branch prediction. In addition, when there are more cache entries, there will less aliasing and less victimizing as a result of the larger cache size. In this condition, the branch prediction schemes should work well because there is a large amount of information available in the cache and it has a high probability of being the correct data because of the lower aliasing rates. Therefore, when as the cache size is increased, the overall prediction accuracy should increase. The prediction accuracy will eventually saturate because other variables such as the predictability of the program and its data will come into play. This behavior is shown in the following simulation where the cache size is swept from a cache size of 2^6 to a cache size of 2^18.

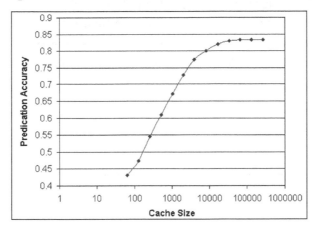

Cache Initialization

The cache initialization time will also affect the overall prediction rates. Every prediction scheme has a unique cache initialization time. This initialization time depends on a number of variables. One of the variables it is most dependent on is the size of the cache. A 4-way associative 16 entry cache is going to take approximately 4 times the as long as a 16 entry non-associative cache. At first glance, both caches appear to have 16 entries. One of the cache sizes in the previous example has 64 entries because of its 4-way associativity. As a result, the algorithm is going to take longer to initialize than the simple direct mapped 16-entry cache.

This problem of initialization is compounded by issues such as context switching. When the processor switches to another task or program, the cache is flushed. This is because the processor is starting a new task. If the cache was to use its current prediction bits, the prediction rates would be poor unless there is a correlation between the two tasks.

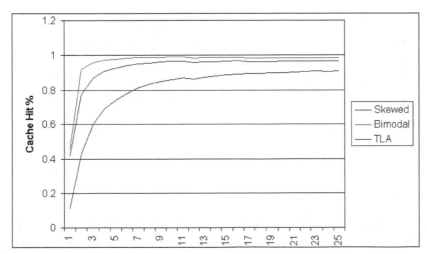

Shown above is a graph of the cache initialization algorithms for several prediction algorithms. As you can see Bimodal, the most simple algorithm, initializes itself within a few hundred cycles. Whereas, the Two Level Adaptive approach takes on the order of a few thousand cycles to initialize.

Hashing Technique

There are many different hashing techniques for branch prediction. One of the simplest techniques involves using the PC of the branch instruction. Then truncating off bits larger than the cache size. Therefore, if the design used a cache of 2^6, there would be 6 bits remaining after the truncation. After this truncation, the remaining 6 bits would be used to directly address the prediction bits. The truncation technique is shown here:

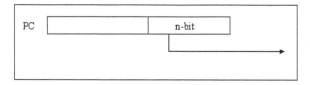

Here is another,

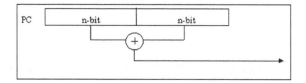

There is an unlimited number of hashing techniques. Creative hashing techniques use as much information as possible that is available at the time of the branch prediction for best results. The hashing technique is included into the prediction scheme. Therefore, the hashing technique used depends on the prediction type that used in the simulation.

Prediction Bits

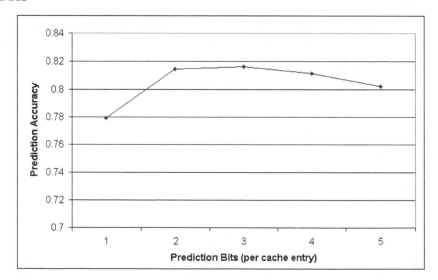

The number of prediction bits used per cache entry effects the branch prediction accuracy. The following graph depicts the prediction accuracy for different number of prediction bits. The state machine used for this simulation is an n-bit saturating counter. Some other standard state machines that can be include n-bit short cut, n-bit taken bias, n-bit taken short cut. As you can see, increasing the number of prediction bits does not necessarily improve the branch prediction accuracy. In the simulation, the highest prediction rates were found by using 3 prediction bits. Although, this number can vary greatly depending on the type of state machine you are running on those bits and also what benchmark, cache sizes, etc. The graph depicts decreasing prediction rates as prediction bits are increased. This is a result of using an n-bit saturating counter. It is possible to continue to increase the prediction accuracy as the number of prediction bits is increased. The designer must use creativity when designing the state machine (DFA) to use in accordance with the number of prediction bits.

Associativity

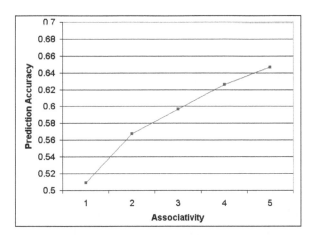

Simulations showed that using a smaller associative cache with approximately the same hardware requirements as a larger non-associative cache is a more effective branch prediction technique. The following graph shows how increasing the associativity will in turn increase the overall prediction accuracy. Below, I have shown a simulation, and varied the associativity of the cache. As you can see, as the associativity is increased, the prediction accuracy increases.

Deterministic Finite Automata

Deterministic Finite Automata (DFA) refers to the type of state machine architecture used on the prediction bits. There is an unlimited number of state machines that can be used with the prediction bits. It is important to obtain the best use of the limited number of prediction bits. Here we has implemented a number of DFA as listed below:

- n-Bit Saturating Counter.

- 2-Bit Short Cut.

- 2-Bit Taken Short Cut.

- 2-Bit Taken Bias.

These different state machines produce different prediction rates. Below I have shown a graph of DFA type vs. prediction accuracy. As you can see, the most common state machine 2-bit saturating counter predicts the outcome of the branches very well. It is also apparent that using a more creative scheme such as 2-bit taken short cut and 2-bit short cut can provide even better results. It's important to design the DFA scheme around the types of software that will be executed on the processor as well as the type of branch prediction method used.

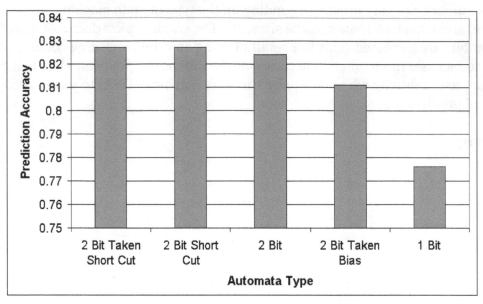

History Bits

Some prediction schemes attempt to retain additional information about the branch history in order to achieve a higher prediction accuracy. Two Level Adaptive prediction does just that by retaining local history bits. We have found that the prediction accuracy varies as a result of the number of history bits. Below I have shown a graph of the prediction accuracy as a function of the number of local history bits for TLA. As you can see, the prediction accuracy increases as a result of increasing the number of local history bits. Unfortunately, increasing the number of local history bits for this implementation increases the overall size of the cache and the complexity of the branch prediction unit.

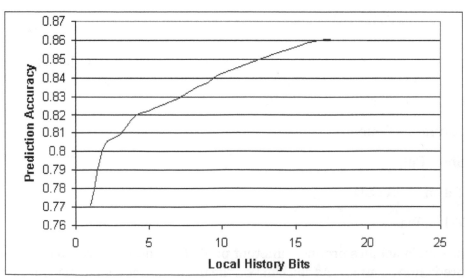

Prediction Scheme

Our group has implemented a number of branch prediction schemes. The schemes included into the modified `sim-inorder` software are:

- Static Predictor.

- Bimodal.

- Branch History Table (BHT).

- Combination.

- Correlation.

- Two Level Adaptive.

- Skewed.

- Gshare.

When designing branch prediction it is important to run many simulations. It is important to test prediction schemes is many environments. Some prediction schemes work very well in a given situation and then very poorly in another. Whereas, other prediction schemes have a well-rounded behavior below, we have shown all the branch prediction techniques simulated with the gcc Spec95 benchmark. As you can see, the prediction results greatly vary from one scheme to the next.

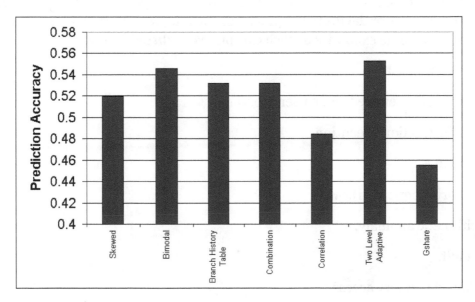

The Program and its Data

One of the most important factors in branch prediction accuracy is the type of software executed on the processor. Some software contains very predictable branches. Whereas other software contains very unpredictable branches. Also, the prediction accuracy depends on the type of data used as input to the software. Below I have shown all the Spec95 benchmarks simulated against a single bimodal predictor. As you can see, the prediction accuracy varies dramatically from one benchmark to the next.

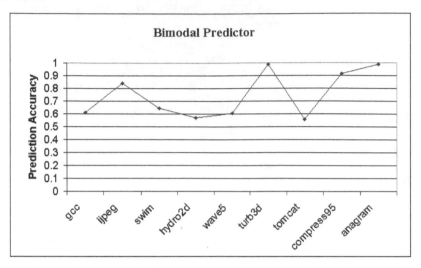

Exception Handling and Floating Point Pipelines

Exceptions or interrupts are unexpected events that require change in flow of control. Different ISAs use the terms differently. Exceptions generally refer to events that arise within the CPU, for example, undefined opcode, overflow, system call, etc. Interrupts point to requests coming from an external I/O controller or device to the processor. Dealing with these events without sacrificing performance is hard. Some examples of such exceptions are listed below:

- I/O device request.

- Invoking an OS service from a user program.

- Tracing instruction execution.

- Breakpoint.

- Integer arithmetic overflow.

- FP arithmetic anomaly.

- Page fault.

- Misaligned memory access.

- Memory protection violation.

- Using an undefined or unimplemented instruction.

- Hardware malfunctions.

- Power failure.

There are different characteristics for exceptions. They are as follows:

- Synchronous Vs Asynchronous:

  - Some exceptions may be synchronous, whereas others may be asynchronous. If the same exception occurs in the same place with the same data and memory allocation, then it is a synchronous exception. They are more difficult to handle.

  - Devices external to the CPU and memory cause asynchronous exceptions. They can be handled after the current instruction and hence easier than synchronous exceptions.

- User Requested Vs Coerced:

  - Some exceptions may be user requested and not automatic. Such exceptions are predictable and can be handled after the current instruction.

  - Coerced exceptions are generally raised by hardware and not under the control of the user program. They are harder to handle.

- User Maskable Vs Unmaskable:

  - Exceptions can be maskable or unmaskable. They can be masked or unmasked by a user task. This decides whether the hardware responds to the exception or not. You may have instructions that enable or disable exceptions.

- Within Vs between Instructions:

  - Exceptions may have to be handled within the instruction or between instructions. Within exceptions are normally synchronous and are harder since the instruction has to be stopped and restarted. Catastrophic exceptions like hardware malfunction will normally cause termination.

  - Exceptions that can be handled between two instructions are easier to handle.

- Resume Vs Terminate:

  - Some exceptions may lead to the program to be continued after the exception and some of them may lead to termination. Things are much more complicated if we have to restart.

  - Exceptions that lead to termination are much more easier, since we just have to terminate and need not restore the original status. Therefore, exceptions that occur within instructions and exceptions that must be re-startable are much more difficult to handle.

Exceptions are just another form of control hazard. For example, consider that an overflow occurs on the ADD instruction in the EX stage:

```
ADD $1, $2, $1
```

We have to basically prevent $1 from being written into, complete the previous instructions that did not have any problems, flush the ADD and subsequent instructions and handle the exception. This is somewhat similar to a mis-predicted branch and we can use much of the same hardware. Normally, once an exception is raised, we force a trap instruction into the pipeline on the next IF and turn off all writes for the faulting instruction and for all instructions that follow in the pipeline, until the trap is taken. This is done by placing zeros in the latches, thus preventing any state changes till the exception is handled. The exception-handling routine saves the PC of the faulting instruction in order to return from the exception later. But if we use delayed branching, it is not possible to re-create the state of the processor with a single PC because the instructions in the pipeline may not be sequentially related. So we need to save and restore as many PCs as the length of the branch delay plus one. This is pictorially depicted in Figure below.

```
Here's what happens on a data page fault
       1  2  3  4  5  6  7  8  9
i      F  D  X  M  W
i+1       F  D  X  M  W < page fault
i+2          F  D  X  M  W < squash
i+3             F  D  X  M  W < squash
i+4                F  D  X  M  W < squash
i+5    trap >           F  D  X  M  W
i+6    trap handler >      F  D  X  M  W
```

Once the exception has been handled, control must be transferred back to the original program in the case of a re-startable exception. ISAs support special instructions that return the processor from the exception by reloading the PCs and restarting the instruction stream. For example, MIPS uses the instruction RFE.

If the pipeline can be stopped so that the instructions just before the faulting instruction are completed and those after it can be restarted from scratch, the pipeline is said to have precise exceptions. Generally, the instruction causing a problem is prevented from changing the state. But, for some exceptions, such as floating-point exceptions, the faulting instruction on some processors writes its result before the exception can be handled. In such cases, the hardware must be equipped to retrieve the source operands, even if the destination is identical to one of the source operands. Because floating-point operations may run for many cycles, it is highly likely that some other instruction may have written the source operands. To overcome this, many recent processors have introduced two modes of operation. One mode has precise exceptions and the other (fast or performance mode) does not. The precise exception mode is slower, since it allows less overlap among floating point instructions. In some high-performance CPUs, including Alpha 21064, Power2, and MIPS R8000, the precise mode is often much slower (> 10 times) and thus useful only for debugging of codes.

Having looked at the general issues related to exceptions; let us now look at the MIPS architecture in particular. The exceptions that can occur in a MIPS pipeline are:

- IF – Page fault, misaligned memory access, memory protection violation.

- ID – Undefined or illegal opcode.

- EX – Arithmetic exception.

- MEM – Page fault on data, misaligned memory access, memory protection violation.

- WB – None.

In MIPS, exceptions are managed by a System Control Coprocessor (CP0). It saves the PC of the offending or interrupted instruction. A register called the Exception Program Counter (EPC) is used for this purpose. We should also know the cause of the exception. This gives an indication of the problem. MIPS uses a register called the Cause Register to record the cause of the exception. Let us assume two different types of exceptions alone, identified by one bit – undefined instruction = 0 and arithmetic overflow = 1. In order to handle these two registers, we will need to add two control signals EPCWrite and CauseWrite. Additionally, we will need a 1-bit control signal to set the low-order bit of the Cause register appropriately, say, signal IntCause. In the MIPS architecture, the exception handler address is 8000 0180.

The other way to handle exceptions is by Vectored Interrupts, where the handler address is determined by the cause. In a vectored interrupt, the address to which control is transferred is determined by the cause of the exception. For example, if we consider two different types of exceptions, we can define the two exception vector addresses as Undefined opcode: C0000000, Overflow: C0000020. The operating system knows the reason for the exception by the address at which it is initiated. To summarize, the instructions either deal with the interrupt, or jump to the real handler. This handler reads the cause and transfers control to the relevant handler which determines the action required. If it is a restartable exception, corrective action is taken and the EPC is used to return to the program. Otherwise, the program is terminated and error is reported. Figure below shows the MIPS pipeline with the EPC and Cause registers added and the exception handler address added to the multiplexor feeding the PC.

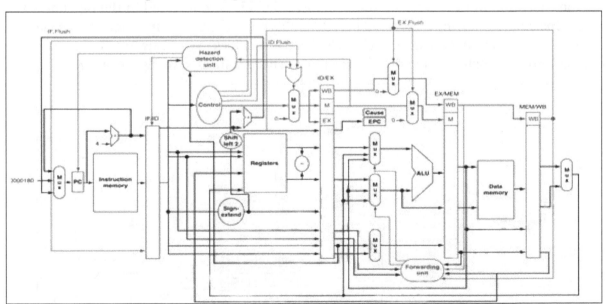

Let us look at an example scenario and discuss what happens in the MIPS pipeline when an exception occurs. Consider the following code snippet and assume that the add instruction raises an exception in the execution stage. This is illustrated in figure. During the 6th clock cycle, the add instruction is in the execution stage, the slt instruction is in the decode stage and the lw instruction is in the fetch stage.

```
40  sub $11, $2, $4

44  and $12, $2, $5

48  or  $13, $2, $6

4C add $1,  $2, $1

50  slt $15, $6, $7

54  lw  $16, 50($7)
```

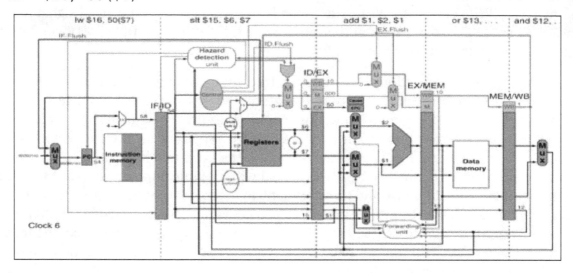

Once the exception in the execution stage is raised, bubbles are inserted in the pipeline starting from the instruction causing a problem, i.e. add in this case. The earlier instructions are allowed to proceed normally. During the next clock cycle, i.e. the 7th clock cycle, a sw $25, 1000($0) instruction is let into the pipeline to handle the exception. This is indicated in Figure below.

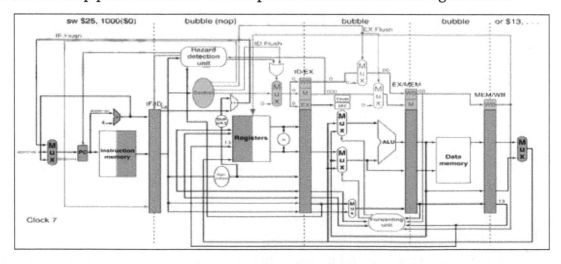

Another complication that we need to consider is the fact that multiple exceptions may occur simultaneously, say in the IF and MEM stage and also exceptions may happen out of order. The instruction in the earlier stage, say, IF may raise an exception and then an instruction in the EX stage may raise an exception. Since pipelining overlaps multiple instructions, we could have multiple exceptions at once and also out of order. However, exceptions will have to be handled in order. Normally, the hardware maintains a status vector and posts all exceptions caused by a given instruction in a status vector associated with that instruction. This exception status vector is carried along as the instruction moves down the pipeline. Once an exception indication is set in the exception status vector, any control signal that may cause a data value to be written is turned off (this includes both register writes and memory writes). Because a store can cause an exception during MEM, the hardware must be prepared to prevent the store from completing if it raises an exception. When an instruction enters the WB stage, the exception status vector is checked. If there are any exceptions posted, they are handled in the order in which they would occur in time on an unpipelined processor. Thus, the hardware always deals with the exception from the earliest instruction and if it is a terminating exception, flushes the subsequent instructions. This is how precise exceptions are maintained.

However, in complex pipelines where multiple instructions are issued per cycle, or those that lead to Out-of-order completion because of long latency instructions, maintaining precise exceptions is difficult. In such cases, the pipeline can just be stopped and the status including the cause of the exception is saved. Once the control is transferred to the handler, the handler will determine which instruction(s) had exceptions and whether each instruction is to be completed or flushed. This may require manual completion. This simplifies the hardware, but the handler software becomes more complex.

Apart from the complications caused by exceptions, there are also issues that the ISA can bring in. In the case of the MIPS architecture, all instructions do a write to the register file (except store) and that happens in the last stage only. But is some ISAs, things may be more complicated. For example, when there is support for auto-increment addressing mode, a register write happens in the middle of the instruction. Now, if the instruction is aborted because of an exception, it will leave the processor state altered. Although we know which instruction caused the exception, without additional hardware support the exception will be imprecise because the instruction will be half finished. Restarting the instruction stream after such an imprecise exception is difficult. A similar problem arises from instructions that update memory state during execution, such as the string copy operations on the VAX or IBM 360. If these instructions don't run to completion and are interrupted in the middle, they leave the state of some of the memory locations altered. To make it possible to interrupt and restart these instructions, these instructions are defined to use the general-purpose registers as working registers. Thus, the state of the partially completed instruction is always in the registers, which are saved on an exception and restored after the exception, allowing the instruction to continue. In the VAX an additional bit of state records when an instruction has started updating the memory state, so that when the pipeline is restarted, the CPU knows whether to restart the instruction from the beginning or from the middle of the instruction. The IA-32 string instructions also use the registers as working storage, so that saving and restoring the registers saves and restores the state of such instructions.

Yet another problem arises because of condition codes. Many processors set the condition codes implicitly as part of the instruction. This approach has advantages, since condition codes decouple the evaluation of the condition from the actual branch.

However, implicitly set condition codes can cause difficulties in scheduling any pipeline delays between setting the condition code and the branch, since most instructions set the condition code and cannot be used in the delay slots between the condition evaluation and the branch. Additionally, in processors with condition codes, the processor must decide when the branch condition is fixed. This involves finding out when the condition code has been set for the last time before the branch. In most processors with implicitly set condition codes, this is done by delaying the branch condition evaluation until all previous instructions have had a chance to set the condition code. In effect, the condition code must be treated as an operand that requires hazard detection for RAW hazards with branches, just as MIPS must do on the registers.

Last of all, we shall look at how the MIPS pipeline can be extended to handle floating point operations. A typical floating point pipeline is shown in Figure. There are multiple execution units, like FP adder, FP multiply, etc. and they have different latencies. These functional units may or may not be pipelined. We normally define two terms with respect to floating point pipelines. The latency is the number of intervening cycles between an instruction that produces a result and an instruction that uses the result. The initiation or repeat interval is the number of cycles that must elapse between issuing two operations of a given type. The structure of the floating point pipeline requires the introduction of the additional pipeline registers (e.g., A1/A2, A2/A3, A3/A4) and the modification of the connections to those registers. The ID/EX register must be expanded to connect ID to EX, DIV, M1, and A1.

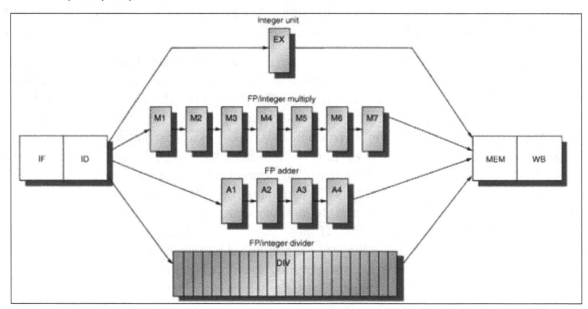

The long latency floating point instructions lead to a more complex pipeline. Since there is more number of instructions in the pipeline, there are frequent RAW hazards. Also, since these floating point instructions have varying latencies, multiple instructions might finish at the same time and there will be potentially multiple writes to the register file in a cycle. This might lead to structural hazards as well as WAW hazards. To handle the multiple writes to the register file, we need to increase the number of ports, or stall one of the writes during ID, or stall one of the writes during WB (the stall will propagate). WAW hazards will have to be detected during ID and the later instruction will have to be stalled. WAR hazards of course, are not possible since all reads happen earlier. The variable latency instructions and hence out-of-order completion will also lead to imprecise exceptions. You either have to buffer the results if they complete early or save more pipeline state so that you can return to exactly the same state that you left at.

References

- Pipelining, computer-architecture: studytonight.com, Retrieved 07, February 2020

- Pipelining-Hazards, pipelining-in-computer-architecture: binaryterms.com, Retrieved 16, August 2020

- Handling-data-hazards: cs.umd.edu, Retrieved 09, July 2020

- Branch-pred, Projects: web.engr.oregonstate.edu, Retrieved 13, June 2020

- Exception-handling-and-floating-point-pipelines: cs.umd.edu, Retrieved 05, May 2020

Computer Memory: Hierarchy, Cache and Virtual

All the different types of data storage technologies used by a computer, fall under computer memory including RAM, ROM and Flash memory. Memory hierarchy separates the computer storage on the basis of speed as well as use. This chapter discusses in detail the theories and methodologies related to computer memory.

Computer memory is a generic term for all of the different types of data storage technology that a computer may use, including RAM, ROM, and flash memory. Some types of computer memory are designed to be very fast, meaning that the central processing unit (CPU) can access data stored there very quickly. Other types are designed to be very low cost, so that large amounts of data can be stored there economically.

Another way that computer memory can vary is that some types are non-volatile, which means they can store data on a long term basis even when there is no power. And some types are volatile, which are often faster, but which lose all the data stored on them as soon as the power is switched off.

A computer system is built using a combination of these types of computer memory, and the exact configuration can be optimized to produce the maximum data processing speed or the minimum cost, or some compromise between the two.

Types of Computer Memory: Primary and Secondary

Although many types of memory in a computer exist, the most basic distinction is between primary memory, often called system memory, and secondary memory, which is more commonly called storage. The key difference between primary and secondary memory is speed of access.

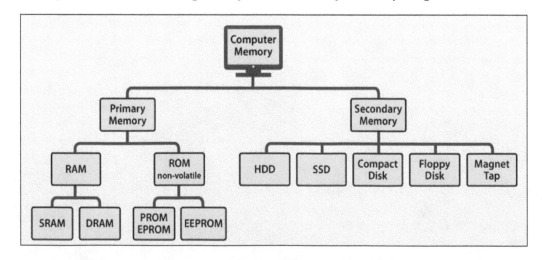

- Primary memory includes ROM and RAM, and is located close to the CPU on the computer motherboard, enabling the CPU to read data from primary memory very quickly indeed. It is used to store data that the CPU needs imminently so that it does not have to wait for it to be delivered.

- Secondary memory by contrast, is usually physically located within a separate storage device, such as a hard disk drive or solid state drive (SSD), which is connected to the computer system either directly or over a network. The cost per gigabyte of secondary memory is much lower, but the read and write speeds are significantly slower.

Over several periods of computer evolution, a wide of array of computer memory types has been deployed, each with its own strengths and weaknesses.

Primary Memory Types: RAM and ROM

There are two key types of primary memory:

- RAM, or random access memory.

- ROM, or read-only memory.

Let's look in-depth at both types of memory:

RAM Computer Memory

The acronym RAM stems from the fact that data stored in random access memory can be accessed – as the name suggests – in any random order. Or, put another way, any random bit of data can be accessed just as quickly as any other bit.

The most important things to understand about RAM are that RAM memory is very fast, it can be written to as well as read, it is volatile (so all data stored in RAM memory is lost when it loses power) and, finally, it is very expensive compared to all types of secondary memory in terms of cost per gigabyte. It is because of the relative high cost of RAM compared to secondary memory types that most computer systems use both primary and secondary memory.

Data that is required for imminent processing is moved to RAM where it can be accessed and modified very quickly, so that the CPU is not kept waiting. When the data is no longer required it is shunted out to slower but cheaper secondary memory, and the RAM space that has been freed up is filled with the next chunk of data that is about to be used.

Types of RAM

- DRAM: DRAM stands for Dynamic RAM, and it is the most common type of RAM used in computers. The oldest type is known as single data rate (SDR) DRAM, but newer computers use faster dual data rate (DDR) DRAM. DDR comes in several versions including DDR2 , DDR3, and DDR4, which offer better performance and are more energy efficient than DDR. However different versions are incompatible, so it is not possible to mix DDR2 with DDR3 DRAM in a computer system. DRAM consists of a transistor and a capacitor in each cell.

- SRAM: SRAM stands for Static RAM, and it is a particular type of RAM which is faster than DRAM, but more expensive and bulker, having six transistors in each cell. For those reasons SRAM is generally only used as a data cache within a CPU itself or as RAM in very high-end server systems. A small SRAM cache of the most imminently-needed data can result in significant speed improvements in a system.

The key differences between DRAM and SRAM are that SRAM is faster than DRAM - perhaps two to three times faster - but more expensive and bulkier. SRAM is usually available in megabytes, while DRAM is purchased in gigabytes.

DRAM uses more energy than SRAM because it constantly needs to be refreshed to maintain data integrity, while SRAM - though volatile – does not need constant refreshing when it is powered up.

ROM Computer Memory

ROM stands for read-only memory, and the name stems from the fact that while data can be read from this type of computer memory, data cannot normally be written to it. It is a very fast type of computer memory which is usually installed close to the CPU on the motherboard.

ROM is a type of non-volatile memory, which means that the data stored in ROM persists in the memory even when it receives no power – for example when the computer is turned off. In that sense it is similar to secondary memory, which is used for long term storage.

When a computer is turned on, the CPU can begin reading information stored in ROM without the need for drivers or other complex software to help it communicate. The ROM usually contains "bootstrap code" which is the basic set of instructions a computer needs to carry out to become aware of the operating system stored in secondary memory, and to load parts of the operating system into primary memory so that it can start up and become ready to use. ROM is also used in simpler electronic devices to store firmware which runs as soon as the device is switched on.

Types of ROM

ROM is available in several different types, including PROM, EPROM, and EEPROM.

- PROM: PROM stands for Programmable Read-Only Memory, and it is different from true ROM in that while a ROM is programmed (i.e. has data written to it) during the manufacturing process, a PROM is manufactured in an empty state and then programmed later using a PROM programmer or burner.

- EPROM: EPROM stands for Erasable Programmable Read-Only Memory, and as the name suggests, data stored in an EPROM can be erased and the EPROM reprogrammed. Erasing an EPROM involves removing it from the computer and exposing it to ultraviolet light before re-burning it.

- EEPROM: EEPROM stands for Electrically Erasable Programmable Read-Only Memory, and the distinction between EPROM and EEPROM is that the latter can be erased and written to by the computer system it is installed in. In that sense EEPROM is not strictly read-only. However in many cases the write process is slow, so it is normally only done to update program code such as firmware or BIOS code on an occasional basis.

Confusingly, NAND flash memory (such as that found in USB memory sticks and solid state disk drives) is a type of EEPROM, but NAND flash is considered to be secondary memory.

Secondary Memory Types

Secondary memory comprises many different storage media which can be directly attached to a computer system. These include:

- Hard disk drives.

- Solid state drives (SSDs).

- Optical (CD or DVD) drives.

- Tape drives.

Secondary memory also includes:

- Storage arrays including 3D NAND flash arrays connected over a storage area network (SAN).

- Storage devices which may be connected over a conventional network (known as network attached storage or NAS).

Arguably cloud storage can also be called secondary memory.

Differences between RAM and ROM

ROM:

- Non-volatile.

- Fast to read.

- Usually used in small quantities.

- Cannot be written to quickly.

- Used to store boot instructions or firmware.

- Relatively expensive per megabyte stored compared to RAM.

RAM:

- Volatile.

- Fast to read and write.

- Used as system memory to store data (including program code) that the CPU needs to process imminently.

- Relatively cheap per megabyte stored compared to ROM, but relatively expensive compared to secondary memory.

Memory Hierarchy

The memory in a computer can be divided into five hierarchies based on the speed as well as use. The processor can move from one level to another based on its requirements. The five hierarchies in the memory are registers, cache, main memory, magnetic discs, and magnetic tapes. The first three hierarchies are volatile memories which mean when there is no power, and then automatically they lose their stored data. Whereas the last two hierarchies are not volatile which means they store the data permanently. A memory element is the set of storage devices which stores the binary data in the type of bits. In general, the storage of memory can be classified into two categories such as volatile as well as non- volatile.

The memory hierarchy design in a computer system mainly includes different storage devices. Most of the computers were inbuilt with extra storage to run more powerfully beyond the main memory capacity. The following memory hierarchy diagram is a hierarchical pyramid for computer memory. The designing of the memory hierarchy is divided into two types such as primary (Internal) memory and secondary (External) memory.

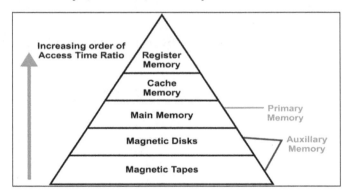

- Primary Memory: The primary memory is also known as internal memory, and this is accessible by the processor straightly. This memory includes main, cache, as well as CPU registers.

- Secondary Memory: The secondary memory is also known as external memory, and this is accessible by the processor through an input/output module. This memory includes an optical disk, magnetic disk, and magnetic tape.

Characteristics of Memory Hierarchy

The memory hierarchy characteristics mainly include the following:

- Performance: Previously, the designing of a computer system was done without memory hierarchy, and the speed gap among the main memory as well as the CPU registers enhances because of the huge disparity in access time, which will cause the lower performance of the system. So, the enhancement was mandatory. The enhancement of this was designed in the memory hierarchy model due to the system's performance increase.

- Ability: The ability of the memory hierarchy is the total amount of data the memory can store. Because whenever we shift from top to bottom inside the memory hierarchy, then the capacity will increase.

- Access time: The access time in the memory hierarchy is the interval of the time among the data availability as well as request to read or write. Because whenever we shift from top to bottom inside the memory hierarchy, then the access time will increase.

- Cost per bit: When we shift from bottom to top inside the memory hierarchy, then the cost for each bit will increase which means an internal Memory is expensive compared with external memory.

Memory Hierarchy Design

The memory hierarchy in computers mainly includes the following:

- Registers: Usually, the register is a static RAM or SRAM in the processor of the computer which is used for holding the data word which is typically 64 or 128 bits. The program counter register is the most important as well as found in all the processors. Most of the processors use a status word register as well as an accumulator. A status word register is used for decision making, and the accumulator is used to store the data like mathematical operation. Usually, computers like complex instruction set computers have so many registers for accepting main memory, and RISC- reduced instruction set computers have more registers.

- Cache Memory: Cache memory can also be found in the processor, however rarely it may be another IC (integrated circuit) which is separated into levels. The cache holds the chunk of data which are frequently used from main memory. When the processor has a single core then it will have two (or) more cache levels rarely. Present multi-core processors will be having three, 2-levels for each one core, and one level is shared.

- Main Memory: The main memory in the computer is nothing but, the memory unit in the CPU that communicates directly. It is the main storage unit of the computer. This memory is fast as well as large memory used for storing the data throughout the operations of the computer. This memory is made up of RAM as well as ROM.

- Magnetic Disks: The magnetic disks in the computer are circular plates fabricated of plastic otherwise metal by magnetized material. Frequently, two faces of the disk are utilized as well as many disks may be stacked on one spindle by read or write heads obtainable on every plane. All the disks in computer turn jointly at high speed. The tracks in the computer are nothing but bits which are stored within the magnetized plane in spots next to concentric circles. These are usually separated into sections which are named as sectors.

- Magnetic Tape: This tape is a normal magnetic recording which is designed with a slender magnetizable covering on an extended, plastic film of the thin strip. This is mainly used to back up huge data. Whenever the computer requires to access a strip, first it will mount to access the data. Once the data is allowed, then it will be unmounted. The access time of memory will be slower within magnetic strip as well as it will take a few minutes for accessing a strip.

Advantages of Memory Hierarchy

The need for a memory hierarchy includes the following:

- Memory distributing is simple and economical.

- Removes external destruction.

- Data can be spread all over.

- Permits demand paging & pre-paging.

- Swapping will be more proficient.

Cache Memory

Cache memory is a chip-based computer component that makes retrieving data from the computer's memory more efficient. It acts as a temporary storage area that the computer's processor can retrieve data from easily. This temporary storage area, known as a cache, is more readily available to the processor than the computer's main memory source, typically some form of DRAM.

Cache memory is sometimes called CPU (central processing unit) memory because it is typically integrated directly into the CPU chip or placed on a separate chip that has a separate bus interconnect with the CPU. Therefore, it is more accessible to the processor, and able to increase efficiency, because it's physically close to the processor. In order to be close to the processor, cache memory needs to be much smaller than main memory. Consequently, it has less storage space. It is also more expensive than main memory, as it is a more complex chip that yields higher performance.

What it sacrifices in size and price, it makes up for in speed. Cache memory operates between 10 to 100 times faster than RAM, requiring only a few nanoseconds to respond to a CPU request. The name of the actual hardware that is used for cache memory is high-speed static random access memory (SRAM). The name of the hardware that is used in a computer's main memory is dynamic random access memory (DRAM).

Cache memory is not to be confused with the broader term cache. Caches are temporary stores of data that can exist in both hardware and software. Cache memory refers to the specific hardware component that allows computers to create caches at various levels of the network.

Types of Cache Memory

Cache memory is fast and expensive. Traditionally, it is categorized as "levels" that describe its closeness and accessibility to the microprocessor. There are three general cache levels:

- L1 cache, or primary cache, is extremely fast but relatively small, and is usually embedded in the processor chip as CPU cache.

- L2 cache, or secondary cache, is often more capacious than L1. L2 cache may be embedded on the CPU, or it can be on a separate chip or coprocessor and have a high-speed alternative system bus connecting the cache and CPU. That way it doesn't get slowed by traffic on the main system bus.

- Level 3 (L3) cache is specialized memory developed to improve the performance of L1 and L2. L1 or L2 can be significantly faster than L3, though L3 is usually double the speed of

DRAM. With multicore processors, each core can have dedicated L1 and L2 cache, but they can share an L3 cache. If an L3 cache references an instruction, it is usually elevated to a higher level of cache.

In the past, L1, L2 and L3 caches have been created using combined processor and motherboard components. Recently, the trend has been toward consolidating all three levels of memory caching on the CPU itself. That's why the primary means for increasing cache size has begun to shift from the acquisition of a specific motherboard with different chipsets and bus architectures to buying a CPU with the right amount of integrated L1, L2 and L3 cache.

Contrary to popular belief, implementing flash or more dynamic RAM (DRAM) on a system won't increase cache memory. This can be confusing since the terms memory caching (hard disk buffering) and cache memory are often used interchangeably. Memory caching, using DRAM or flash to buffer disk reads, is meant to improve storage I/O by caching data that is frequently referenced in a buffer ahead of slower magnetic disk or tape. Cache memory, on the other hand, provides read buffering for the CPU.

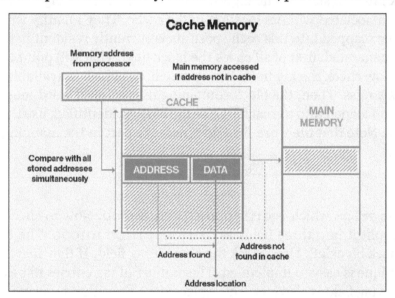

Mapping

There are three types of mapping in cache memory:

Direct Mapping

This is the simplest mapping technique. In this technique, block i of the main memory is mapped onto block j modulo (number of blocks in cache) of the cache. In our example, it is block j mod 32. That is, the first 32 blocks of main memory map on to the corresponding 32 blocks of cache, 0 to 0, 1 to 1, ... and 31 to 31. And remember that we have only 32 blocks in cache. So, the next 32 blocks of main memory are also mapped onto the same corresponding blocks of cache. So, 32 again maps to block 0 in cache, 33 to block 1 in cache and so on. That is, the main memory blocks are grouped as groups of 32 blocks and each of these groups will map on to the corresponding cache blocks.

For example, whenever one of the main memory blocks 0, 32, 64, ... is loaded in the cache, it is stored only in cache block 0. So, at any point of time, if some other block is occupying the cache block, that is removed and the other block is stored. For example, if we want to bring in block 64, and block 0 is already available in cache, block 0 is removed and block 64 is brought in. Similarly, blocks 1, 33, 65, ... are stored in cache block 1, and so on. You can easily see that 2^9 blocks of main memory will map onto the same block in cache. Since more than one memory block is mapped onto a given cache block position, contention may arise for that position even when the cache is not full. That is, blocks, which are entitled to occupy the same cache block, may compete for the block. For example, if the processor references instructions from block 0 and 32 alternatively, conflicts will arise, even though the cache is not full. Contention is resolved by allowing the new block to over-write the currently resident block. Thus, in this case, the replacement algorithm is trivial. There is no other place the block can be accommodated. So it only has to replace the currently resident block.

Placement of a block in the cache is determined from the memory address. The memory address can be divided into three fields, as shown below. The low-order 6 bits select one of 64 words in a block. When a new block enters the cache, the 5-bit cache block field determines the cache position in which this block must be stored. The high-order 9 bits of the memory address of the block are stored in 9 tag bits associated with its location in the cache. They identify which of the 2^9 blocks that are eligible to be mapped into this cache position is currently resident in the cache. As a main memory address is generated, first of all check the block field. That will point to the block that you have to check for. Now check the tag field. If they match, the block is available in cache and it is a hit. Otherwise, it is a miss. Then, the block containing the required word must first be read from the main memory and loaded into the cache. Once the block is identified, use the word field to fetch one of the 64 words. Note that the word field does not take part in the mapping.

Tag	Block	Word
9	5	6

Consider an address 78F28 which is 0111 1000 1111 0010 1000. Now to check whether the block is in cache or not, split it into three fields as 011110001 11100 101000. The block field indicates that you have to check block 28. Now check the nine bit tag field. If they match, it is a hit. The direct-mapping technique is easy to implement. The number of tag entries to be checked is only one and the length of the tag field is also less. The replacement algorithm is very simple. However, it is not very flexible. Even though the cache is not full, you may have to do a lot of thrashing between main memory and cache because of the rigid mapping policy.

Fully Associative Mapping

This is a much more flexible mapping method, in which a main memory block can be placed into any cache block position. This indicates that there is no need for a block field. In this case, 14 tag bits are required to identify a memory block when it is resident in the cache. The tag bits of an address received from the processor are compared to the tag bits of each block of the cache to see if the desired block is present. This is called the associative mapping technique. It gives complete freedom in choosing the cache location in which to place the memory block. Thus, the space in the cache can be used more efficiently. A new block that has to be brought into the cache has to replace (eject) an existing block only if the cache is full. In this case, we need an algorithm to select the block to be replaced. The commonly used algorithms are random, FIFO and LRU. Random replacement does a random choice of the block to be removed. FIFO removes the oldest block, without considering the memory access patterns. So, it is not very effective. On the other hand, the least recently used technique considers the access patterns and removes the block that has not been referenced for the longest period. This is very effective.

Thus, associative mapping is totally flexible. But, the cost of an associative cache is higher than the cost of a direct-mapped cache because of the need to search all the tag patterns to determine whether a given block is in the cache. Also, note that the tag length increases. That is, both the number of tags and the tag length increase. The replacement also is complex. Therefore, it is not practically feasible.

Tag	Word
14	6

Set Associative Mapping

This is a compromise between the above two techniques. Blocks of the cache are grouped into sets, consisting of n blocks, and the mapping allows a block of the main memory to reside in any block of a specific set. It is also called n-way set associative mapping. Hence, the contention problem of the direct method is eased by having a few choices for block placement. At the same time, the hardware cost is reduced by decreasing the size of the associative search. For our example, the main memory address for the set-associative-mapping technique for a cache with two blocks per set (2–way set associative mapping). There are 16 sets in the cache. In this case, memory blocks 0, 16, 32 ... map into cache set 0, and they can occupy either of the two block positions within this set. Having 16 sets means that the 4-bit set field of the address determines which set of the cache might contain the desired block. The 11 bit tag field of the address must then be associatively compared to the tags of the two blocks of the set to check if the desired block is present. This two-way associative search is simple to implement and combines the advantages of both the other techniques. This can be in fact treated as the general case; when n is 1, it becomes direct mapping; when n is the number of blocks in cache, it is associative mapping.

Tag	Set	Word
11	4	6

One more control bit, called the valid bit, must be provided for each block. This bit indicates whether the block contains valid data. It should not be confused with the modified, or dirty, bit mentioned earlier. The dirty bit, which indicates whether the block has been modified during its cache residency, is needed only in systems that do not use the write-through method. The valid bits are all set to 0 when power is initially applied to the system or when the main memory is loaded with new programs and data from the disk. Transfers from the disk to the main memory are carried out by a DMA mechanism. Normally, they bypass the cache for both cost and performance reasons. The valid bit of a particular cache block is set to 1 the first time this block is loaded from the main memory, Whenever a main memory block is updated by a source that bypasses the cache, a check is made to determine whether the block being loaded is currently in the cache. If it is, its valid bit is cleared to 0. This ensures that stale data will not exist in the cache.

A similar difficulty arises when a DMA transfer is made from the main memory to the disk, and the cache uses the write-back protocol. In this case, the data in the memory might not reflect the changes that may have been made in the cached copy. One solution to this problem is to flush the cache by forcing the dirty data to be written back to the memory before the DMA transfer takes place. The operating system can do this easily, and it does not affect performance greatly, because such disk transfers do not occur often. This need to ensure that two different entities (the processor and DMA subsystems in this case) use the same copies of data is referred to as a cache coherence problem.

Read/Write Policies

Last of all, we need to also discuss the read/write policies that are followed. The processor does not need to know explicitly about the existence of the cache. It simply issues Read and Write requests using addresses that refer to locations in the memory. The cache control circuitry determines whether the requested word currently exists in the cache. If it does, the Read or Write operation is performed on the appropriate cache location. In this case, a read or write hit is said to have occurred. In a Read operation, no modifications take place and so the main memory is not affected. For a write hit, the system can proceed in two ways. In the first technique, called the write-through protocol, the cache location and the main memory location are updated simultaneously. The second technique is to update only the cache location and to mark it as updated with an associated flag bit, often called the dirty or modified bit. The main memory location of the word is updated later, when the block containing this marked word is to be removed from the cache to make room for a new block. This technique is known as the write-back, or copy-back protocol. The write-through protocol is simpler, but it results in unnecessary write operations in the main memory when a given cache word is updated several times during its cache residency. Note that the write-back protocol may also result in unnecessary write operations because when a cache block is written back to the memory all words of the block are written back, even if only a single word has been changed while the block was in the cache. This can be avoided if you maintain more number of dirty bits per block. During a write operation, if the addressed word is not in the cache, a write miss occurs.

Then, if the write-through protocol is used, the information is written directly into the main memory. In the case of the write-back protocol, the block containing the addressed word is first brought into the cache, and then the desired word in the cache is overwritten with the new information. When a write miss occurs, we use the write allocate policy or no write allocate policy. That is, if we use the write back policy for write hits, then the block is anyway brought to cache (write allocate) and the dirty bit is set. On the other hand, if it is write through policy that is used, then the block is not allocated to cache and the modifications happen straight away in main memory.

Irrespective of the write strategies used, processors normally use a write buffer to allow the cache to proceed as soon as the data is placed in the buffer rather than wait till the data is actually written into main memory.

Virtual Memory

Virtual memory is a valuable concept in computer architecture that allows you to run large, sophisticated programs on a computer even if it has a relatively small amount of RAM. A computer with virtual memory artfully juggles the conflicting demands of multiple programs within a fixed amount of physical memory. A PC that's low on memory can run the same programs as one with abundant RAM, although more slowly.

Physical Vs Virtual Addresses

A computer accesses the contents of its RAM through a system of addresses, which are essentially numbers that locate each byte. Because the amount of memory varies from PC to PC, determining which software will work on a given computer becomes complicated. Virtual memory solves this problem by treating each computer as if it has a large amount of RAM and each program as if it uses the PC exclusively. The operating system, such as Microsoft Windows or Apple's OS X, creates a set of virtual addresses for each program. The OS translates virtual addresses into physical ones, dynamically fitting programs into RAM as it becomes available.

Address Mapping using Paging

The address mapping is simplified if the information in the address space and the memory space are each divided into groups of fixed size. The physical memory is broken down into groups of equal size called page frames and the logical memory is divided into pages of the same size. The programs are also considered to be split into pages. Pages commonly range from 2K to 16K bytes in length. They constitute the basic unit of information that is moved between the main memory and the disk whenever the translation mechanism determines that a move is required. Pages should not be too small, because the access time of a magnetic disk is much longer than the access time of the main memory. The reason for this is that it takes a considerable amount of time to locate the data on the disk, but once located, the data can be transferred at a rate of several megabytes per second. On the other hand, if pages are too large it is possible that a substantial portion of a page may not be used, yet this unnecessary data will occupy valuable space in the main memory. If you consider a computer with an address space of 1M and a memory space of 64K, and if you split each into groups of 2K words, you will obtain 2^9 (512) pages and thirty-two page frames. At any given time, up to thirty-two pages of address space may reside in main memory in anyone of the thirty-two blocks.

In order to do the mapping, the virtual address is represented by two numbers: a page number and an offset or line address within the page. In a computer with 2^p words per page, p bits are used to specify an offset and the remaining high-order bits of the virtual address specify the page number. In the example above, we considered a virtual address of 20 bits. Since each page consists of 2^{11} = 2K words, the high order nine bits of the virtual address will specify one of the 512 pages and the low-order 11 bits give the offset within the page. Note that the line address in address space and memory space is the same; the only mapping required is from a page number to a block number.

The mapping information between the pages and the page frames is available in a page table. The page table consists of as many pages that a virtual address can support. The base address of the page table is stored in a register called the Page Table Base Register (PTBR). Each process can have one or more of its own page tables and the operating system switches from one page table to another on a context switch, by loading a different address into the PTBR. The page number, which is part of the virtual address, is used to index into the appropriate page table entry. The page table entry contains the physical page frame address, if the page is available in main memory. Otherwise, it specifies wherein secondary storage, the page is available. This generates a page fault and the operating system brings the requested page from secondary storage to main storage. Along with this address information, the page table entry also provides information about the privilege level associated with the page and the access rights of the page. This helps in providing protection to the page. The mapping process is indicated in Figure below shows a typical page table entry. The dirty or modified bit indicates whether the page was modified during the cache residency period.

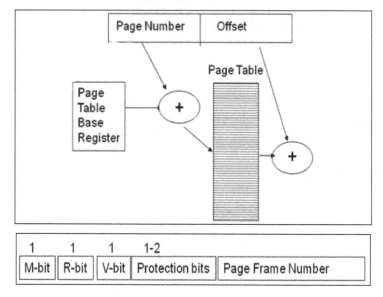

- M – Indicates whether the page has been written (dirty).

- R – Indicates whether the page has been referenced (useful for replacement).

- V – Valid bit.

- Protection bits – Indicate what operations are allowed on this page.

- Page Frame Number says where in memory is the page.

A virtual memory system is thus a combination of hardware and software techniques. The memory management software system handles all the software operations for the efficient utilization of memory space. It must decide the answers to the usual four questions in a hierarchical memory system:

- Where can a block be placed in the upper level?

- How is a block found if it is in the upper level?

- Which block should be replaced on a miss?

- What happens on a write? The hardware mapping mechanism and the memory management software together constitute the architecture of a virtual memory and answer all these questions.

When a program starts execution, one or more pages are transferred into main memory and the page table is set to indicate their position. Thus, the page table entries help in identifying a page. The program is executed from main memory until it attempts to reference a page that is still in auxiliary memory. This condition is called a page fault. When a page fault occurs, the execution of the present program is suspended until the required page is brought into main memory. Since loading a page from auxiliary memory to main memory is basically an I/O operation, the operating system assigns this task to the I/O processor. In the meantime, control is transferred to the next program in memory that is waiting to be processed in the CPU. Later, when the memory block has been assigned and the transfer completed, the original program can resume its operation. It should be noted that it is always a write back policy that is adopted, because of the long access times associated with the disk access. Also, when a page fault is serviced, the memory may already be full.

In this case, as we discussed for caches, a replacement has to be done. The replacement policies are again FIFO and LRU. The FIFO replacement policy has the advantage of being easy to implement. !t has the disadvantage that under certain circumstances pages are removed and loaded from memory too frequently. The LRU policy is more difficult to implement but has been more attractive on the assumption that the least recently used page is a better candidate for removal than the least recently loaded page as in FIFO. The LRU algorithm can be implemented by associating a counter with every page that is in main memory. When a page is referenced, its associated counter is set to zero. At fixed intervals of time, the counters associated with all pages presently in memory are incremented by 1. The least recently used page is the page with the highest count. The counters are often called aging registers, as their count indicates their age, that is, how long ago their associated pages have been referenced.

Drawback of Virtual Memory

So far we have assumed that the page tables are stored in memory. Since, the page table information is used by the MMU, which does the virtual to physical address translation, for every read and write access, every memory access by a program can take at least twice as long: one memory access to obtain the physical address and a second access to get the data. So, ideally, the page table should be situated within the MMU. Unfortunately, the page table may be rather large, and since the MMU is normally implemented as part of the processor chip, it is impossible to include a complete page table on this chip. Therefore, the page table is kept in the main memory. However, a copy of a small portion of the page table can be accommodated within the MMU. This portion consists of the page table entries that correspond to the most recently accessed pages. A small cache, usually called the Translation Lookaside Buffer (TLB) is incorporated into the MMU for this purpose. The TLB stores the most recent logical to physical address translations. The operation of the TLB with respect to the page table in the main memory is essentially the same as the operation we have discussed in conjunction with the cache memory. Figure shows a possible organization of a TLB where the associative mapping technique is used. Set associative mapped TLBs are also found in commercial products. The TLB gives information about the validity of the page, status of whether it is available in physical memory, protection information, etc. apart from the physical address.

Virtual page number	Physical page frame address	Valid	Dirty	Reference	Access

An essential requirement is that the contents of the TLB be coherent with the contents of page tables in the memory. When the operating system changes the contents of page tables, it must simultaneously invalidate the corresponding entries in the TLB. The valid bit in the TLB is provided for this purpose. When an entry is invalidated, the TLB will acquire the new information as part of the MMU's normal response to access misses.

With the introduction of the TLB, the address translation proceeds as follows. Given a virtual address, the MMU looks in the TLB for the referenced page. If the page table entry for this page is found in the TLB, the physical address is obtained immediately. If there is a miss in the TLB, then the required entry is obtained from the page table in the main memory and the TLB is updated.

Recall that the caches need a physical address, unless we use virtual caches. As discussed with respect to cache optimizations, machines with TLBs go one step further to reduce the number of cycles/cache access. They overlap the cache access with the TLB access. That is, the high order bits of the virtual address are used to look in the TLB while the low order bits are used as index into the cache. The flow is as shown below.

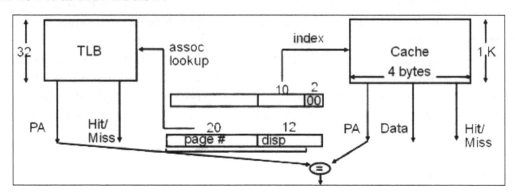

```
IF cache hit AND (cache tag = PA) then deliver data to CPU

ELSE IF [cache miss OR (cache tag = PA)and TLB hit THEN]

     access memory with the PA from the TLB

ELSE do standard VA translation
```

The overlapped access only works as long as the address bits used to index into the cache do not change as the result of VA translation. This usually limits things to small caches, large page sizes, or high n-way set associative caches if you want a large cache.

Address Mapping using Segments

A segment is a set of logically related instructions or data elements associated with a given name. Segments may be generated by the programmer or by the operating system. Examples of segments are a subroutine, an array of data, a table of symbols, or a user's program. As in paging, the address generated by a segmented program is called a logical address. This is similar to a virtual address except that logical address space is associated with variable-length segments rather than fixed-length pages. The logical address consists of the segment number and the offset. The segment number is mapped to a physical address using segment descriptor tables. These tables do the same function as the page tables in paging. Because the segments can vary is size, a bounds check is also needed to make sure that the offset is within the segment. The function of the memory management unit is to map logical addresses into physical addresses similar to the virtual memory mapping concept. The segmentation concept is illustrated in Figure below.

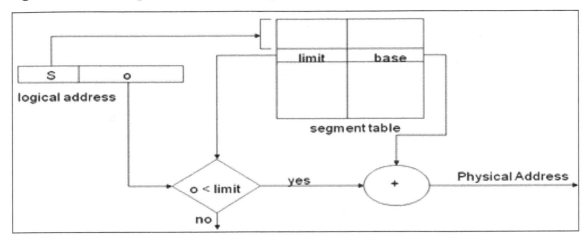

In addition to relocation information, each segment descriptor entry has protection information associated with it. Segmentation offers the advantage of sharing commonly used data and programs. Shared programs are placed in a unique segment in each user's logical address space so that a single physical copy can be shared.

Segments cannot be broken further and the entire segment has to be either in memory or on disk. The variable sizes of the segments leads to external fragmentation in memory, whereas, in paging we have only internal fragmentation, where the last page alone may not be completely filled. When it comes to bringing in a new segment into main memory also, we have more complications. In the case of paging, all the blocks are of the same size. Therefore, any block can replace any block. However, as segments are of varying sizes, the operating system has to identify a segment large enough to accommodate the incoming segment. This is done with the following techniques:

- First fit: The first segment that is big enough to accommodate the incoming segment is chosen.

- Best fit: The best fitting segment, that is, the one leaving the least amount of free space is chosen. For example, if the segment size is 4K, and the available segments are of sizes 5K and 8K, the 5K segment will be chosen.

- Worst fit: The one that is the worst fit, leaving the maximum space will be chosen. In the previous example, the segment of size 8K will be chosen.

Note that the TLB is used in the case of segmentation also to speed up the memory access.

Address Mapping using Segmented Paging

It is also possible to have a third memory management technique called segmented paging. As the name suggests, this is a combination of both segmentation and paging. It was already mentioned that the property of logical space is that it uses variable-length segments. The length of each segment is allowed to grow and contract according to the needs of the program being executed. One way of specifying the length of a segment is by associating with it a number of equal-sized pages. To see how this is done, consider the logical address shown in figure. The logical address is partitioned into three fields. The segment field specifies a segment number. The page field specifies the page within the segment and the word field gives the specific word within the page. A page field of k bits can specify up to 2^k pages. A segment number may be associated with just one page or with as many as 2^k pages. Thus the length of a segment would vary according to the number of pages that are assigned to it.

The mapping of the logical address into a physical address is done by means of two tables. The segment number of the logical address specifies the address for the segment table. The entry in the segment table is a pointer address for a page table base. This new address is often referred to as a linear address. The page table base is added to the page number given in the logical address. The sum produces a pointer address to an entry in the page table. The value found in the page table provides the block number in physical memory. The concatenation of the block field with the word field produces the final physical mapped address.

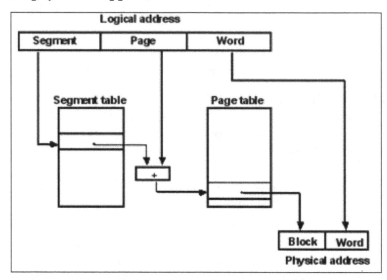

We thus use pages to describe components of the segments. This makes segments easy to manage and we can swap memory between segments. We need to allocate page table entries only for those pieces of the segments that have themselves been allocated. Segments that are shared can be represented with shared page tables. The two mapping tables may be stored in main memory. Therefore, a memory reference from the CPU will require three accesses to memory - one from the segment table, one from the page table, and the third from main memory. This would slow the system even more. To avoid this speed penalty, the TLB is used in this case also.

Memory Management System

In a multiprogramming environment where many programs reside in memory, it becomes necessary to move programs and data around the memory, to vary the amount of memory in use by a given program, and to prevent a program from changing other programs. The demands on computer memory brought about by multiprogramming have created the need for a memory management system. A memory management system is a collection of hardware and software procedures for managing the various programs residing in memory. The memory management software is part of an overall operating system available in many computers. The hardware includes the page tables, segment tables and TLBs in the MMU as pointed out in the previous section. Putting everything together, we can say that the basic components of a memory management system are:

- A facility for dynamic storage relocation that maps logical memory references into physical memory addresses.

- A provision for sharing common programs stored in memory by different users.

- Protection of information against unauthorized access between users and preventing users from changing operating system functions.

The sharing of common programs is an integral part of a multiprogramming system. For example, several users wishing to compile their C programs should be able to share a single copy of the compiler rather than each user having a separate copy in memory. Other system programs residing in memory are also shared by all users in a multiprogramming system without having to produce multiple copies.

The third issue in multiprogramming is protecting one program from unwanted interaction with another. An example of unwanted interaction is one user's unauthorized copying of another user's program. Another aspect of protection is concerned with preventing the occasional user from performing operating system functions and thereby interrupting the orderly sequence of operations in a computer installation. The secrecy of certain programs must be kept from unauthorized personnel to prevent abuses in the confidential activities of an organization. This feature is again supported in virtual memory by providing support for the addition of protection and access rights information in every page/ segment. The following features are supported by the architecture in order to provide protection:

- Provide at least two modes, indicating whether the running process is a user process or an operating system process, called a kernel process or a supervisor process.

- Provide a portion of the processor state that a user process can use but not modify. This state includes an user/supervisor mode bit(s), an exception enable/disable bit, and memory protection information. Users are prevented from writing this state because the operating system cannot control user processes if users can give themselves supervisor privileges, disable exceptions, or change memory protection.

- Provide mechanisms whereby the processor can go from user mode to supervisor mode and vice versa. The first direction is typically accomplished by a system call, implemented as a special instruction that transfers control to a dedicated location in supervisor code space. The PC is saved from the point of the system call, and the processor is placed in supervisor mode. The return to user mode is like a subroutine return that restores the previous user/supervisor mode.

- Provide mechanisms to limit memory accesses to protect the memory state of a process without having to swap the process to disk on a context switch.

Thus, the above discussion clearly shows that we can enforce protection through the operating system with the support of architecture. However, the operating systems consist of tens of millions of lines of code and there are quite a lot of bugs here. Flaws in the OS have led to vulnerabilities that are routinely exploited. This problem, and the possibility that not enforcing protection could be much more costly than in the past, has led some to look for a protection model with a much smaller code base than the full OS, such as Virtual Machines.

Virtual Machines and Protection

Although virtual machines were not very popular in single-user computers, they have recently gained popularity due to the following reasons:

- The increasing importance of isolation and security in modern systems.

- The failures in security and reliability of standard operating systems.

- The sharing of a single computer among many unrelated users.

- The dramatic increases in raw speed of processors, which makes the overhead of VMs more acceptable.

VMs provide a complete system-level environment at the binary instruction set architecture (ISA) level. They present the illusion that the users of a VM have an entire computer to themselves, including a copy of the operating system. A single computer runs multiple VMs and can support a number of different operating systems. On a conventional platform, a single OS "owns" all the hardware resources, but with a VM, multiple operating systems share the hardware resources. The software that supports VMs is called a virtual machine monitor (VMM) or hypervisor; the VMM is the heart of Virtual Machine technology. The underlying hardware platform is called the host, and its resources are shared among the guest VMs. The VMM determines how to map virtual resources to physical resources. A physical resource may be time-shared, partitioned, or even emulated in software. The VMM is much smaller than a traditional OS. Each guest OS maintains its own set of page tables. The VMM adds a level of memory between physical and virtual memory called "real memory" and the VMM maintains shadow page table that maps guest virtual addresses to physical addresses.

Improving the Access Times of Main Memory

Last of all, we shall look at various techniques that are used to improve the performance of main memory. Figure shows various methods used to increase the bandwidth of main memory. The first method is a simple one where the CPU, cache, bus and memory have the same width, say 32 or 64 bits. The second one shows a wide memory organization, where the CPU/Mux width is 1 word. However, the Mux/Cache, bus and memory width are N words. The Alpha processor uses 64 bits & 256 bits and the UtraSPARC uses 64 bits and 512 bits. The third organization shows an interleaved organization, where the CPU, cache and bus have a width of 1 word, but the memory has N Modules; for example, word interleaved. First-level caches are often organized with a physical width of 1 word because most CPU accesses are of that size. There is additional cost involved in the wider connection between the CPU and memory, typically called a memory bus. This may help for the second-level caches, since the multiplexing can be between the first and second level caches, and not on the critical path.

Memory chips can be organized in banks to read or write multiple words at a time rather than a single word. The mapping of the addresses to banks affects the behavior of the memory system. This mapping is called the Interleaving Factor. Interleaving Memory normally means banks of memory that are word interleaved. It is used to optimize sequential memory accesses. A cache read miss is an ideal match to word-interleaved memory, because the words in a block are read sequentially. Write back caches make writes as well as reads sequential, getting even more efficiency from word-interleaved memory. However, the disadvantages are the shrinking number of chips and the difficulty of main memory expansion.

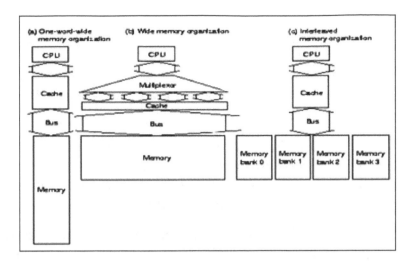

We can also look at independent memory banks, where each bank needs separate address lines and possibly a separate data bus. This is particularly useful with non-blocking caches that allow the CPU to proceed beyond a cache miss, potentially allowing multiple cache misses to be serviced simultaneously. Otherwise, the multiple reads will be serviced by a single memory port and will get only a small benefit of overlapping access with transmission. Normally, independent of memory technology, higher bandwidth is made available using memory banks, by making memory and its bus wider, or doing both.

References

- Types-of-computer-memory, storage-hardware: enterprisestorageforum.com, Retrieved 10, May 2020

- Memory-hierarchy-in-computer-architecture: elprocus.com, Retrieved 21, February 2020

- Cache-memory: techtarget.com, Retrieved 19, July 2020

- Concept-virtual-memory-computer-architecture-65904: Retrieved 03, January 2020

Components of Central Processing Unit

Central Processing Unit is the main electronic circuitry within the computer that executes instructions that make up a computer program. The arithmetic and bitwise operations on integer binary numbers are performed by Arithmetic Logic Unit. All the diverse principles related to the central processing unit are carefully analyzed in this chapter.

Central processing unit (CPU) is the central component of the computer system. Sometimes it is called as microprocessor or processor. It is the brain that runs the show inside the computer. All functions and processes that is done on a computer is performed directly or indirectly by the processor. Obviously, computer processor is one of the most important elements of the computer system. CPU is consist of transistors, that receives inputs and produces output. Transistors perform logical operations which is called processing. It is also, scientifically, not only one of the most amazing parts of the PC, but one of the most amazing devices in the world of technology.

In terms of computing power, the *computer processor* is the most important element of a computer system. It add and compare its data in CPU chip.

CPU speed of executing an instruction depends on its clock frequency which is measured in MHz (megahertz) or GHz (gigahertz), more the clock frequency, more is the speed of computer's instruction execution.

Actual Working

Now let's try to understand the working of the CPU. Whenever a data or some instruction or program is requested by the user, the CPU draws it from the RAM (Random Access Memory) and might some other hardware for the purpose.

Now before sending the information back to the RAM, the CPU reads the information associated with the task given to it. After reading the information, the CPU starts its calculation and transporting the data.

Before the data is further executed, it has to travel through the System BUS. A bus in the computer is a communication system that is used to transfer the data among all the components of the computer.

The duty of the CPU is to make sure that the data is processed and is on the system bus. The CPU manages data to make it in a correct order while arranging the data on the system bus. Thus, the action requested by the user is done and the user gets the processed and calculated information. Now when the data is processed, the CPU is required to store it in the system's memory.

So, this is how actually a CPU works.

Components of CPU

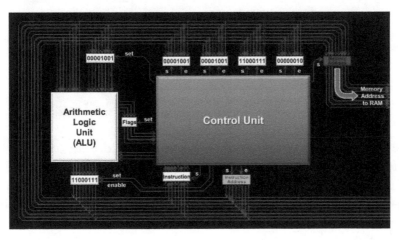

A Typical CPU Consists Of 2 Parts:

- Control Unit
- Logic Unit

Control Unit: This part of CPU is used to manage the operation of the CPU. It commands the various computer components to react according to the program's instruction. The computer programs are stored in the storage devices (hard disks and SSDs) and when a user run those programs, they load directly into the primary memory (RAM) for their execution. No program can be able to run without loading into primary memory. The control unit of the CPU is used to direct the whole computer system to process program's instruction using electrical signals. The control unit of a CPU communicates with ALU and memory to carry out the process instructions. Actually the control unit does not carry out the instruction of the program, instead, it commands the other part of the process. Without the control unit, the respective components will not be able to execute the program as they don't know what to do and when to do.

Logic Unit: Logic unit is also referred as Arithmetic Logic Unit (ALU). The ALU is a digital electronic circuit placed inside the CPU. Logic Unit is the basic building block of the CPU. The function of the ALU is to perform integer calculation and bitwise logic operations. Calculation of ALU includes addition, subtraction, shifting operations and Boolean comparisons (like AND, OR, XOR and NOT operations). The ALUs of different processor models may differ in design and functioning. In some simple computer, the processor may contain only one ALU while in the complex computer; the processor may have more than one ALU which work simultaneously to perform all the calculations. But we should remember that the main job of ALU is to calculate integer operations.

More Basic Elements of CPU

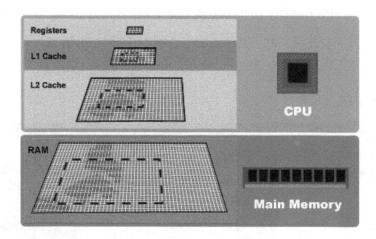

Register: A register is a very small place which is used to hold data of the processor. A register is used to store information such as instruction, storage address and any kind of data like bit sequence or any characters etc. A processor's register should be large enough to store all the given information. A 64-bit processor should have at least 64-bit registers and 32-bit register for a 32-bit processor. The register is the fastest of all the memory devices.

L1 and L2 Cache Memory: Cache Memory is a type of memory which is placed in the processor's chip or may be placed separately connected by a bus. The use of Cache Memory is to store program instructions which are again and again used by software for an operation. When the CPU processes data, the data is first looked into the cache memory. If the data is found, then it uses the data accordingly and if not, then the processor start to look in the larger memory, which is actually time-consuming. Cache memory is costly but it's really lightning fast.

There are levels of cache memory, they are as follows:

- L1 cache: L1 cache is extraordinary fast but it is very small. It is mainly placed on the CPU chip.

- L2 cache: L2 cache has more data holding capacity than L1 cache. It is situated in CPU chip or in the separate chip but connected to CPU with the high-speed alternative data bus.

Something about Multi-core CPUs

Nowadays computer comes with a multi-core processor. The multi-core processor means that more than one processor is embedded in the CPU Chip. Those multi-core processors work simultaneously and the main advantages of using the multi-core CPU is that it quickly achieved the high performance, consuming less energy power and the multi-tasking or parallel processing is really efficient. Since all the processor is plugged into the same plug so the connection between them is also actually fast.

Different Multi Core Processor Difference

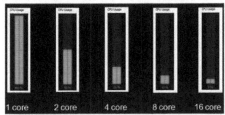

Dual Core Processor: In this, Dual or 2 processors are embedded in the chip and they work simultaneously. Multi-tasking is more than the single core processor.

Quad Core Processor: In this, Quad or 4 processors are embedded in the chip and work simultaneously. They are faster than dual core processor. Multi-tasking is more than the dual core processor.

Hexa Core Processor: In this, Hexa or 6 processors are embedded in the chip and work simultaneously. They are faster than quad core processor. Multi-tasking is more than the quad core processor.

Octa Core Processor: In this, Octa or 8 processors are embedded in the chip and they work simultaneously. They are faster than the hexacore processor.

Control Unit

A control unit (CU) handles all processor control signals. It directs all input and output flow, fetches code for instructions from micro programs and directs other units and models by providing control and timing signals. A CU component is considered the processor brain because it issues orders to just about everything and ensures correct instruction execution.

CU functions are as follows:

- Controls sequential instruction execution
- Interprets instructions
- Guides data flow through different computer areas
- Regulates and controls processor timing

- Sends and receives control signals from other computer devices
- Handles multiple tasks, such as fetching, decoding, execution handling and storing results

Design of Control Unit

Control unit generates timing and control signals for the operations of the computer. The control unit communicates with ALU and main memory. It also controls the transmission between processor, memory and the various peripherals. It also instructs the ALU which operation has to be performed on data.

Control unit can be designed by two methods which are given below.

Hardwired Control Unit

It is implemented with the help of gates, flip flops, decoders etc. in the hardware. The inputs to control unit are the instruction register, flags, timing signals etc. This organization can be very complicated if we have to make the control unit large.

If the design has to be modified or changed, all the combinational circuits have to be modified which is a very difficult task.

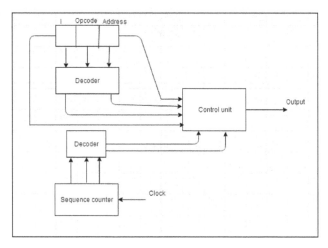

Microprogrammed Control Unit

It is implemented by using programming approach. A sequence of micro operations is carried out by executing a program consisting of micro-instructions. In this organization any modifications or changes can be done by updating the micro program in the control memory by the programmer.

Difference between Hardwired Control and Microprogrammed Control

Hardwired Control	Microprogrammed Control
Technology is circuit based.	Technology is software based.
It is implemented through flip-flops, gates, decoders etc.	Microinstructions generate signals to control the execution of instructions.

Fixed instruction format.	Variable instruction format (16-64 bits per instruction).
Instructions are register based.	Instructions are not register based.
ROM is not used.	ROM is used.
It is used in RISC.	It is used in CISC.
Faster decoding.	Slower decoding.
Difficult to modify.	Easily modified.
Chip area is less.	Chip area is large.

Arithmetic Logic Unit

An arithmetic-logic unit (ALU) is the part of a computer processor (CPU) that carries out arithmetic and logic operations on the operands in computer instruction words. In some processors, the ALU is divided into two units, an arithmetic unit (AU) and a logic unit (LU). Some processors contain more than one AU - for example, one for *fixed-point* operations and another for *floating-point* operations. (In personal computers floating point operations are sometimes done by a floating point unit on a separate chip called a numeric coprocessor.)

Typically, the ALU has direct input and output access to the processor controller, main memory (random access memory or RAM in a personal computer), and input/output devices. Inputs and outputs flow along an electronic path that is called a bus. The input consists of an instruction word (sometimes called a machine instruction word) that contains an operation code (sometimes called an "op code"), one or more operands, and sometimes a format code. The operation code tells the ALU what operation to perform and the operands are used in the operation. (For example, two operands might be added together or compared logically.) The format may be combined with the op code and tells, for example, whether this is a fixed-point or a floating-point instruction. The output consists of a result that is placed in a storage *register* and settings that indicate whether the operation was performed successfully. (If it isn't, some sort of status will be stored in a permanent place that is sometimes called the machine status word).

In general, the ALU includes storage places for input operands, operands that are being added, the accumulated result (stored in an *accumulator*), and shifted results. The flow of bits and the operations performed on them in the subunits of the ALU is controlled by gated circuits. The gates in these circuits are controlled by a sequence logic unit that uses a particular algorithm or sequence for each operation code. In the arithmetic unit, multiplication and division are done by a series of adding or subtracting and shifting operations. There are several ways to represent negative numbers. In the logic unit, one of 16 possible logic operations can be performed - such as comparing two operands and identifying where bits don't match.

The design of the ALU is obviously a critical part of the processor and new approaches to speeding up instruction handling are continually being developed.

The three fundamental attributes of an ALU are its operands and results, functional organization, and algorithms.

Operands and Results

The operands and results of the ALU are machine words of two kinds: *arithmetic words,* which represent numerical values in digital form, and *logic words,* which represent arbitrary sets of digitally encoded symbols. Arithmetic words consist of digit vectors (strings of digits).

Operator: Operator is arithmetic or logical operation that is performed on the operand given in instructions.

Flag: ALU uses many types of the flag during processing instructions. All these bits are stored in status or flag registers.

Functional Organization of an ALU

A typical ALU consists of three types of functional parts: storage registers, operations logic, and sequencing logic.

Arithmetic Logical Unit (ALU) Architecture

ALU is formed through the combinational circuit. The combinational circuit used logical gates like AND, OR, NOT, XOR for their construction. The combinational circuit does not have any memory element to store a previous data bit. Adders are the main part of the arithmetic logic unit to perform addition, subtraction by 2's complement.

Control unit generates the selection signals for selecting the function performed by ALU.

Registers: Registers are a very important component in ALU to store instruction, intermediate data, output, and input.

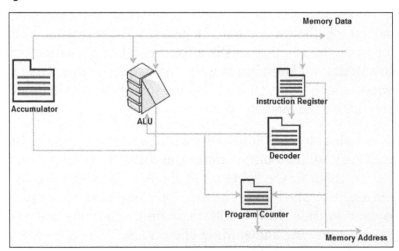

Logic Gates

Logic gates are building a block of ALU. Logic gates are constructed from diode, resistors or transistors. These gates are used in Integrated circuit represent binary input as 'ON' and 'OFF' state. Binary number 0 is represented by 'OFF' and Binary Number '1' is represented by 'ON' state in an integrated circuit.

OR gate: OR gate can take two or more inputs. The output of OR gate is always 1 if any of the inputs is 1 and 0 if all the inputs are false. OR gate performs an addition operation on all operand given in instructions. It can be expressed as X=A+B or X=A+B+C.

OR

Inputs		Output
A	B	C
0	0	0
0	1	1
1	0	1
1	1	1

AND gate: AND gate takes two or more inputs. The output of AND gate is 1 if all inputs are 1. AND gate gives 0 results if any one of input in given data is 0. AND gate performs multiplication option on all inputs operands. It is represented by '.' symbol. We can write it as- X=A.B or X=A.B.C.

AND

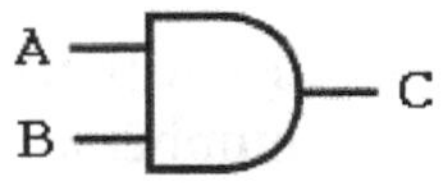

Inputs		Output
A	B	C
0	0	0
0	1	0
1	0	0
1	1	1

NOT gate: NOT gate is used to reverse the result of gates or reverse Boolean state from 0 to 1 and 1 to 0. NOT gate is also used with 'AND' and 'OR' gate. While using with AND or 'OR' gate, NOT gate is representing an as small circle in front of both gates. After using NOT gate, AND gates convert into NAND or 'OR' gate convert into NOR.

NOT

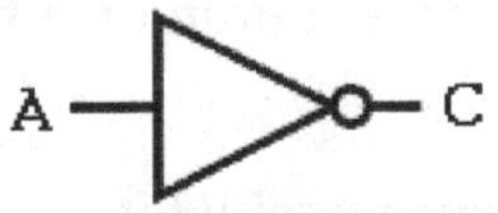

Input	Output
A	C
0	1
1	0

Registers: Registers provide fast memory access as a comparison to cache, RAM, hard disk. They are built on CPU. Register are small in size. Processing Intermediate data stored in registers. A number of registers used for specific purpose. ALU used four general purpose register. All these four registers are 16-bit register is divided into registers. 16-bit register implies that register can store maximum 16 bit of data.

Accumulator: Accumulator is 16 bit by default and general purpose register. By default means that any operand in instruction does not specify a particular register for holding the operand. That time operand will automatically store in AC. AC is used as two separate registers of 7 bit AL and AH. AC located inside the ALU. Intermediate data and result after execution will store in AC.AC used MBR to deal with memory.

Program counter: PC stands for program counter. *It is 16-bit register.* It counts the number of instruction left for execution. It acts as a pointer for instructions and also known as Instruction pointer register. PC holds the address of next instruction to be executed. When an instruction is fetched from the register. Register get automatically incremented by one and point to the address of next instruction.

Flag register: it is also known as a Status register or Program Status register. Flag register holds the Boolean value of status word used by the process.

Auxiliary flag: if two numbers are to be added such that if in the beginning of higher bit there is a carry. This is known as auxiliary bit.

Carry bit: Carry bit is indicate the most significant borrow or carry bit by subtracting a greater number than a smaller number or adding two numbers.

Sign Bit: Sign bit is a most significant bit in 2's complement to show that result is negative or positive. It is also known as negative bit. If the final carry over here after the sum of last most significant bit is 1, it is dropped and the result is positive.

If there is no carry over here then 2's complement will negative and negative bit set as 1.

Overflow bit: Overflow bit used to indicate that stack is overflow or not after processing the instruction. It is set to be 1 means that stack is overflow if it is 0 then its reverse to happen.

Parity bit: Parity bit represent odd or even set of '1' bits in given string. It is used as error detecting code. Parity bit has two types: Even parity bit and an Odd parity bit.

In even parity bit, we count the occurrence of I's in the string. If a number of 1 bit is odd in counting than we will add even parity bit to make it even or if the number of 1 bit are even then even parity bit is 0.

Data	*Number of 1 bits*	*even parity bit*	*Data including Even Parity bit*
1010111	*5*	*1*	*11010111*

Memory Address register: Address register holds the address of memory where data is residing. CPU fetches the address from the register and access the location to acquire data. In the same way, MAR is used to write the data into memory.

Data register: Data registers also Known as Memory Data Register. It holds the content or instruction fetched from memory location for reading and writing purpose. It is 16-bit register means that can store 2^{16} bytes of data. From Data, register instruction moves in Instruction register and data content moves to AC for manipulation.

Instruction register: Instruction holds the instruction to be executed. Control unit of CPU fetch the instruction, decode it and execute the instruction by accessing appropriate content.IR is 16-bit register. It has two fields – Opcode and operand.

PC holds the address of the instruction to be executed. Once the address is fetched it gets incremented by 1.PC hold the address of next instructions. In this situation, IR holds the address of the current instruction.

Input /output register: Input register holds the input from input devices and output register hold the output that has to give to output devices.

Memory Management Unit

A computer's memory management unit (MMU) is the physical hardware that handles its virtual memory and caching operations. The MMU is usually located within the computer's central processing unit (CPU), but sometimes operates in a separate integrated chip (IC). All data request inputs are sent to the MMU, which in turn determines whether the data needs to be retrieved from RAM or ROM storage.

A memory management unit is also known as a paged memory management unit.

The memory management unit performs three major functions:

- Hardware memory management

- Operating system (OS) memory management

- Application memory management

Hardware memory management deals with a system's RAM and cache memory, OS memory management regulates resources among objects and data structures, and application memory management allocates and optimizes memory among programs.

The MMU also includes a section of memory that holds a table that matches virtual addresses to physical addresses, called the translation look a side buffer (TLB).

Many microprocessors and microcontrollers incorporate a memory management unit (MMU) or have one available as an option. Equally, there are some devices that have no MMU support and many systems are built without one anyway.

We need to think in terms of logical addresses, which are what the software deals with, and physical addresses, which are seen by the hardware (the memory system). If there is no MMU, logical and physical addresses are the same. An MMU changes the mapping between logical and physical addresses.

Obviously, the simplest thing an MMU can do is map the logical addresses straight on to their physical counterparts.

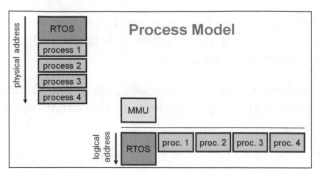

A common use of an MMU is to implement an operating system using process model – like Linux. In this case, each task has one or more dedicated areas of memory for its code and data. When a task is made current by the scheduler, the MMU maps these physical addresses onto a logical address area starting from 0. All the physical memory belonging to other tasks (processes) and to the OS itself is hidden from view and, thus, protected. Each process behaves as if it has free use of the entire CPU. Although this mechanism is safe and elegant, it has the drawback that there is an overhead – the MMU remapping – on every context switch.

Another approach is to implement a lightweight process model (also called "thread protected mode"). In most RTOSes, an MMU has not been traditionally used (or available) and all memory is visible at all times. If the MMU is set up in the trivial way I mentioned earlier, parts of the mapping may be switched off as each task is scheduled. Thus, no remapping of addresses occurs, but only the memory for the current task, and relevant parts of the OS, is visible at any one time. This provides much of the protection of process model, with a lower overhead on each context switch.

CPU Modes

Processor Mode also called as CPU modes or CPU "privilege level". The CPU modes are used by processor to create an operating environment for automatic. Specifically, the CPU mode controls how the processor sees and manages the system memory and task that use it. There are three different modes of operation but one more mode is added for new 64 bit processor:

1. Real Mode.

2. Protected Mode.

3. Virtual Mode Real Mode.

4. 64 bit extension Mode.

Real Mode

The original IBM PC could only address 1MB of system memory and the original versions of DOS created to work on it were designed with this in mind. DOS is it's by nature a single tasking operating system meaning it can only handle one program running at a time. The decision made in this early days have carried forward until now and in each new processor care had to be taken to be able to put the processor in a mode that would be compatible with the original Intel 8088 chip. This is called Real Mode. Real mode is of course used by DOS and "standard" DOS application.

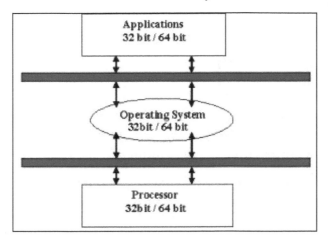

Protected Mode

Starting with the 80286 chip in the IBM AT, a new CPU mode was published called protected mode. This is much more powerful mode of operation than real mode and is used in all modern multitasking operating systems. The advantages of protected mode (compared to real mode) are:

- Full access to all of the system memory. There is no1 MB limitation in mode.

- Ability to multiple tasking meaning having the operating system manages the execution of multiple programs simultaneously.

- Preference to for virtual memory which gives the permission the system to use the hard disk to emulate additional system memory when needed.

- Faster (32 bit) access to memory and faster 32 bit drivers to do I/O transfer.

The name of this mode comes from its primary use which is multitasking operating system. Each program that is running has its own assigned memory location which is protected from conflict with other programs. If a program tries to access a memory address that it isn't allowed to a "protection fault" is generated.

Protected mode is now used by the most people use their PCs.

Virtual Mode

This mode is also called virtual 8086 mode. The third mode of operation is actually an some more capability, an enhancement of protected mode. The use Protected mode is for to run graphical multitasking operating system such as the various types of windows. There is often desire to be able to run DOS program under the window, but DOS programs need to be run in the real mode not protected mode. Virtual real mode is used to solve this problem. Virtual real mode is also used when you use a DOS box or run a DOS game in Windows 95.

64 Bit Extension Mode

This mode is also called Long Mode. 64 bit extension mode is the mode where a 64 bit application can access the 64 bit instruction and registers while 32 bit and 16 bit programs are executed in a compatibility sub mode.

Multi-core Processor

A multicore processor is a single integrated circuit (a.k.a., chip multiprocessor or CMP) that contains multiple core processing units, more commonly known as *cores*. There are many different multicore processor architectures, which vary in terms of:

- Number of cores: Different multicore processors often have different numbers of cores. For example, a quad-core processor has four cores. The number of cores is usually a power of two.

- Number of core types:

    o Homogeneous (symmetric) cores. All of the cores in a homogeneous multicore processor are of the same type; typically the core processing units are general-purpose central processing units that run a single multicore operating system.

    o Heterogeneous (asymmetric) cores. Heterogeneous multicore processors have a mix of core types that often run different operating systems and include graphics processing units.

- Number and level of caches: Multicore processors vary in terms of their instruction and data caches, which are relatively small and fast pools of local memory.

- How cores are interconnected: Multicore processors also vary in terms of their bus architectures.

- Isolation. The amount, typically minimal, of in-chip support for the spatial and temporal isolation of cores:

    o Physical isolation ensures that different cores cannot access the same physical hardware (e.g., memory locations such as caches and RAM).

    o Temporal isolation ensures that the execution of software on one *core* does not impact the temporal behavior of software running on another *core*.

Homogeneous Multicore Processor

The following figure notionally shows the architecture of a system in which 14 software applications are allocated by a single host operating system to the cores in a homogeneous quad-core processor. In this architecture, there are three levels of cache, which are progressively larger but slower: L1 (consisting of an instruction cache and a data cache), L2, and L3. Note that the L1 and L2 caches are local to a single core, whereas L3 is shared among all four cores.

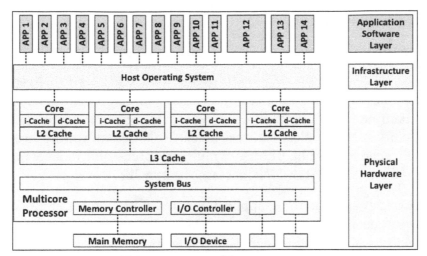

Heterogeneous multicore processor.

The following figure notionally shows how these 14 applications could be allocated to four different operating systems, which in turn are allocated to four different cores, in a heterogeneous, quad-core processor. From left to right, the cores include a general-purpose central processing unit core running Windows; a graphical processing unit (GPU) core running graphics-intensive applications on Linux; a digital signal processing (DSP) core running a real-time operating system (RTOS); and a high-performance core also running an RTOS.

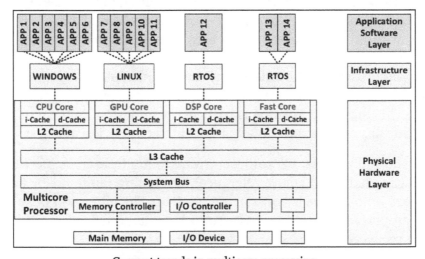

Current trends in multicore processing.

Multicore processors are replacing traditional, single-core processors so that fewer single-core processors are being produced and supported. Consequently, single-core processors are becoming technologically obsolete. Heterogeneous multicore processors, such as computer-on-a-chip processors, are becoming more common.

Although multicore processors have largely saturated some application domains (e.g., cloud computing, data warehousing, and on-line shopping), they are just starting to be used in real-time, safety- and security-critical, cyber-physical systems. One area in which multicore processing is becoming popular is in environments constrained by size, weight, and power, and cooling (SWAP-C), in which significantly increased performance is required.

Pros of Multicore Processing

Multicore processing is typically commonplace because it offers advantages in the following seven areas:

1. Energy Efficiency: By using multicore processors, architects can decrease the number of embedded computers. They overcome increased heat generation due to Moore's Law (i.e., smaller circuits increase electrical resistance, which creates more heat), which in turn decreases the need for cooling. The use of multicore processing reduces power consumption (less energy wasted as heat), which increases battery life.

2. True Concurrency: By allocating applications to different cores, multicore processing increases the intrinsic support for actual (as opposed to virtual) parallel processing within individual software applications across multiple applications.

3. Performance: Multicore processing can increase performance by running multiple applications concurrently. The decreased distance between cores on an integrated chip enables shorter resource access latency and higher cache speeds when compared to using separate processors or computers. However, the size of the performance increase depends on the number of cores, the level of real concurrency in the actual software, and the use of shared resources.

4. Isolation: Multicore processors *may* improve (but do *not* guarantee) spatial and temporal isolation (segregation) compared to single-core architectures. Software running on one core is less likely to affect software on another core than if both are executing on the same single core. This decoupling is due to both spatial isolation (of data in core-specific cashes) and temporal isolation, because threads on one core are not delayed by threads on another core. Multicore processing may also improve robustness by localizing the impact of defects to single core. This increased isolation is particularly important in the independent execution of mixed-criticality applications (mission-critical, safety critical, and security-critical).

5. Reliability and Robustness: Allocating software to multiple cores increases reliability and robustness (i.e., fault and failure tolerance) by limiting fault and/or failure propagation from software on one core to software on another. The allocation of software to multiple cores also supports failure tolerance by supporting failover from one core to another (and subsequent recovery).

6. Obsolescence Avoidance: The use of multicore processors enables architects to avoid technological obsolescence and improve maintainability. Chip manufacturers are applying the latest technical advances to their multicore chips. As the number of cores continues to increase, it becomes increasingly hard to obtain single-core chips.

7. Hardware Costs: By using multicore processors, architects can produce systems with fewer computers and processors.

Cons of Multicore Processing

Although there are many advantages to moving to multicore processors, architects must address disadvantages and associated risks in the following six areas:

1. Shared Resources: Cores on the same processor share both *processor-internal* resources (L3 cache, system bus, memory controller, I/O controllers, and interconnects) and *processor-external* resources (main memory, I/O devices, and networks). These shared resources imply (1) the existence of single points of failure, (2) two applications running on the *same* core can interfere with each other, and (3) software running on one core can impact software running on *another* core (i.e., interference can violate spatial and temporal isolation because multicore support for isolation is limited). The diagram below uses the color red to illustrate six shared resources.

2. Interference: Interference occurs when software executing on one core impacts the behavior of software executing on other cores in the same processor. This interference includes failures of both *spatial* isolation (due to shared memory access) and failure of *temporal* isolation (due to interference delays and/or penalties). Temporal isolation is a bigger problem than spatial isolation since multicore processors may have special hardware that can be used to enforce spatial isolation (to prevent software running on different cores from accessing the same processor-internal memory). The number of interference paths increases rapidly with the number of cores and the exhaustive analysis of all interference paths is often impossible. The impracticality of exhaustive analysis necessitates the selection of representative interference paths when analyzing isolation. The following diagram uses the color red to illustrate three possible interference paths between pairs of applications involving six shared resources.

3. Concurrency Defects: Cores execute concurrently, creating the potential for concurrency defects including deadlock, livelock, starvation, suspension, (data) race conditions, priority inversion, order violations, and atomicity violations. Note that these are essentially the same types of concurrency defects that can occur when software is allocated to multiple threads on a single core.

4. Non-determinism: Multicore processing increases non-determinism. For example, I/O Interrupts have top-level hardware priority (also a problem with single core processors). Multicore processing is also subject to lock trashing, which stems from excessive lock conflicts due to simultaneous access of kernel services by different cores (resulting in decreased concurrency and performance). The resulting non-deterministic behavior can be unpredictable, can cause related faults and failures, and can make testing more difficult (e.g., running the same test multiple times may not yield the same test result).

5. Analysis Difficulty: The real concurrency due to multicore processing requires different memory consistency models than virtual interleaved concurrency. It also breaks traditional analysis approaches for work on single core processors. The analysis of maximum time limits is harder and may be overly conservative. Although interference analysis becomes more complex as the number of cores-per-processor increases, overly-restricting the core number may not provide adequate performance.

6. Accreditation and Certification: Interference between cores can cause missed deadlines and excessive jitter, which in turn can cause faults (hazards) and failures (accidents). Verifying a multicore system requires proper real-time scheduling and timing analysis and/or specialized performance testing. Moving from a single-core to a multicore architecture

may require recertification. Unfortunately, current safety policy guidelines are based on single-core architectures and must be updated based on the recommendations that will be listed in the final blog entry in this series.

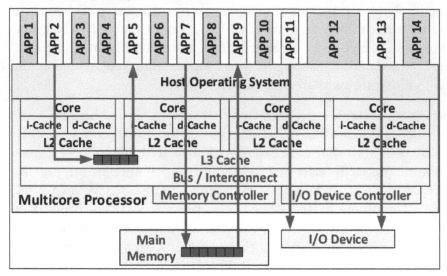

SEI-research on Multicore Processing

Real-time scheduling on multicore processing platforms is a Department of Defense (DoD) technical area of urgent concern for unmanned aerial vehicles (UAVs) and other systems that demand ever-increasing computational power. SEI researchers have provided a range of techniques and tools that improve scheduling on multicore processors. We developed a mode-change protocol for multicores with several operational modes, such as aircraft taxi, takeoff, flight, and landing modes. The SEI developed the first protocol to allow multicore software to switch modes while meeting all timing requirements, thereby allowing software designers add or remove software functions while ensuring safety.

Clock Rate

In a computer, clock speed refers to the number of pulses per second generated by an oscillator that sets the tempo for the processor. Clock speed is usually measured in MHz(megahertz, or millions of pulses per second) or GHz (gigahertz, or billions of pulses per second). Today's personal computers run at a clock speed in the hundreds of megahertz and some exceed one gigahertz. The clock speed is determined by a quartz-crystal circuit, similar to those used in radio communications equipment.

Computer clock speed has been roughly doubling every year. The Intel 8088, common in computers around the year 1980, ran at 4.77 MHz. The 1 GHz mark was passed in the year 2000.

Clock speed is one measure of computer "power," but it is not always directly proportional to the performance level. If you double the speed of the clock, leaving all other hardware unchanged, you will not necessarily double the processing speed. The type of microprocessor, the bus architecture, and the nature of the instruction set all make a difference. In some applications, the amount of random access memory (RAM) is important, too.

Some processors execute only one instruction per clock pulse. More advanced processors can perform more than one instruction per clock pulse. The latter type of processor will work faster at a given clock speed than the former type. Similarly, a computer with a 32-bit bus will work faster at a given clock speed than a computer with a 16-bit bus. For these reasons, there is no simplistic, universal relation among clock speed, "bus speed," and millions of instructions per second (MIPS).

Excessive clock speed can be detrimental to the operation of a computer. As the clock speed in a computer rises without upgrades in any of the other components, a point will be reached beyond which a further increase in frequency will render the processor unstable. Some computer users deliberately increase the clock speed, hoping this alone will result in a proportional improvement in performance, and are disappointed when things don't work out that way.

Megahertz Myth

The megahertz myth addresses the fallacy that higher clock speed translates to better performance. In reality, this picture isn't quite accurate. When assessing CPU performance, certain contributing factors outweigh clock rate. For instance, instruction sets and pipeline depth are valuable in determining performance. However, before you throw clock speed out the window, as it's a valuable metric for comparing CPUs from the same family.

The origins of the myth came about with the competing Apple II and IBM computers, both running PowerPC CPUs. PowerPC CPUs exhibited varying performance yields, despite having the same clock speed. The x86 architecture, with longer pipelines, actually aided CPUs to reach higher frequencies. The Apple variant was significantly slower than the IBM iteration.

To the uninformed consumer, clock speed is the ultimate metric when comparing CPUs. Yet, various factors mean that, say, a 2 GHz CPU can outperform a 2.6 GHz processor. Microarchitecture plays a key role, as does pipeline, and even program design. Thus, clock rate isn't nearly as reliable an indicator of potential performance. Benchmarks instead provide better insight when comparing CPUs.

Modern Adaptations of the Myth

With the advent of multithreading and multicore processors, the myth has stirred up more misconceptions regarding the measurement of performance in multi-core processors. Many people believe that a quad-core processor running at 3 GHz would result in an overall performance of 12 GHz worth of CPU. Others may say that the overall performance is in fact 3 GHz, with each core running at 750 MHz. Both of these ideas are incorrect. Often the same user making these comparisons will be comparing multiple brands of CPU, which will not do the same amount of work per cycle in any case. While micro-architecture traits such as pipeline depth play the same role in performance, the design of parallel processing brings other factor into the picture: software efficiency.

It is true that a poorly written program will run poorly on even a single-core system, but even a well written program that was designed in a linear fashion, will often (if not always) perform better on a single-core system than a multi-core one when run by itself. A system's overall performance cannot be judged by simply comparing the amount of processor cores and clock rates, the software running on the system is also a major factor of observed speed. The myth of the importance of clock rate has confused many people as to how they judge the speed of a computer system.

Challenges to the Myth

Comparisons between PowerPC and Pentium had become a staple of Apple presentations. At the New York City Macworld Expo *Keynote* on July 18, 2001, Steve Jobs described an 867 MHz G4 as completing a task in 45 seconds while a 1.7 GHz Pentium 4 took 82 seconds for the same task, saying that «the name that we've given it is the megahertz myth». He then introduced senior hardware VP Jon Rubinstein who gave a tutorial describing how shorter pipelines gave better performance at half the clock rate. The online cartoon Joy of Tech subsequently presented a series of cartoons inspired by Rubinstein's tutorial.

Intel Reaches its own Speed Limit

From approximately 1995 to 2005, Intel advertised its Pentium mainstream processors primarily on the basis of clock speed alone, in comparison to competitor products such as from AMD. Press articles had predicted that computer processors may eventually run as fast as 10 to 20 gigahertz in the next several decades.

This continued up until about 2005, when the Pentium Extreme Edition was reaching thermal dissipation limits running at speeds of nearly 4 gigahertz. The processor could go no faster without requiring complex changes to the cooling design, such as microfluidic cooling channels embedded within the chip itself to remove heat rapidly.

This was followed by the introduction of the Core 2 desktop processor in 2006, which was a major change from previous Intel desktop processors, allowing nearly a 50% decrease in processor clock while retaining the same performance.

Core 2 had its beginnings in the Pentium M mobile processor, where energy efficiency was more important than raw power, and initially offered power-saving options not available in the Pentium 4 and Pentium D.

Microprocessor

Microprocessor is a controlling unit of a micro-computer, fabricated on a small chip capable of performing ALU (Arithmetic Logical Unit) operations and communicating with the other devices connected to it.

Microprocessor consists of an ALU, register array, and a control unit. ALU performs arithmetical and logical operations on the data received from the memory or an input device. Register array consists of registers identified by letters like B, C, D, E, H, L and accumulator. The control unit controls the flow of data and instructions within the computer.

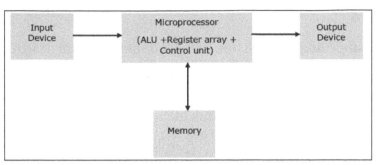

Work of Microprocessor.

The microprocessor follows a sequence: Fetch, Decode, and then Execute.

Initially, the instructions are stored in the memory in a sequential order. The microprocessor fetches those instructions from the memory, then decodes it and executes those instructions till STOP instruction is reached. Later, it sends the result in binary to the output port. Between these processes, the register stores the temporarily data and ALU performs the computing functions.

List of Terms used in a Microprocessor

Here is a list of some of the frequently used terms in a microprocessor:

- Instruction Set: It is the set of instructions that the microprocessor can understand.

- Bandwidth: It is the number of bits processed in a single instruction.

- Clock Speed: It determines the number of operations per second the processor can perform. It is expressed in megahertz (MHz) or gigahertz (GHz).It is also known as Clock Rate.

- Word Length: It depends upon the width of internal data bus, registers, ALU, etc. An 8-bit microprocessor can process 8-bit data at a time. The word length ranges from 4 bits to 64 bits depending upon the type of the microcomputer.

- Data Types: The microprocessor has multiple data type formats like binary, BCD, ASCII, signed and unsigned numbers.

Features of a Microprocessor

Here is a list of some of the most prominent features of any microprocessor:

- Cost-effective: The microprocessor chips are available at low prices and results its low cost.

- Size: The microprocessor is of small size chip, hence is portable.

- Low Power Consumption: Microprocessors are manufactured by using metal oxide semiconductor technology, which has low power consumption.

- Versatility: The microprocessors are versatile as we can use the same chip in a number of applications by configuring the software program.

- Reliability: The failure rate of an IC in microprocessors is very low, hence it is reliable.

Microarchitecture

Microarchitecture, abbreviated as µarch or uarch, is the fundamental design of a microprocessor.

Microarchitecture is the logical representation of how a microprocessor is designed so that the interconnections between components – the control unit, the arithmetic logic unit, registers and others – interact in an optimized manner. This includes how buses, the data pathways between components, are laid out to dictate the shortest paths and proper connections. In modern microprocessors there are often several layers to deal with complexity. The basic idea is to lay out a circuit that could execute commands and operations that are defined in an instruction set.

A technique that is currently used in microarchitecture is the pipelined datapath. It is a technique that allows a form of parallelism that is applied in data processing by allowing several instructions to overlap in execution. This is done by having multiple execution pipelines that run in parallel or close to parallel.

Execution units are also a crucial aspect of microarchitecture. Execution units perform the operations or calculations of the processor. The choice of the number of execution units, their latency and throughput is a central micro architectural design consideration. The size, latency, throughput and connectivity of memories within the system are also micro architectural decisions.

Another part of microarchitecture is system-level design. This includes decisions on performance such as level and connectivity of input, as well as output and I/O devices.

Micro architectural design pays closer attention to restrictions than capability. A microarchitecture design decision directly affects what goes into a system; it heeds to issues such as:

- Performance
- Chip area/cost
- Logic complexity
- Ease of debugging
- Testability
- Ease of connectivity
- Power consumption
- Manufacturability

A good microarchitecture is one that caters to all of these criteria.

Scalar Processor

A scalar processor is a normal processor, which works on simple instruction at a time, which operates on single data items. But in today's world, this technique will prove to be highly inefficient, as the overall processing of instructions will be very slow.

Vector (Array) Processing

There is a class of computational problems that are beyond the capabilities of a conventional computer. These problems require vast number of computations on multiple data items, that will take a conventional computer (with scalar processor) days or even weeks to complete.

Such complex instruction, which operates on multiple data at the same time, requires a better way of instruction execution, which was achieved by Vector processors.

Scalar CPUs can manipulate one or two data items at a time, which is not very efficient. Also, simple instructions like ADD A to B, and store into C are not practically efficient.

Addresses are used to point to the memory location where the data to be operated will be found, which leads to added overhead of data lookup. So until the data is found, the CPU would be sitting ideal, which is a big performance issue.

Hence, the concept of Instruction Pipeline comes into picture, in which the instruction passes through several sub-units in turn. These sub-units perform various independent functions, for example: the first one decodes the instruction, the second sub-unit fetches the data and the third sub-unit performs the math itself. Therefore, while the data is fetched for one instruction, CPU does not sit idle, it rather works on decoding the next instruction set, ending up working like an assembly line.

Vector processor, not only use Instruction pipeline, but it also pipelines the data, working on multiple data at the same time.

A normal scalar processor instruction would be ADD A, B, which leads to addition of two operands, but what if we can instruct the processor to ADD a group of numbers(from 0 to n memory location) to another group of numbers (let's say, n to k memory location). This can be achieved by vector processors.

In vector processor a single instruction, can ask for multiple data operations, which saves time, as instruction is decoded once, and then it keeps on operating on different data items.

Applications of Vector Processors

Computer with vector processing capabilities are in demand in specialized applications. The following are some areas where vector processing is used:

1. Petroleum exploration.

2. Medical diagnosis.

3. Data analysis.

4. Weather forecasting.

5. Aerodynamics and space flight simulations.

6. Image processing.

7. Artificial intelligence.

Superscalar Processors

It was first invented in 1987. It is a machine which is designed to improve the performance of the scalar processor. In most applications, most of the operations are on scalar quantities. Superscalar approach produces the high performance general purpose processors.

The main principle of superscalar approach is that it executes instructions independently in different pipelines. As we already know, that Instruction pipelining leads to parallel processing thereby speeding up the processing of instructions. In Superscalar processor, multiple such pipelines are introduced for different operations, which further improves parallel processing.

There are multiple functional units each of which is implemented as a pipeline. Each pipeline consists of multiple stages to handle multiple instructions at a time which support parallel execution of instructions.

It increases the throughput because the CPU can execute multiple instructions per clock cycle. Thus, superscalar processors are much faster than scalar processors.

A scalar processor works on one or two data items, while the vector processor works with multiple data items. A superscalar processor is a combination of both. Each instruction processes one data item, but there are multiple execution units within each CPU thus multiple instructions can be processing separate data items concurrently.

While a superscalar CPU is also pipelined, there are two different performance enhancement techniques. It is possible to have a non-pipelined superscalar CPU or pipelined non-superscalar CPU. The superscalar technique is associated with some characteristics, these are:

1. Instructions are issued from a sequential instruction stream.

2. CPU must dynamically check for data dependencies.

3. Should accept multiple instructions per clock cycle.

Superscalar Example

Assume 2-way superscalar processor with the following pipeline:

- 1 ADD/SUB ALU pipeline (1-Cycle INT-OP)

- 1 MULT/DIV ALU pipelines (4-Cycle INT-OP such as MULT)

- 2 MEM pipelines (1-Cycle (L1 hit) and 4-Cycle (L1 miss) MEM OP)

Show the pipeline diagram for the following codes assuming the bypass network:

- LD R1 <- A (L1 hit); LD R2 <- B (L1 miss)

- MULT R3, R1, R2; ADD R4, R1, R2

- SUB R5, R3, R4; ADD R4, R4, 1

- ST C <- R5; ST D <- R4

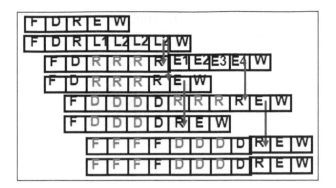

Coprocessor

A coprocessor is an auxiliary processing unit that is used to supplement the processing power of a microprocessor. In short, a coprocessor is an add-on that provides functionally that could not be incorporated in a processor for either economic or technical reasons.

Early microprocessors struggled to provide sufficient functionality on a single silicon chip you got a device that fetched instructions and executed instructions on integers. Floating-point operations, string processing, memory management and many of the functions we expect a processor to perform did not exist.

A processor can be designed to delegate certain operations to one or more external coprocessors. This takes requires two elements: a means of incorporating new instructions into the existing coprocessor architecture and a means of communicating between the processor and coprocessor. Ideally, these tasks should be invisible to the user and a processor-coprocessor pair should appear just as a processor with an enhanced instruction set architecture.

Note that there is a difference between an accelerator and a coprocessor, although both have the same function that is, to enhance performance. The accelerator improves the performance of a system exactly like the coprocessor, but the accelerator is not an extension of the processor's architecture. It is usually a memory-mapped peripheral that can be accessed from the system bus.

The microprocessor itself fetches instructions from memory, and, if an instruction is a coprocessor instruction, the CPU passes it to the coprocessor by means of a bus (which may or may not be dedicated). Moreover, the processor is normally responsible for fetching any data required by the coprocessor.

ARM Coprocessors

Coprocessors for the ARM are connected to it via its data and control buses. When the ARM first encounters an instruction that is not part of its current instruction set, the ARM regards it as a potential coprocessor operation. It is treated only as an illegal instruction exception after it has failed to be accepted buy a coprocessor.

Moreover, because the ARM offers predicated instruction, an op-code that would not be executed because of the predicated condition and state of the condition flags, is not executed irrespective of whether it is a valid coprocessor instruction or not.

When the ARM detects a potential coprocessor instruction, is asserts CPI, coprocessor instruction, which is monitored by all coprocessors in the system. A coprocessor can read the instruction from the data bus and check for both a valid coprocessor ID and a tag (one of 16). If there's a match, the coprocessor responds by asserting CPA, coprocessor absent. Now the coprocessor can assert, CPB, to take control until its operation has been completed.

Hardware Multithreading

A multithreading processor is able to pursue two or more threads of control in parallel within the processor pipeline. The contexts of two or more threads are often stored in separate on-chip register sets.

Formally speaking, CMT(Chip Multi-Threading), is a processor technology that allows multiple hardware threads of execution (also known as strands) on the same chip, through multiple cores per chip, multiple threads per core, or a combination of both.

Multiple Cores per Chip

CMP (Chip Multi-Processing, a.k.a. Multicore), is a processor technology that combines multiple processors (a.k.a. cores) on the same chip.

The idea is very similar to SMP, but implemented within a single chip. Is the most famous paper about this technology?

Multiple Threads per Core

- Vertical Multithreading – Instructions can be issued only from a single thread in any given CPU cycle.

    o Interleaved Multithreading (a.k.a. Fine Grained Multithreading), the instructions of other threads is fetched and fed into the execution pipelines at each processor cycle. So context switches at every CPU cycle.

    o Blocked Multithreading (a.k.a. Coarse Grained Multithreading), the instructions of other threads is executed successively until an event in current execution thread occurs that may cause latency. This delay event induces a context switch.

- Horizontal Multithreading – Instructions can be issued from multiple threads in any given cycle.

    This is so called Simultaneous multithreading (SMT): Instructions are simultaneously issued from multiple threads to the execution units of a superscalar processor. Thus, the wide superscalar instruction issue is combined with the multiple-context approach.

Unused instruction slots, which arise from latencies during the pipelined execution of single-threaded programs by a contemporary microprocessor, are filled by instructions of other threads within a multithreaded processor. The executions units are multiplexed among those thread contexts that are loaded in the register sets.

o   Underutilization of a superscalar processor due to missing instruction-level parallelism can be overcome by simultaneous multithreading, where a processor can issue multiple instructions from multiple threads in each cycle. Simultaneous multithreaded processors combine the multithreading technique with a wide-issue superscalar processor to utilize a larger part of the issue bandwidth by issuing instructions from different threads simultaneously.

Types of Multithreading

Block Multi-threading

The simplest type of multi-threading occurs when one thread runs until it is blocked by an event that normally would create a long latency stall. Such a stall might be a cache-miss that has to access off-chip memory, which might take hundreds of CPU cycles for the data to return. Instead of waiting for the stall to resolve, a threaded processor would switch execution to another thread that was ready to run. Only when the data for the previous thread had arrived, would the previous thread be placed back on the list of ready to-run threads.

For example:

1.   Cycle i: instruction j from thread A is issued

2.   Cycle i+1: instruction j+1 from thread A is issued

3.   Cycle i+2: instruction j+2 from thread A is issued, load instruction which misses in all caches

4.   Cycle i+3: thread scheduler invoked, switches to thread B

5.   Cycle i+4: instruction k from thread B is issued

6.   Cycle i+5: instruction k+1 from thread B is issued

Conceptually, it is similar to cooperative multi-tasking used in real-time operating systems in which tasks voluntarily give up execution time when they need to wait upon some type of the event.

Terminology:

This type of multi-threading is known as Block or Cooperative or Coarse-grained multithreading.

Hardware Cost

The goal of multi-threading hardware support is to allow quick switching between a blocked thread and another thread ready to run. To achieve this goal, the hardware cost is to replicate the program visible registers as well as some processor control registers (such as the program counter). Switching from one thread to another thread means the hardware switches from using one register set to another.

Such additional hardware has these benefits:

- The thread switch can be done in one CPU cycle.

- It appears to each thread that it is executing alone and not sharing any hardware resources with any other threads. This minimizes the amount of software changes needed within the application as well as the operating system to support multithreading.

In order to switch efficiently between active threads, each active thread needs to have its own register set. For example, to quickly switch between two threads, the register hardware needs to be instantiated twice.

Examples:

- Many families of microcontrollers and embedded processors have multiple register banks to allow quick context switching for interrupts. Such schemes can be considered a type of block multithreading among the user program thread and the interrupt threads.

Interleaved Multi-threading

1. Cycle i+1: an instruction from thread B is issued.

2. Cycle i+2: an instruction from thread C is issued.

The purpose of this type of multithreading is to remove all data dependency stalls from the execution pipeline. Since one thread is relatively independent from other threads, there's less chance of one instruction in one pipe stage needing an output from an older instruction in the pipeline.

Conceptually, it is similar to pre-emptive multi-tasking used in operating systems. One can make the analogy that the time-slice given to each active thread is one CPU cycle.

Terminology:

This type of multithreading was first called Barrel processing, in which the staves of a barrel represent the pipeline stages and their executing threads. Interleaved or Pre-emptive or Fine-grained or time-sliced multithreading are more modern terminology.

Hardware Costs

In addition to the hardware costs discussed in the Block type of multithreading, interleaved multithreading has an additional cost of each pipeline stage tracking the thread ID of the instruction it is processing. Also, since there are more threads being executed concurrently in the pipeline, shared resources such as caches and TLBs need to be larger to avoid thrashing between the different threads.

Simultaneous Multi-threading

Simultaneous multithreading (SMT) is a technique for improving the overall efficiency of superscalar CPUs with hardware multithreading. SMT permits multiple independent threads of execution to better utilize the resources provided by modern processor architectures.

The most advanced type of multi-threading applies to superscalar processors. A normal superscalar processor issues multiple instructions from a single thread every CPU cycle. In Simultaneous Multi-threading (SMT), the superscalar processor can issue instructions from multiple threads every CPU cycle. Recognizing that any single thread has a limited amount of instruction level parallelism, this type of multithreading tries to exploit parallelism available across multiple threads to decrease the waste associated with unused issue slots.

For example:

1. Cycle i : instructions j and j+1 from thread A; instruction k from thread B all simultaneously issued

2. Cycle i+1: instruction j+2 from thread A; instruction k+1 from thread B; instruction m from thread C all simultaneously issued

3. Cycle i+2: instruction j+3 from thread A; instructions m+1 and m+2 from thread C all simultaneously issued

Terminology:

To distinguish the other types of multithreading from SMT, the term Temporal multithreading is used to denote when instructions from only one thread can be issued at a time.

Hardware Costs

In addition to the hardware costs discussed for interleaved multithreading, SMT has the additional cost of each pipeline stage tracking the Thread ID of each instruction being processed. Again, shared resources such as caches and TLBs have to be sized for the large number of active threads being processed.

- Fixed interleave

  o Each of N threads executes one instruction every N cycles

  o If thread not ready to go in its slot, insert pipeline bubble

- Software-controlled interleave

  o OS allocates S pipeline slots amongst N threads

  o Hardware performs fixed interleave over S slots executing whichever thread is in that slot

- Hardware-controlled thread scheduling

  o Hardware keeps track of which threads are ready to go

  o Picks next thread to execute based on hardware priority scheme

CPU Registers

In *computer architecture*, a processor register is a very fast computer memory used to speed the execution of computer programs by providing quick access to commonly used values-typically, the values being in the midst of a calculation at a given point in time.

These registers are the top of the memory hierarchy, and are the fastest way for the system to manipulate data. In a very simple *microprocessor*, it consists of a single memory location, usually called an *accumulator*. Registers are built from fast multi-ported memory cell. They must be able to drive its data onto an internal bus in a single clock cycle. The result of ALU operation is stored here and could be re-used in a subsequent operation or saved into memory.

Registers are normally measured by the number of bits they can hold, for example, an "8-bit register" or a "32-bit register". Registers are now usually implemented as a register file, but they have also been implemented using individual flip-flops, high speed core memory, thin film memory, and other ways in various machines.

CPU Register.

The term is often used to refer only to the group of registers that can be directly indexed for input or output of an instruction, as defined by the instruction set. More properly, these are called the *"architected registers"*. For instance, the x86 instruction set defines a set of eight 32-bit registers, but a CPU that implements the X86 instruction set will contain many more hardware registers than just these eight.

A brief description of most important CPU's registers and their functions are given below:

1. Memory Address Register (MAR)

This register holds the address of memory where CPU wants to read or write data. When CPU wants to store some data in the memory or reads the data from the memory, it places the address of the required memory location in the MAR.

2. Memory Buffer Register (MBR)

This register holds the contents of data or instruction read from, or written in memory. The contents of instruction placed in this register are transferred to the Instruction Register, while the contents of data are transferred to the accumulator or I/O register.

In other words you can say that this register is used to store data/instruction coming from the memory or going to the memory.

3. I/O Address Register (I/O AR)

I/O Address register is used to specify the address of a particular I/O device

4. I/O Buffer Register (I/O I3R)

I/O Buffer Register is used for exchanging data between the I/O module and the processor

5. Program Counter (PC)

Program Counter register is also known as Instruction Pointer Register. This register is used to store the address of the next instruction to be fetched for execution. When the instruction is fetched, the value of IP is incremented. Thus this register always points or holds the address of next instruction to be fetched.

6. Instruction Register (IR):

Once an instruction is fetched from main memory, it is stored in the Instruction Register. The control unit takes instruction from this register, decodes and executes it by sending signals to the appropriate component of computer to carry out the task.

7. Accumulator Register:

The accumulator register is located inside the ALU, It is used during arithmetic & logical operations of ALU. The control unit stores data values fetched from main memory in the accumulator for arithmetic or logical operation. This register holds the initial data to be operated upon, the intermediate results, and the final result of operation. The final result is transferred to main memory through MBR.

8. Stack Control Register:

A stack represents a set of memory blocks; the data is stored in and retrieved from these blocks in an order, i.e. First In and Last Out (FILO). The Stack Control Register is used to manage the stacks in memory. The size of this register is 2 or 4 bytes.

9. Flag Register:

The Flag register is used to indicate occurrence of a certain condition during an operation of the CPU. It is a special purpose register with size one byte or two bytes. Each bit of the flag register constitutes a flag (or alarm), such that the bit value indicates if a specified condition was encountered while executing an instruction.

References

- Memory-management-unit-mmu-4768: techopedia.com, Retrieved 17, May 2020
- Hardware-Multithreading-115017034: scribd.com, Retrieved 19, June 2020
- What-is-cpu-central-processing-unit-and-how-its-work: deskdecode.com, Retrieved 25, June 2020
- Performance-fundamentals-megahertz: cupofmoe.com, Retrieved 19, July 2020
- Design-of-control-unit, computer-architecture: studytonight.com, Retrieved 10, April 2020

5

Synchronization

Synchronization refers to the orderly sharing of system resources by processes. Synchronization involves two concepts: synchronization of processes and synchronization of data. Barrier is a type of synchronization. In a group of threads; a thread must stop at this point and is unable to proceed until all threads reach this barrier. Synchronization is a vast subject that branches out into significant processes which have been thoroughly discussed in this chapter.

In computer science, synchronization refers to one of two distinct but related concepts: synchronization of processes, and synchronization of data. *Process synchronization* refers to the idea that multiple processes are to join up or handshake at a certain point, in order to reach an agreement or commit to a certain sequence of action. *Data synchronization* refers to the idea of keeping multiple copies of a dataset in coherence with one another, or to maintain data integrity. Process synchronization primitives are commonly used to implement data synchronization.

The Need for Synchronization

The need for synchronization does not arise merely in multi-processor systems but for any kind of concurrent processes; even in single processor systems. Mentioned below are some of the main needs for synchronization:

Forks and Joins: When a job arrives at a fork point, it is split into N sub-jobs which are then serviced by n tasks. After being serviced, each sub-job waits until all other sub-jobs are done processing. Then, they are joined again and leave the system. Thus, in parallel programming, we require synchronization as all the parallel processes wait for several other processes to occur.

Producer-Consumer: In a producer-consumer relationship, the consumer process is dependent on the producer process till the necessary data has been produced.

Exclusive use resources: When multiple processes are dependent on a resource and they need to access it at the same time the operating system needs to ensure that only one processor accesses it at a given point in time.This reduces concurrency.

Thread or Process Synchronization

Thread synchronization is defined as a mechanism which ensures that two or more concurrent processes or threads do not simultaneously execute some particular program segment known as critical section. Processes' access to critical section is controlled by using synchronization techniques. When one thread starts executing the critical section (serialized segment of the program) the other thread should wait until the first thread finishes. If proper synchronization techniques are not applied, it may cause a race condition where the values of variables may be unpredictable and vary depending on the timings of context switches of the processes or threads.

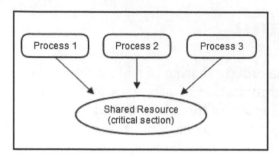

Three processes accessing a shared resource (critical section) simultaneously.

For example, suppose that there are three processes, namely 1, 2, and 3. All three of them are concurrently executing, and they need to share a common resource (critical section) as shown in Figure above. Synchronization should be used here to avoid any conflicts for accessing this shared resource. Hence, when Process 1 and 2 both try to access that resource, it should be assigned to only one process at a time. If it is assigned to Process 1, the other process (Process 2) needs to wait until Process 1 frees that resource (as shown in Figure below).

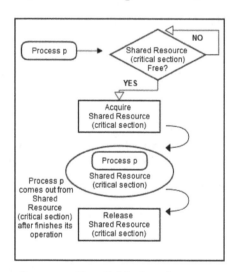

A process accessing a shared resource if available, based on some synchronization technique.

Another synchronization requirement which needs to be considered is the order in which particular processes or threads should be executed. For example, we cannot board a plane until we buy a ticket. Similarly, we cannot check e-mails without validating our credentials (i.e., user name and password). In the same way, an ATM will not provide any service until we provide it with a correct PIN.

Other than mutual exclusion, synchronization also deals with the following:

- deadlock, which occurs when many processes are waiting for a shared resource (critical section) which is being held by some other process. In this case, the processes just keep waiting and execute no further;

- starvation, which occurs when a process is waiting to enter the critical section, but other processes monopolize the critical section, and the first process is forced to wait indefinitely;

- priority inversion, which occurs when a high-priority process is in the critical section, and it is interrupted by a medium-priority process. This violation of priority rules can happen under certain circumstances and may lead to serious consequences in real-time systems;

- busy waiting, which occurs when a process frequently polls to determine if it has access to a critical section. This frequent polling robs processing time from other processes.

Minimizing Synchronization

One of the challenges for exascale algorithm design is to minimize or reduce synchronization. Synchronization takes more time than computation, especially in distributed computing. Reducing synchronization drew attention from computer scientists for decades. Whereas it becomes an increasingly significant problem recently as the gap between the improvement of computing and latency increases. Experiments have shown that (global) communications due to synchronization on a distributed computers takes a dominated share in a sparse iterative solver. This problem is receiving increasing attention after the emergence of a new benchmark metric,the High Performance Conjugate Gradient(HPCG), for ranking the top 500 supercomputers.

Classic Problems of Synchronization

The following are some classic problems of synchronization:

- The Producer–Consumer Problem (also called The Bounded Buffer Problem);

- The Readers–Writers Problem;

- The Dining Philosophers Problem.

These problems are used to test nearly every newly proposed synchronization scheme or primitive.

Hardware Synchronization

Many systems provide hardware support for critical section code.

A single processor or uniprocessor system could disable interrupts by executing currently running code without preemption, which is very inefficient on multiprocessor systems. "The key ability we require to implement synchronization in a multiprocessor is a set of hardware primitives with the ability to atomically read and modify a memory location. Without such a capability, the cost of building basic synchronization primitives will be too high and will increase as the processor count increases. There are a number of alternative formulations of the basic hardware primitives, all of which provide the ability to atomically read and modify a location, together with some way to tell if the read and write were performed atomically. These hardware primitives are the basic building blocks that are used to build a wide variety of user-level synchronization operations, including things such as locks and barriers. In general, architects do not expect users to employ the basic hardware primitives, but instead expect that the primitives will be used by system programmers to build a synchronization library, a process that is often complex and tricky." Many modern hardware provides special atomic hardware instructions by either test-and-set the memory word or compare-and-swap contents of two memory words.

Synchronization Strategies in Programming Languages

In Java, to prevent thread interference and memory consistency errors, blocks of code are wrapped into synchronized *(lock_object)* sections. This forces any thread to acquire the said lock object before it can execute the block. The lock is automatically released when thread leaves the block or enter the waiting state within the block. Any variable updates, made by the thread in synchronized block, become visible to other threads whenever those other threads similarly acquires the lock.

In addition to mutual exclusion and memory consistency, Java *synchronized* blocks enable signaling, sending events from those threads, which have acquired the lock and execute the code block to those which are waiting for the lock within the block. This means that Java synchronized sections combine functionality of mutexes and events. Such primitive is known as synchronization monitor.

Any object is fine to be used as a lock/monitor in Java. The declaring object is implicitly implied as lock object when the whole method is marked with *synchronized*.

The .NET framework has synchronization primitives. "Synchronization is designed to be cooperative, demanding that every thread or process follow the synchronization mechanism before accessing protected resources (critical section) for consistent results." In .NET, locking, signaling, lightweight synchronization types, spinwait and interlocked operations are some of mechanisms related to synchronization.

Implementation of Synchronization

Spinlock

Another effective way of implementing synchronization is by using spinlocks. Before accessing any shared resource or piece of code, every processor checks a flag. If the flag is reset, then the processor sets the flag and continues executing the thread. But, if the flag is set (locked), the threads would keep spinning in a loop and keep checking if the flag is set or not. But, spinlocks are effective only if the flag is reset for lower cycles otherwise it can lead to performance issues as it wastes many processor cycles waiting.

Barriers

Barriers are simple to implement and provide good responsiveness. They are based on the concept of implementing wait cycles to provide synchronization.Consider three threads running simultaneously, starting from barrier 1. After time t, thread1 reaches barrier 2 but it still has to wait for thread 2 and 3 to reach barrier2 as it does not have the correct data. Once, all the threads reach barrier 2 they all start again. After time t, thread 1 reaches barrier3 but it will have to wait for threads 2 and 3 and the correct data again.

Thus, in barrier synchronization of multiple threads there will always be a few threads that will end up waiting for other threads as in the above example thread 1 keeps waiting for thread 2 and 3. This results in severe degradation of the process performance.

The barrier synchronization wait function for i^{th} thread can be represented as:

(Wbarrier)i = f ((Tbarrier)i, (Rthread)i)

Where Wbarrier is the wait time for a thread, Tbarrier is the number of threads has arrived, and Rthread is the arrival rate of threads.

Experiments show that 34% of the total execution time is spent in waiting for other slower threads.

Semaphores

Semaphores are signalling mechanisms which can allow one or more threads/processors to access a section. A Semaphore has a flag which has a certain fixed value associated with it and each time a thread wishes to access the section, it decrements the flag. Similarly, when the thread leaves the section, the flag is incremented. If the flag is zero, the thread cannot access the section and gets blocked if it chooses to wait.

Some semaphores would allow only one thread or process in the code section. Such Semaphores are called binary semaphore and are very similar to Mutex. Here, if the value of semaphore is 1, the thread is allowed to access and if the value is 0, the access is denied.

Mathematical Foundations

Synchronization was originally a process-based concept whereby a lock could be obtained on an object. Its primary usage was in databases. There are two types of (file) lock; read-only and read–write. Read-only locks may be obtained by many processes or threads. Readers–writer locks are exclusive, as they may only be used by a single process/thread at a time.

Although locks were derived for file databases, data is also shared in memory between processes and threads. Sometimes more than one object (or file) is locked at a time. If they are not locked simultaneously they can overlap, causing a deadlock exception.

Java and Ada only have exclusive locks because they are thread based and rely on the compare-and-swap processor instruction.

An abstract mathematical foundation for synchronization primitives is given by the history monoid. There are also many higher-level theoretical devices, such as process calculi and Petri nets, which can be built on top of the history monoid.

Synchronization Examples

Following are some synchronization examples with respect to different platforms.

Synchronization in Windows

Windows provides:

- interrupt masks, which protect access to global resources (critical section) on uniprocessor systems;

- spinlocks, which prevent, in multiprocessor systems, spinlocking-thread from being pre-empted;

- dispatchers, which act like mutexes, semaphores, events, and timers.

Synchronization in Linux

Linux provides:

- semaphores

- spinlock

- barriers

- mutex

- readers–writer locks, for the longer section of codes which are accessed very frequently but don't change very often

- Read-copy-update (RCU)

Enabling and disabling of kernel preemption replaced spinlocks on uniprocessor systems. Prior to kernel version 2.6, Linux disabled interrupt to implement short critical sections. Since version 2.6 and later, Linux is fully preemptive.

Synchronization in Solaris

Solaris provides:

- semaphores;

- condition variables;

- adaptive mutexes, binary semaphores that are implemented differently depending upon the conditions;

- readers–writer locks:

- turnstiles, queue of threads which are waiting on acquired lock.

Pthreads Synchronization

Pthreads is a platform-independent API that provides:

- mutexes;

- condition variables;

- readers–writer locks;

- spinlocks;

- barriers.

Data Synchronization

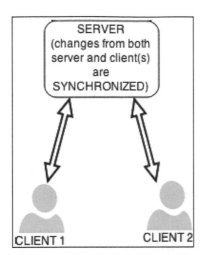

Changes from both server and client(s) are synchronized.

A distinctly different (but related) concept is that of data synchronization. This refers to the need to keep multiple copies of a set of data coherent with one another or to maintain data integrity, Figure above. For example, database replication is used to keep multiple copies of data synchronized with database servers that store data in different locations.

Examples include:

- File synchronization, such as syncing a hand-held MP3 player to a desktop computer;

- Cluster file systems, which are file systems that maintain data or indexes in a coherent fashion across a whole computing cluster;

- Cache coherency, maintaining multiple copies of data in sync across multiple caches;

- RAID, where data is written in a redundant fashion across multiple disks, so that the loss of any one disk does not lead to a loss of data;

- Database replication, where copies of data on a database are kept in sync, despite possible large geographical separation;

- Journaling, a technique used by many modern file systems to make sure that file metadata are updated on a disk in a coherent, consistent manner.

Challenges in Data Synchronization

Some of the challenges which user may face in data synchronization:

- data formats complexity;

- real-timeliness;

- data security;

- data quality;

- performance.

Data Formats Complexity

When we start doing something, the data we have usually is in a very simple format. It varies with time as the organization grows and evolves and results not only in building a simple interface between the two applications (source and target), but also in a need to transform the data while passing them to the target application. ETL (extraction transformation loading) tools can be very helpful at this stage for managing data format complexities.

Real-timeliness

This is an era of real-time systems. Customers want to see the current status of their order in e-shop, the current status of a parcel delivery—a real time parcel tracking—, the current balance on their account, etc. This shows the need of a real-time system, which is being updated as well to enable smooth manufacturing process in real-time, e.g., ordering material when enterprise is running out stock, synchronizing customer orders with manufacturing process, etc. From real life, there exist so many examples where real-time processing gives successful and competitive advantage.

Data Security

There are no fixed rules and policies to enforce data security. It may vary depending on the system which you are using. Even though the security is maintained correctly in the source system which captures the data, the security and information access privileges must be enforced on the target systems as well to prevent any potential misuse of the information. This is a serious issue and particularly when it comes for handling secret, confidential and personal information. So because of the sensitivity and confidentiality, data transfer and all in-between information must be encrypted.

Data Quality

Data quality is another serious constraint. For better management and to maintain good quality of data, the common practice is to store the data at one location and share with different people and different systems and/or applications from different locations. It helps in preventing inconsistencies in the data.

Performance

There are five different phases involved in the data synchronization process:

- data extraction from the source (or master, or main) system;
- data transfer;
- data transformation;
- data load to the target system.

Each of these steps is very critical. In case of large amounts of data, the synchronization process needs to be carefully planned and executed to avoid any negative impact on performance.

Fork–join Model

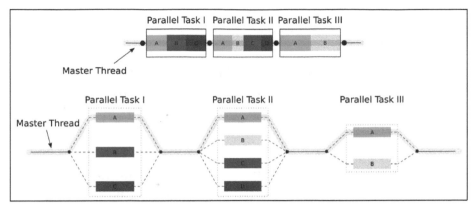

An illustration of the fork–join paradigm, in which three regions of the program permit parallel execution of the variously colored blocks. Sequential execution is displayed on the top, while its equivalent fork–join execution is on the bottom.

In parallel computing, the fork–join model is a way of setting up and executing parallel programs, such that execution branches off in parallel at designated points in the program, to "join" (merge) at a subsequent point and resume sequential execution. Parallel sections may fork recursively until a certain task granularity is reached. Fork–join can be considered a parallel design pattern. It was formulated as early as 1963.

By nesting fork–join computations recursively, one obtains a parallel version of the divide and conquer paradigm, expressed by the following generic pseudocode:

```
solve(problem):

    if problem is small enough:

        solve problem directly (sequential algorithm)

    else:

        for part in subdivide(problem)

            fork subtask to solve part

        join all subtasks spawned in previous loop

        combine results from subtasks
```

Examples

The simple parallel merge sort of CLRS is a fork–join algorithm.

```
mergesort(A, lo, hi):

    if lo < hi:                      // at least one element of input

        mid = ⌊lo+ (hi - lo) / 2⌋

        fork mergesort(A, lo, mid)   // process (potentially) in parallel with
main task
```

```
mergesort(A, mid, hi)        // main task handles second recursion

join

merge(A, lo, mid, hi)
```

The first recursive call is "forked off", meaning that its execution may run in parallel (in a separate thread) with the following part of the function, up to the join that causes all threads to synchronize. While the join may look like a barrier, it is different because the threads will continue to work after a barrier, while after a join only one thread continues.

The second recursive call is not a fork in the pseudocode above; this is intentional, as forking tasks may come at an expense. If both recursive calls were set up as subtasks, the main task would not have any additional work to perform before being blocked at the join.

Implementations

Implementations of the fork–join model will typically fork *tasks*, *fibers* or *lightweight threads*, not operating-system-level "heavyweight" threads or processes, and use a thread pool to execute these tasks: the fork primitive allows the programmer to specify *potential* parallelism, which the implementation then maps onto actual parallel execution. The reason for this design is that creating new threads tends to result in too much overhead.

The lightweight threads used in fork–join programming will typically have their own scheduler (typically a work stealing one) that maps them onto the underlying thread pool. This scheduler can be much simpler than a fully featured, preemptive operating system scheduler: general-purpose thread schedulers must deal with blocking for locks, but in the fork–join paradigm, threads only block at the join point.

Fork–join is the main model of parallel execution in the OpenMP framework, although OpenMP implementations may or may not support nesting of parallel sections. It is also supported by the Java concurrency framework, the Task Parallel Library for .NET, and Intel's Threading Building Blocks (TBB). The Cilk programming language has language-level support for fork and join, in the form of the spawn and sync keywords, or cilk_spawn and cilk_sync in Cilk Plus.

Producer–consumer Problem

In computing, the producer–consumer problem (also known as the bounded-buffer problem) is a classic example of a multi-process synchronization problem. The problem describes two processes, the producer and the consumer, who share a common, fixed-size buffer used as a queue. The producer's job is to generate data, put it into the buffer, and start again. At the same time, the consumer is consuming the data (i.e., removing it from the buffer), one piece at a time. The problem is to make sure that the producer won't try to add data into the buffer if it's full and that the consumer won't try to remove data from an empty buffer.

The solution for the producer is to either go to sleep or discard data if the buffer is full. The next time the consumer removes an item from the buffer, it notifies the producer, who starts to fill the buffer again. In the same way, the consumer can go to sleep if it finds the buffer to be empty. The next time the producer puts data into the buffer, it wakes up the sleeping consumer. The solution can be reached by means of inter-process communication, typically using semaphores. An inadequate solution could result in a deadlock where both processes are waiting to be awakened. The problem can also be generalized to have multiple producers and consumers.

Inadequate Implementation

To solve the problem, a less experienced programmer might come up with a solution shown below. In the solution two library routines are used, sleep and wakeup. When sleep is called, the caller is blocked until another process wakes it up by using the wakeup routine. The global variable itemCount holds the number of items in the buffer.

```
int itemCount = 0;


procedure producer() {

    while (true) {

        item = produceItem();


        if (itemCount == BUFFER_SIZE) {

            sleep();

        }


        putItemIntoBuffer(item);

        itemCount = itemCount + 1;


        if (itemCount == 1) {

            wakeup(consumer);

        }

    }

}


procedure consumer() {

    while (true) {


        if (itemCount == 0) {
```

```
        sleep();

    }


    item = removeItemFromBuffer();

    itemCount = itemCount - 1;


    if (itemCount == BUFFER_SIZE - 1) {

        wakeup(producer);

    }


    consumeItem(item);

    }

}
```

The problem with this solution is that it contains a race condition that can lead to a deadlock. Consider the following scenario:

1. The consumer has just read the variable itemCount, noticed it's zero and is just about to move inside the if block.

2. Just before calling sleep, the consumer is interrupted and the producer is resumed.

3. The producer creates an item, puts it into the buffer, and increases itemCount.

4. Because the buffer was empty prior to the last addition, the producer tries to wake up the consumer.

5. Unfortunately the consumer wasn't yet sleeping, and the wakeup call is lost. When the consumer resumes, it goes to sleep and will never be awakened again. This is because the consumer is only awakened by the producer when itemCount is equal to 1.

6. The producer will loop until the buffer is full, after which it will also go to sleep.

Since both processes will sleep forever, we have run into a deadlock. This solution therefore is unsatisfactory.

An alternative analysis is that if the programming language does not define the semantics of concurrent accesses to shared variables (in this case itemCount) without use of synchronization, then the solution is unsatisfactory for that reason, without needing to explicitly demonstrate a race condition.

Using Semaphores

Semaphores solve the problem of lost wakeup calls. In the solution below we use two semaphores, fillCount and emptyCount, to solve the problem. fillCount is the number of items already in the buffer and available to be read, while emptyCount is the number of available spaces in the buffer where items could be written. fillCount is incremented and emptyCount decremented when a new item is put into the buffer. If the producer tries to decrement emptyCount when its value is zero, the producer is put to sleep. The next time an item is consumed, emptyCount is incremented and the producer wakes up. The consumer works analogously.

```
semaphore fillCount = 0; // items produced

semaphore emptyCount = BUFFER_SIZE; // remaining space


procedure producer() {

    while (true) {

        item = produceItem();

        down(emptyCount);

        putItemIntoBuffer(item);

        up(fillCount);

    }

}


procedure consumer() {

    while (true) {

        down(fillCount);

        item = removeItemFromBuffer();

        up(emptyCount);

        consumeItem(item);

    }

}
```

The solution above works fine when there is only one producer and consumer. With multiple producers sharing the same memory space for the item buffer, or multiple consumers sharing the same memory space, this solution contains a serious race condition that could result in two or more processes reading or writing into the same slot at the same time. To understand how this is possible, imagine how the procedure put ItemIntoBuffer() can be implemented. It could contain two actions, one determining the next available slot and the other writing into it. If the procedure can be executed concurrently by multiple producers, then the following scenario is possible:

1. Two producers decrement emptyCount

2. One of the producers determines the next empty slot in the buffer

3. Second producer determines the next empty slot and gets the same result as the first producer

4. Both producers write into the same slot

To overcome this problem, we need a way to make sure that only one producer is executing putItemIntoBuffer() at a time. In other words, we need a way to execute a critical section with mutual exclusion. The solution for multiple producers and consumers is shown below.

```
mutex buffer_mutex; // similar to "semaphore buffer_mutex = 1", but different

semaphore fillCount = 0;


semaphore emptyCount = BUFFER_SIZE;


procedure producer() {

    while (true) {

        item = produceItem();

        down(emptyCount);

            down(buffer_mutex);

                putItemIntoBuffer(item);

            up(buffer_mutex);

        up(fillCount);

    }

}


procedure consumer() {

    while (true) {

        down(fillCount);

            down(buffer_mutex);

                item = removeItemFromBuffer();

            up(buffer_mutex);

        up(emptyCount);

        consumeItem(item);

    }

}
```

Notice that the order in which different semaphores are incremented or decremented is essential: changing the order might result in a deadlock. It is important to note here that though mutex seems to work as a semaphore with value of 1 (binary semaphore), but there is difference in the fact that mutex has ownership concept. Ownership means that mutex can only be "incremented" back (set to 1) by the same process that "decremented" it (set to 0), and all others tasks wait until mutex is available for decrement (effectively meaning that resource is available), which ensures mutual exclusivity and avoids deadlock. Thus using mutexes improperly can stall many processes when exclusive access is not required, but mutex is used instead of semaphore.

Using Monitors

The following pseudo code shows a solution to the producer–consumer problem using monitors. Since mutual exclusion is implicit with monitors, no extra effort is necessary to protect the critical section. In other words, the solution shown below works with any number of producers and consumers without any modifications. It is also noteworthy that using monitors makes race conditions much less likely than when using semaphores.

```
monitor ProducerConsumer {

    int itemCount;

    condition full;

    condition empty;


    procedure add(item) {

        while (itemCount == BUFFER_SIZE) {

            wait(full);

        }


        putItemIntoBuffer(item);

        itemCount = itemCount + 1;


        if (itemCount == 1) {

            notify(empty);

        }

    }

    procedure remove() {

        while (itemCount == 0) {
```

```
            wait(empty);

        }


        item = removeItemFromBuffer();

        itemCount = itemCount - 1;


        if (itemCount == BUFFER_SIZE - 1) {

            notify(full);

        }



        return item;

    }

}


procedure producer() {

    while (true) {

        item = produceItem();

        ProducerConsumer.add(item);

    }

}


procedure consumer() {

    while (true) {

        item = ProducerConsumer.remove();

        consumeItem(item);

    }

}
```

Note the use of while statements in the above code, both when testing if the buffer is full or empty. With multiple consumers, there is a race condition where one consumer gets notified that an item has been put into the buffer but another consumer is already waiting on the monitor so removes it from the buffer instead. If the while was instead an if, too many items might be put into the buffer or a remove might be attempted on an empty buffer.

Without Semaphores or Monitors

The producer–consumer problem, particularly in the case of a single producer and single consumer, strongly relates to implementing a FIFO or a channel. The producer–consumer pattern can provide highly efficient data communication without relying on semaphores, mutexes, or monitors *for data transfer*. Use of those primitives can give performance issues as they are expensive to implement. Channels and FIFOs are popular just because they avoid the need for end-to-end atomic synchronization. A basic example coded in C is shown below. Note that:

- Atomic read-modify-write access to shared variables is avoided, as each of the two Count variables is updated only by a single thread. Also, these variables stay incremented all the time; the relation remains correct when their values wrap around on an integer overflow.

- This example does not put threads to sleep, which may be acceptable depending on the system context. The sched_yield() is there just to behave nicely and could be removed. Thread libraries typically require semaphores or condition variables to control the sleep/ wakeup of threads. In a multi-processor environment, thread sleep/wakeup would occur much less frequently than passing of data tokens, so avoiding atomic operations on data passing is beneficial.

- This example does not work for multiple producers and/or consumers because there is a race condition when checking the state. For example, if only one token is in the storage buffer and two consumers find the buffer non-empty, then both will consume the same token and possibly increase the count of consumed tokens over produced counter.

- This example, as written, requires that UINT_MAX + 1 is evenly divisible by BUFFER_ SIZE; if it is not evenly divisible, [Count % BUFFER_SIZE] produces the wrong buffer index after Count wraps past UINT_MAX back to zero. An alternate solution without this restriction would employ two additional Idx variables to track the current buffer index for the head (producer) and tail (consumer). These Idx variables would be used in place of [Count % BUFFER_SIZE], and each of them would have to be incremented at the same time as the respective Count variable is incremented, as follows: Idx = (Idx + 1) % BUF-FER_SIZE.

```c
volatile unsigned int produceCount = 0, consumeCount = 0;

TokenType buffer[BUFFER_SIZE];


void producer(void) {

    while (1) {

        while (produceCount - consumeCount == BUFFER_SIZE)
```

```
            sched_yield(); /* `buffer` is full */
        /* You must update the field in the buffer _before_ incrementing your
         * pointer.
         */
        buffer[produceCount % BUFFER_SIZE] = produceToken();
        ++produceCount;
    }
}

void consumer(void) {
    while (1) {
        while (produceCount - consumeCount == 0)
            sched_yield(); /* `buffer` is empty */


        consumeToken(&buffer[consumeCount % BUFFER_SIZE]);
        ++consumeCount;
    }
}
```

Waiting Algorithms

Complication with Stores

- In OOO execution instructions issue out of program order:

  o A store may issue out of program order

  o But it cannot write its value to cache until it retires i.e. comes to the head of ROB; Why? (assume 1p)

  o So its value is kept in a store buffer (this is normally part of the store queue entry occupied by the store)

  o If it hits in the cache (i.e. a write hit), nothing happens

  o If it misses in the cache, either a ReadX or an Upgrade request is issued on the bus depending on the state of the requested cache line

  o Until the store retires subsequent loads from the same processor to the same address can steal the value from store buffer (why not the old value?)

What about others?

- Take the following example (assume invalidation-based protocol):

  o P0 writes x, P1 reads x

  o P0 issues store, assume that it hits in cache, but it commits much later (any simple reason?)

  o P1 issues BusRd (Can it hit in P1's cache?)

  o Snoop logic in P0's cache controller finds that it is responsible for sourcing the cache line (M state)

  o What value of x does the launched cache line contain? New value or the old value?

  o After this BusRd what is the state of P0's line?

  o After this BusRd can the loads from P0 still continue to use the value written by the store?

  o What happens when P0 ultimately commits the store?

- Take the following example (assume invalidation-based protocol):

  o P0 writes x, P1 reads x

  o P0 issues store, assume that it hits in cache, but it commits much later (any simple reason?)

  o P1 issues BusRd (Can it hit in P1's cache?)

  o Snoop logic in P0's cache controller finds that it is responsible for sourcing the cache line (M state)

  o What value of x does the launched cache line contain? New value or the old value? OLD VALUE

  o After this BusRd what is the state of P0's line? S

  o After this BusRd can the matching loads from P0 still continue to use the value written by the store? YES

  o What happens when P0 ultimately commits the store? UPGRADE MISS

More Example

- In the previous example same situation may arise even if P0 misses in the cache; the timing of P1's read decides whether the race happens or not;

- Another example:

  o P0 writes x, P1 writes x

- o   Suppose the race does happen i.e. P1 launches BusRdX before P0's store commits (Can P1 launch upgrade?)

- o   Surely the launched cache line will have old value of x as before

- o   Is it safe for the matching loads from P0 to use the new value of x from store buffer?

- o   What happens when P0's store ultimately commits?

- •   In the previous example same situation may arise even if P0 misses in the cache; the timing of P1's read decides whether the race happens or not;

- •   Another example:

  - o   P0 writes x, P1 writes x

  - o   Suppose the race does happen i.e. P1 launches BusRdX before P0's store commits (Can P1 launch upgrade?)

  - o   Surely the launched cache line will have old value of x as before

  - o   Is it safe for the matching loads from P0 to use the new value of x from store buffer? YES

  - o   What happens when P0 's store ultimately commits? READ-EXCLUSIVE MISS

Yet Another Example

- •   Another example:

  - o   P0 reads x, P0 writes x, P1 writes x

  - o   Suppose the race does happen i.e. P1 launches BusRdX before P0's store commits

  - o   Surely the launched cache line will have old value of x as before

  - o   What value does P0's load commit?

Synchronization Types

- •   Mutual exclusion:

  - o   Synchronize entry into critical sections

  - o   Normally done with locks

- •   Point-to-point synchronization:

  - o   Tell a set of processors (normally set cardinality is one) that they can proceed

  - o   Normally done with flags

- •   Global synchronization:

- o   Bring every processor to sync

- o   Wait at a point until everyone is there

- o   Normally done with barriers

Synchronization

- Normally a two-part process: acquire and release; acquire can be broken into two parts: intent and wait:

  - o   Intent: express intent to synchronize (i.e. contend for the lock, arrive at a barrier)

  - o   Wait: wait for your turn to synchronization (i.e. wait until you get the lock)

  - o   Release: proceed past synchronization and enable other contenders to synchronize

  - o   Waiting algorithms do not depend on the type of synchronization

Waiting Algorithms

- Busy wait (common in multiprocessors):

  - o   Waiting processes repeatedly poll a location (implemented as a load in a loop)

  - o   Releasing process sets the location appropriately

  - o   May cause network or bus transactions

- Block:

  - o   Waiting processes are de-scheduled

  - o   Frees up processor cycles for doing something else

- Busy waiting is better if:

  - o   De-scheduling and re-scheduling take longer than busy waiting

  - o   No other active process

  - o   Does not work for single processor

- Hybrid policies: busy wait for some time and then block

Implementation

- Popular trend:

  - o   Architects offer some simple atomic primitives

  - o   Library writers use these primitives to implement synchronization algorithms

- o Normally hardware primitives for acquire and possibly release are provided

- o Hard to offer hardware solutions for waiting

- o Also hardwired waiting may not offer that much of flexibility

Hardwired Locks

- Not popular today:

  - o Less flexible

  - o Cannot support large number of locks

- Possible designs:

  - o Dedicated lock line in bus so that the lock holder keeps it asserted and waiters snoop the lock line in hardware

  - o Set of lock registers shared among processors and lock holder gets a lock register (Cray Xmp)

Software Locks

- Bakery algorithm;

```
Shared: choosing[P] = FALSE, ticket[P] = 0;

Acquire: choosing[i] = TRUE; ticket[i] = max(ticket,…,ticket[P-1]) + 1;
choosing[i] = FALSE;

  for j = 0 to P-1

  while (choosing[j]);

  while (ticket[j] && ((ticket[j], j) < (ticket[i], i)));

  endfor

Release: ticket[i] = 0;
```

- Does it work for multiprocessors?

  - o Assume sequential consistency

  - o Performance issues related to coherence?

- Too much overhead: need faster and simpler lock algorithms;

  - o Need some hardware support

Hardware Support

- Start with a simple software lock;

```
Shared: lock = 0;

Acquire: while (lock); lock = 1;

Release or Unlock: lock = 0;
```

- Assembly translation;

```
Lock: lw register, lock_addr  /* register is any processor register */
       bnez register, Lock
       addi register, register, 0x1
       sw register, lock_addr


Unlock: xor register, register, register
          sw register, lock_addr
```

- Does it work?

    o What went wrong?

    o We wanted the read-modify-write sequence to be atomic

Atomic Exchange

- We can fix this if we have an atomic exchange instruction;

```
          addi register, r0, 0x1          /* r0 is hardwired to 0 */
  Lock:   xchg register, lock_addr    /* An atomic load and store */
          bnez register, Lock

Unlock remains unchanged
```

- Various processors support this type of instruction:

    o Intel x86 has xchg, Sun UltraSPARC has ldstub (load-store-unsigned byte), UltraS-
       PARC also has swap

    o Normally easy to implement for bus-based systems: whoever wins the bus for xchg can
       lock the bus

    o Difficult to support in distributed memory systems

Test and Set

- Less general compared to exchange;

```
  Lock:   ts register, lock_addr
             bnez register, Lock

Unlock remains unchanged
```

- Loads current lock value in a register and sets location always with 1;

  o Exchange allows to swap any value

- A similar type of instruction is fetch & op;

  o Fetch memory location in a register and apply op on the memory location

  o Op can be a set of supported operations e.g. add, increment, decrement, store etc.

  o In Test & set op=set

Fetch and Op

- Possible to implement a lock with fetch & clear then add (used to be supported in BBN Butterfly 1);

```
          addi reg1, r0, 0x1

Lock:  fetch & clr then add reg1, reg2, lock_addr            /* fetch in
reg2, clear, add reg1 */

          bnez reg2, Lock
```

- Butterfly 1 also supports fetch & clear then xor,

- Sequent Symmetry supports fetch & store,

- More sophisticated: compare & swap;

  o Takes three operands: reg1, reg2, memory address

  o Compares the value in reg1 with address and if they are equal swaps the contents of reg2 and address

  o Not in line with RISC philosophy (same goes for fetch & add)

Compare and Swap

```
          addi reg1, r0, 0x0          /* reg1 has 0x0 */

          addi reg2, r0, 0x1          /* reg2 has 0x1 */

Lock: compare & swap reg1, reg2, lock_addr

          bnez reg2, Lock
```

Traffic of Test and Set

- In some machines (e.g., SGI Origin 2000) uncached fetch & op is supported,

  o every such instruction will generate a transaction (may be good or bad depending on the support in memory controller; will discuss later)

- Let us assume that the lock location is cacheable and is kept coherent,

- o Every invocation of test & set must generate a bus transaction; Why? What is the transaction? What are the possible states of the cache line holding lock_addr?

- o Therefore all lock contenders repeatedly generate bus transactions even if someone is still in the critical section and is holding the lock

- Can we improve this?

- o Test & set with backoff

Backoff Test and Set

- Instead of retrying immediately wait for a while,

- o How long to wait?

- o Waiting for too long may lead to long latency and lost opportunity

- o Constant and variable backoff

- o Special kind of variable backoff: exponential backoff (after the i th attempt the delay is k*ci where k and c are constants)

- o Test & set with exponential backoff works pretty well

```
          delay = k
Lock:   ts register, lock_addr
            bez register, Enter_CS
            pause (delay)              /* Can be simulated as a timed loop */
            delay = delay*c
            j Lock
```

Test and Test and Set

- Reduce traffic further,

- o Before trying test & set make sure that the lock is free

```
    Lock: ts register, lock_addr
            bez register, Enter_CS
    Test:   lw register, lock_addr
            bnez register, Test
            j Lock
```

- How good is it?

o   In a cacheable lock environment the Test loop will execute from cache until it receives an invalidation (due to store in unlock); at this point the load may return a zero value after fetching the cache line

o   If the location is zero then only everyone will try test & set

TTS Traffic Analysis

- Recall that unlock is always a simple store,

- In the worst case everyone will try to enter the CS at the same time,

    o   First time P transactions for ts and one succeeds; every other processor suffers a miss on the load in Test loop; then loops from cache

    o   The lock-holder when unlocking generates an upgrade (why?) and invalidates all others

    o   All other processors suffer read miss and get value zero now; so they break Test loop and try ts and the process continues until everyone has visited the CS

    o $(P+(P-1)+1+(P-1))+((P-1)+(P-2)+1+(P-2))+... = (3P-1) + (3P-4) + (3P-7) + ... \sim 1.5P2$ asymptotically

    o   For distributed shared memory the situation is worse because each invalidation becomes a separate message (more later)

Goals of a Lock Algorithm

- Low latency: if no contender the lock should be acquired fast,

- Low traffic: worst case lock acquire traffic should be low; otherwise it may affect unrelated transactions,

- Scalability: Traffic and latency should scale slowly with the number of processors,

- Low storage cost: Maintaining lock states should not impose unrealistic memory overhead,

- Fairness: Ideally processors should enter CS according to the order of lock request (TS or TTS does not guarantee this),

Ticket Lock

- Similar to Bakery algorithm but simpler,

- A nice application of fetch & inc,

- Basic idea is to come and hold a unique ticket and wait until your turn comes,

    o   Bakery algorithm failed to offer this uniqueness thereby increasing complexity

```
Shared:   ticket = 0, release_count = 0;
```

```
Lock:       fetch & inc reg1, ticket_addr

Wait:       lw reg2, release_count_addr            /* while (release_count
!= ticket); */

            sub reg3, reg2, reg1

            bnez reg3, Wait


Unlock: addi reg2, reg2, 0x1  /* release_count++ */

        sw reg2, release_count_addr
```

- Initial fetch & inc generates O(P) traffic on bus-based machines (may be worse in DSM depending on implementation of fetch & inc),

- But the waiting algorithm still suffers from 0.5P2 messages asymptotically,

  o Researchers have proposed proportional backoff i.e. in the wait loop put a delay proportional to the difference between ticket value and last read release_count

- Latency and storage-wise better than Bakery,

- Traffic-wise better than TTS and Bakery (I leave it to you to analyze the traffic of Bakery),

- Guaranteed fairness: the ticket value induces a FIFO queue,

Array-based Lock

- Solves the $O(P^2)$ traffic problem,

- The idea is to have a bit vector (essentially a character array if boolean type is not supported),

- Each processor comes and takes the next free index into the array via fetch & inc,

- Then each processor loops on its index location until it becomes set,

- On unlock a processor is responsible to set the next index location if someone is waiting,

- Initial fetch & inc still needs O(P) traffic, but the wait loop now needs O(1) traffic,

- Disadvantage: storage overhead is O(P),

- Performance concerns,

  o Avoid false sharing: allocate each array location on a different cache line

  o Assume a cache line size of 128 bytes and a character array: allocate an array of size 128P bytes and use every 128th position in the array

o   For distributed shared memory the location a processor loops on may not be in its local memory: on acquire it must take a remote miss; allocate P pages and let each processor loop on one bit in a page? Too much wastage; better solution: MCS lock (Mellor-Crummey & Scott)

- Correctness concerns,

    o   Make sure to handle corner cases such as determining if someone is waiting on the next location (this must be an atomic operation) while unlocking

    o   Remember to reset your index location to zero while unlocking

RISC Processors

- All these atomic instructions deviate from the RISC line,

    o   Instruction needs a load as well as a store

- Also, it would be great if we can offer a few simple instructions with which we can build most of the atomic primitives,

    o   Note that it is impossible to build atomic fetch & inc with xchg instruction

- MIPS, Alpha and IBM processors support a pair of instructions: LL and SC,

    o   Load linked and store conditional

LL/SC

- Load linked behaves just like a normal load with some extra tricks,

    o   Puts the loaded value in destination register as usual

    o   Sets a load_linked bit residing in cache controller to 1

    o   Puts the address in a special lock_address register residing in the cache controller

- Store conditional is a special store,

    o   sc reg, addr stores value in reg to addr only if load_linked bit is set; also it copies the value in load_linked bit to reg and resets load_linked bit

- Any intervening "operation" (e.g., bus transaction or cache replacement) to the cache line containing the address in lock_address register clears the load_linked bit so that subsequent sc fails,

Locks with LL/SC

- Test & set

```
Lock:  LL r1, lock_addr              /* Normal read miss/BusRead */
       addi r2, r0, 0x1
```

```
       SC r2, lock_addr            /* Possibly upgrade miss */

       beqz r2, Lock               /* Check if SC succeeded */

       bnez r1, Lock               /* Check if someone is in CS */
```

- LL/SC is best-suited for test & test & set locks

```
Lock:  LL r1, lock_addr

       bnez r1, Lock

       addi r1, r0, 0x1

       SC r1, lock_addr

       beqz r1, Lock
```

Fetch and Op with LL/SC

- Fetch & inc,

```
Try:   LL r1, addr

       addi r1, r1, 0x1

       SC r1, addr

       beqz r1, Try
```

- Compare & swap: Compare with r1, swap r2 and memory location (here we keep on trying until comparison passes),

```
Try:   LL r3, addr

       sub r4, r3, r1

       bnez r4, Try

       add r4, r2, r0

       SC r4, addr

       beqz r4, Try

       add r2, r3, r0
```

Store Conditional and OOO

- Execution of SC in an OOO pipeline,

  o Rather subtle

  o For now assume that SC issues only when it comes to the head of ROB i.e. non-speculative execution of SC

  o It first checks the load_linked bit; if reset doesn't even access cache (saves cache bandwidth and unnecessary bus transactions) and returns zero in register

o If load_linked bit is set, it accesses cache and issues bus transaction if needed (Bus-ReadX if cache line in I state and BusUpgr if in S state)

o Checks load_linked bit again before writing to cache (note that cache line goes to M state in any case)

o Can wake up dependents only when SC graduates (a case where a store initiates a dependence chain)

Speculative SC?

- What happens if SC is issued speculatively?

  o Actual store happens only when it graduates and issuing a store early only starts the write permission process

  o Suppose two processors are contending for a lock

  o Both do LL and succeed because nobody is in CS

  o Both issue SC speculatively and due to some reason the graduation of SC in both of them gets delayed

  o So although initially both may get the line one after another in M state in their caches, the load_linked bit will get reset in both by the time SC tries to graduate

  o They go back and start over with LL and may issue SC again speculatively leading to a livelock (probability of this type of livelock increases with more processors)

  o Speculative issue of SC with hardwired backoff may help

  o Better to turn off speculation for SC

- What about the branch following SC?

  o Can we speculate past that branch?

  o Assume that the branch predictor tells you that the branch is not taken i.e. fall through: we speculatively venture into the critical section

  o We speculatively execute the critical section

  o This may be good and bad

  o If the branch prediction was correct we did great

  o If the predictor went wrong, we might have interfered with the execution of the processor that is actually in CS: may cause unnecessary invalidations and extra traffic

  o Any correctness issues?

Point-to-point Synch

- Normally done in software with flags,

```
P0: A = 1; flag = 1;

P1: while (!flag); print A;
```

- Some old machines supported full/empty bits in memory,

    o Each memory location is augmented with a full/empty bit

    o Producer writes the location only if bit is reset

    o Consumer reads location if bit is set and resets it

    o Lot less flexible: one producer-one consumer sharing only (one producer-many consumers is very popular); all accesses to a memory location become synchronized (unless compiler flags some accesses as special)

- Possible optimization for shared memory,

    o Allocate flag and data structures (if small) guarded by flag in same cache line e.g., flag and A in above example

Barrier

In parallel computing, a barrier is a type of synchronization method. A barrier for a group of threads or processes in the source code means any thread/process must stop at this point and cannot proceed until all other threads/processes reach this barrier.

Many collective routines and directive-based parallel languages impose implicit barriers. For example, a parallel *do* loop in Fortran with OpenMP will not be allowed to continue on any thread until the last iteration is completed. This is in case the program relies on the result of the loop immediately after its completion. In message passing, any global communication (such as reduction or scatter) may imply a barrier.

Implementation

The basic barrier has mainly two variables, one of which records the pass/stop state of the barrier, the other of which keeps the total number of threads that have entered in the barrier. The barrier state was initialized to be "stop" by the first threads coming into the barrier. Whenever a thread enters, based on the number of threads already in the barrier, only if it is the last one, the thread set the barrier state to be "pass" so that all the threads can get out of the barrier. On the other hand, when the incoming thread is not the last one, it is trapped in the barrier and keeps testing if the barrier state is changed from "stop" to "pass" and it gets out only when the barrier state changes to be "pass". The pseudocode below demonstrate this.

```
int barrierCounter = 0

int barrierFlag = 0
```

```
function barrier()

{

    Lock()


    if (barrierCounter == 0)

        barrierFlag = 0                         // reset flag is first


    barrierCounter = barrierCounter + 1

    myCount = barrierCounter                    // myCount local


    UnLock()


    if (myCount == numProcessors)               // last thread

        barrierCounter = 0                      // reset

        barrierFlag = 1                         // release

    else

        wait for barrierFlag == 1

}
```

The potential problems are as follows:

1. When sequential barriers using the same pass/block state variable are implemented, a deadlock could happen in the first barrier whenever a thread reaches the second and there are still some threads have not got out of the first barrier.

2. Due to all the threads repeatedly accessing the global variable for pass/stop, the communication traffic is rather high, which decreases the scalability.

The following Sense-Reversal Centralized Barrier is designed to resolve the first problem. And the second problem can be resolved by regrouping the threads and using multi-level barrier, e.g. Combining Tree Barrier. Also hardware implementations may have the advantage of higher scalability.

Sense-Reversal Centralized Barrier

A Sense-Reversal Centralized Barrier solves the potential deadlock problem arising when sequential barriers are used. Instead of using the same value to represent pass/stop, sequential barriers use opposite values for pass/stop state. For example, if barrier 1 uses 0 to stop the threads, barrier 2 will use 1 to stop threads and barrier 3 will use 0 to stop threads again and so on. The pseudo code below demonstrates this.

```
int barrierCounter
int barrierFlag


function barrier()
{
    sense = !sense                          //toggle private sense


    Lock()


    barrierCounter = barrierCounter + 1
    myCount = barrierCounter                //myCount local


    UnLock()


    if (myCount == numProcessors)           //last thread
        barrierCounter = 0                  //reset
        barrierFlag = sense                 //release
    else
        wait for barrierFlag != sense



}
```

Combining Tree Barrier

A Combining Tree Barrier is a hierarchical way of implementing barrier to resolve the scalability by avoiding the case that all threads spinning on a same location.

In k-Tree Barrier, all threads are equally divided into subgroups of k threads and a first-round synchronizations are done within these subgroups. Once all subgroups have done their synchronizations, the first thread in each subgroup enters the second level for further synchronization. In the second level, like in the first level, the threads form new subgroups of k threads and synchronize within groups, sending out one thread in each subgroup to next level and so on. Eventually, in the final level there is only one subgroup to be synchronized. After the final-level synchronization, the releasing signal is transmitted to upper levels and all threads get past the barrier.

Hardware Barrier Implementation

The hardware barrier uses hardware to implement the above basic barrier model.

The simplest hardware implementation uses dedicated wires to transmit signal to implement barrier. This dedicated wire performs OR/AND operation to act as the pass/block flags and thread counter. For small systems, such a model works and communication speed is not a major concern. In large multiprocessor systems this hardware design can make barrier implementation have high latency. The network connection among processors is one implementation to lower the latency, which is analogous to Combining Tree Barrier.

Memory Barrier

A memory barrier, also known as a membar, memory fence or fence instruction, is a type of barrier instruction that causes a central processing unit (CPU) or compiler to enforce an ordering constraint on memory operations issued before and after the barrier instruction. This typically means that operations issued prior to the barrier are guaranteed to be performed before operations issued after the barrier.

Memory barriers are necessary because most modern CPUs employ performance optimizations that can result in out-of-order execution. This reordering of memory operations (loads and stores) normally goes unnoticed within a single thread of execution, but can cause unpredictable behaviour in concurrent programs and device drivers unless carefully controlled. The exact nature of an ordering constraint is hardware dependent and defined by the architecture's memory ordering model. Some architectures provide multiple barriers for enforcing different ordering constraints.

Memory barriers are typically used when implementing low-level machine code that operates on memory shared by multiple devices. Such code includes synchronization primitives and lock-free data structures on multiprocessor systems, and device drivers that communicate with computer hardware.

An Illustrative Example

When a program runs on a single-CPU machine, the hardware performs the necessary bookkeeping to ensure that the program executes as if all memory operations were performed in the order specified by the programmer (program order), so memory barriers are not necessary. However, when the memory is shared with multiple devices, such as other CPUs in a multiprocessor system, or memory mapped peripherals, out-of-order access may affect program behavior. For example, a second CPU may see memory changes made by the first CPU in a sequence which differs from program order.

The following two-processor program gives an example of how such out-of-order execution can affect program behavior:

Initially, memory locations x and f both hold the value 0. The program running on processor #1 loops while the value of f is zero, then it prints the value of x. The program running on processor #2 stores the value 42 into x and then stores the value 1 into f. Pseudo-code for the two program fragments is shown below. The steps of the program correspond to individual processor instructions.

Processor #1:

```
while (f == 0);
```

```
// Memory fence required here
print x;
Processor #2:
x = 42;
// Memory fence required here
f = 1;
```

One might expect the print statement to always print the number "42"; however, if processor #2's store operations are executed out-of-order, it is possible for f to be updated *before* x, and the print statement might therefore print "0". Similarly, processor #1's load operations may be executed out-of-order and it is possible for x to be read *before* f is checked, and again the print statement might therefore print an unexpected value. For most programs neither of these situations are acceptable. A memory barrier can be inserted before processor #2's assignment to f to ensure that the new value of x is visible to other processors at or prior to the change in the value of f. Another can be inserted before processor #1's access to x to ensure the value of x is not read prior to seeing the change in the value of f.

Low-level Architecture-specific Primitives

Memory barriers are low-level primitives and part of an architecture's memory model, which, like instruction sets, vary considerably between architectures, so it is not appropriate to generalize about memory barrier behavior. The conventional wisdom is that using memory barriers correctly requires careful study of the architecture manuals for the hardware being programmed. That said, the following paragraph offers a glimpse of some memory barriers which exist in contemporary products.

Some architectures, including the ubiquitous x86/x64, provide several memory barrier instructions including an instruction sometimes called "full fence". A full fence ensures that all load and store operations prior to the fence will have been committed prior to any loads and stores issued following the fence. Other architectures, such as the Itanium, provide separate "acquire" and "release" memory barriers which address the visibility of read-after-write operations from the point of view of a reader (sink) or writer (source) respectively. Some architectures provide separate memory barriers to control ordering between different combinations of system memory and I/O memory. When more than one memory barrier instruction is available it is important to consider that the cost of different instructions may vary considerably.

Multithreaded Programming and Memory Visibility

Multithreaded programs usually use synchronization primitives provided by a high-level programming environment, such as Java and .NET Framework, or an application programming interface (API) such as POSIX Threads or Windows API. Synchronization Primitives such as mutexes and semaphores are provided to synchronize access to resources from parallel threads of execution. These primitives are usually implemented with the memory barriers required to provide the expected memory visibility semantics. In such environments explicit use of memory barriers is not generally necessary.

Each API or programming environment in principle has its own high-level memory model that defines its memory visibility semantics. Although programmers do not usually need to use memory barriers in such high level environments, it is important to understand their memory visibility semantics, to the extent possible. Such understanding is not necessarily easy to achieve because memory visibility semantics are not always consistently specified or documented.

Just as programming language semantics are defined at a different level of abstraction than machine language opcodes, a programming environment's memory model is defined at a different level of abstraction than that of a hardware memory model. It is important to understand this distinction and realize that there is not always a simple mapping between low-level hardware memory barrier semantics and the high-level memory visibility semantics of a particular programming environment. As a result, a particular platform's implementation of (say) POSIX Threads may employ stronger barriers than required by the specification. Programs which take advantage of memory visibility as implemented rather than as specified may not be portable.

Out-of-order Execution Versus Compiler Reordering Optimizations

Memory barrier instructions address reordering effects only at the hardware level. Compilers may also reorder instructions as part of the program optimization process. Although the effects on parallel program behavior can be similar in both cases, in general it is necessary to take separate measures to inhibit compiler reordering optimizations for data that may be shared by multiple threads of execution. Note that such measures are usually necessary only for data which is not protected by synchronization primitives such as those discussed in the prior section.

In C and C++, the volatile keyword was intended to allow C and C++ programs to directly access memory-mapped I/O. Memory-mapped I/O generally requires that the reads and writes specified in source code happen in the exact order specified with no omissions. Omissions or reorderings of reads and writes by the compiler would break the communication between the program and the device accessed by memory-mapped I/O. A C or C++ compiler may not omit reads from and writes to volatile memory locations, nor may it reorder read/writes relative to other such actions for the same volatile location (variable). The keyword volatile *does not guarantee a memory barrier* to enforce cache-consistency. Therefore, the use of "volatile" alone is not sufficient to use a variable for inter-thread communication on all systems and processors.

The C and C++ standards prior to C11 and C++11 do not address multiple threads (or multiple processors), and as such, the usefulness of volatile depends on the compiler and hardware. Although volatile guarantees that the volatile reads and volatile writes will happen in the exact order specified in the source code, the compiler may generate code (or the CPU may re-order execution) such that a volatile read or write is reordered with regard to non-volatile reads or writes, thus limiting its usefulness as an inter-thread flag or mutex. Preventing such is compiler specific, but some compilers, like gcc, will not reorder operations around in-line assembly code with volatile and "memory" tags, like in: asm volatile ("" : : : "memory"). Moreover, it is not guaranteed that volatile reads and writes will be seen in the same order by other processors or cores due to caching, cache coherence protocol and relaxed memory ordering, meaning volatile variables alone may not even work as inter-thread flags or mutexes.

Some languages and compilers may provide sufficient facilities to implement functions which address both the compiler reordering and machine reordering issues. In Java version 1.5 (also known as version 5), the volatile keyword is now guaranteed to prevent certain hardware *and* compiler re-orderings, as part of the new Java Memory Model. C++11 standardizes special atomic types and operations with semantics similar to those of volatile in the Java Memory Model.

Barrier

- High-level classification of barriers,

  o Hardware and software barriers

- Will focus on two types of software barriers,

  o .Centralized barrier: every processor polls a single count

  o Distributed tree barrier: shows much better scalability

- Performance goals of a barrier implementation,

  o Low latency: after all processors have arrived at the barrier, they should be able to leave quickly

  o Low traffic: minimize bus transaction and contention

  o Scalability: latency and traffic should scale slowly with the number of processors

  o Low storage: barrier state should not be big

  o Fairness: Preserve some strict order of barrier exit (could be FIFO according to arrival order); a particular processor should not always be the last one to exit

Centralized Barrier

```
struct bar_type {

   int counter;

   struct lock_type lock;

   int flag = 0;

} bar_name;


BARINIT (bar_name) {

   LOCKINIT(bar_name.lock);

   bar_name.counter = 0;
```

```
}

BARRIER (bar_name, P) {

   int my_count;

   LOCK (bar_name.lock);

   if (!bar_name.counter) {

      bar_name.flag = 0; /* first one */

   }

   my_count = ++bar_name.counter;

   UNLOCK (bar_name.lock);

   if (my_count == P) {

      bar_name.counter = 0;

      bar_name.flag = 1; /* last one */

   }

   else {

       while (!bar_name.flag);

   }

}
```

Sense Reversal

- The last implementation fails to work for two consecutive barrier invocations,

  o Need to prevent a process from entering a barrier instance until all have left the previous instance

  o Reverse the sense of a barrier i.e. every other barrier will have the same sense: basically attach parity or sense to a barrier

```
BARRIER (bar_name, P) {

   local sense = !local_sense; /* this is private per processor */

   LOCK (bar_name.lock);

   bar_name.counter++;

   if (bar_name.counter == P) {

       UNLOCK (bar_name.lock);
```

```
            bar_name.counter = 0;

            bar_name.flag = local_sense;

        }

        else {

            UNLOCK (bar_name.lock);

            while (bar_name.flag != local_sense);

        }

    }
```

Centralized Barrier

- How fast is it?

  o Assume that the program is perfectly balanced and hence all processors arrive at the barrier at the same time

  o Latency is proportional to P due to the critical section (assume that the lock algorithm exhibits at most O(P) latency)

  o The amount of traffic of acquire section (the CS) depends on the lock algorithm; after everyone has settled in the waiting loop the last processor will generate a BusRdX during release (flag write) and others will subsequently generate BusRd before releasing: O(P)

  o Scalability turns out to be low partly due to the critical section and partly due to O(P) traffic of release

  o No fairness in terms of who exits first

Tree Barrier

- Does not need a lock, only uses flags,

  o Arrange the processors logically in a binary tree (higher degree also possible)

  o Two siblings tell each other of arrival via simple flags (i.e. one waits on a flag while the other sets it on arrival)

  o One of them moves up the tree to participate in the next level of the barrier

  o Introduces concurrency in the barrier algorithm since independent subtrees can proceed in parallel

  o Takes log(P) steps to complete the acquire

  o A fixed processor starts a downward pass of release waking up other processors that in turn set other flags o Shows much better scalability compared to centralized barriers in DSM multiprocessors; the advantage in small bus-based systems is not much, since all transactions are any way serialized on the bus; in fact the additional log (P) delay may hurt performance in bus-based SMPs

```
TreeBarrier (pid, P) {

    unsigned int i, mask;

    for (i = 0, mask = 1; (mask & pid) != 0; ++i, mask <<= 1) {

        while (!flag[pid][i]);

        flag[pid][i] = 0;

    }

    if (pid < (P - 1)) {

        flag[pid + mask][i] = 1;

        while (!flag[pid][MAX- 1]);

        flag[pid][MAX - 1] = 0;

    }

    for (mask >>= 1; mask > 0; mask >>= 1) {

flag[pid - mask][MAX-1] = 1;

    }

}
```

- Convince yourself that this works,

- Take 8 processors and arrange them on leaves of a tree of depth 3,

- You will find that only odd nodes move up at every level during acquire (implemented in the first for loop),

- The even nodes just set the flags (the first statement in the if condition): they bail out of the first loop with mask=1,

- The release is initiated by the last processor in the last for loop; only odd nodes execute this loop (7 wakes up 3, 5, 6; 5 wakes up 4; 3 wakes up 1, 2; 1 wakes up 0),

- Each processor will need at most log (P) + 1 flags,

- Avoid false sharing: allocate each processor's flags on a separate chunk of cache lines,

- With some memory wastage (possibly worth it) allocate each processor's flags on a separate page and map that page locally in that processor's physical memory,

    o Avoid remote misses in DSM multiprocessor

o   Does not matter in bus-based SMPs

Hardware Support

- Read broadcast,

  o   Possible to reduce the number of bus transactions from P-1 to 1 in the best case

  o   A processor seeing a read miss to flag location (possibly from a fellow processor) backs off and does not put its read miss on the bus

  o   Every processor picks up the read reply from the bus and the release completes with one bus transaction

  o   Needs special hardware/compiler support to recognize these flag addresses and resort to read broadcast

Hardware Barrier

- Useful if frequency of barriers is high,

  o   Need a couple of wired-AND bus lines: one for odd barriers and one for even barriers

  o   A processor arrives at the barrier and asserts its input line and waits for the wired-AND line output to go HIGH

  o   Not very flexible: assumes that all processors will always participate in all barriers

  o   Bigger problem: what if multiple processes belonging to the same parallel program are assigned to each processor?

  o   No SMP supports it today

  o   However, possible to provide flexible hardware barrier support in the memory controller of DSM multiprocessors: memory controller can recognize accesses to special barrier counter or barrier flag, combine them in memory and reply to processors only when the barrier is complete (no retry due to failed lock)

Speculative Synch

- Speculative synchronization,

  o   Basic idea is to introduce speculation in the execution of critical sections

  o   Assume that no other processor will have conflicting data accesses in the critical section and hence don't even try to acquire the lock

  o   Just venture into the critical section and start executing

  o   Note the difference between this and speculative execution of critical section due to speculation on the branch following SC: there you still contend for the lock generating network transactions

- Martinez and Torrellas. In ASPLOS 2002,

- Rajwar and Goodman. In ASPLOS 2002,

- We will discuss Martinez and Torrellas,

Why is it good?

- In many cases compiler/user inserts synchronization conservatively,

  o Hard to know exact access pattern

  o The addresses accessed may depend on input

- Take a simple example of a hash table,

  o When the hash table is updated by two processes you really do not know which bins they will insert into

  o So you conservatively make the hash table access a critical section

  o For certain input values it may happen that the processes could actually update the hash table concurrently

How does it work?

- Speculative locks,

  o Every processor comes to the critical section and tries to acquire the lock

  o One of them succeeds and the rest fail

  o The successful processor becomes the safe thread

  o The failed ones don't retry but venture into the critical section speculatively as if they have the lock; at this point a speculative thread also takes a checkpoint of its register state in case a rollback is needed

  o The safe thread executes the critical section as usual

  o The speculative threads are allowed to consume values produced by the safe thread but not by the sp. threads

  o All stores from a speculative thread are kept inside its cache hierarchy in a special "speculative modified" state; these lines cannot be sent to memory until it is known to be safe; if such a line is replaced from cache either it can be kept in a small buffer or the thread can be stalled

- Speculative locks (continued),

  o If a speculative thread receives a request for a cache line that is in speculative M state, that means there is a data race inside the critical section and by design the receiver thread is rolled back to the beginning of critical section

- o Why can't the requester thread be rolled back?

- o In summary, the safe thread is never squashed and the speculative threads are not squashed if there is no cross-thread data race

- o If a speculative thread finishes executing the critical section without getting squashed, it still must wait for the safe thread to finish the critical section before committing the speculative state (i.e. changing speculative M lines to M); why?

- Speculative locks (continued),

    - o Upon finishing the critical section, a speculative thread can continue executing beyond the CS, but still remaining in speculative mode

    - o When the safe thread finishes the CS all speculative threads that have already completed CS, can commit in some non-deterministic order and revert to normal execution

    - o The speculative threads that are still inside the critical section remain speculative; a dedicated hardware unit elects one of them the lock owner and that becomes the safe non-speculative thread; the process continues

    - o Clearly, under favorable conditions speculative synchronization can reduce lock contention enormously

Why is it correct?

- In a non-speculative setting there is no order in which the threads execute the CS,

    - o Even if there is an order that must be enforced by the program itself

- In speculative synchronization some threads are considered safe (depends on time of arrival) and there is exactly one safe thread at a time in a CS,

- The speculative threads behave as if they complete the CS in some order after the safe thread(s),

- A read from a thread (spec. or safe) after a write from another speculative thread to the same cache line triggers a squash,

    - o It may not be correct to consume the speculative value

    - o Same applies to write after write

Performance Concerns

- Maintaining a safe thread guarantees forward progress,

    - o Otherwise if all were speculative, cross-thread races may repeatedly squash all of them

- False sharing?

    - o What if two bins of a hash table belong to the same cache line?

    - o Two threads are really not accessing the same address, but the speculative thread will still suffer from a squash

- Possible to maintain per-word speculative state,

Speculative Flags and Barriers

- Speculative flags are easy to support,
  - o Just continue past an unset flag in speculative mode
  - o The thread that sets the flag is always safe
  - o The thread(s) that read the flag will speculate
- Speculative barriers come for free,
  - o Barriers use locks and flags
  - o However, since the critical section in a barrier accesses a counter, multiple threads venturing into the CS are guaranteed to have conflicts
  - o So just speculate on the flag and let the critical section be executed conventionally

Speculative Flags and Branch Prediction

```
P0: A=1; flag=1;

P1: while (!flag); print A;

Assembly of P1's code

Loop:    lw register, flag_addr

              beqz register, Loop

         ...
```

- What if I pass a hint via the compiler (say, a single bit in each branch instruction) to the branch predictor asking it to always predict not taken for this branch?
  - o Isn't it achieving the same effect as speculative flag, but with a much simpler technique? No.

References

- Hennessy, John L.; Patterson, David A. (September 30, 2011). "Chapter 5: Thread-Level Parallelism". Computer Architecture: A Quantitative Approach (Fifth ed.). Morgan Kauf-mann. ISBN 978-0-123-83872-8

- "Synchronization Primitives in .NET framework". MSDN, The Microsoft Developer Net-work. Microsoft. Retrieved 23, August 2020

- Silberschatz, Abraham; Gagne, Greg; Galvin, Peter Baer (July 11, 2008). "Chapter 6: Process Synchronization". Operating System Concepts (Eighth ed.). John Wiley & Sons. ISBN 978-0-470-12872-5

- Solihin, Yan (2015-01-01). Fundamentals of Parallel Multicore Architecture (1st ed.). Chap-man & Hall/CRC. ISBN 1482211181

- Cormen, Thomas H.; Leiserson, Charles E.; Rivest, Ronald L.; Stein, Clifford (2009). Introduction to Algori-thms (3rd ed.). MIT Press and McGraw-Hill. ISBN 0-262-03384-4

- M. M., Rahman (2012). "Process synchronization in multiprocessor and multi-core pro-cessor". Informatics, Electronics & Vision (ICIEV), 2012 International Conference. doi:10.1109/ICIEV.2012.6317471

- Boehm, Hans (June 2005). Threads cannot be implemented as a library. Proceedings of the 2005 ACM SIGPLAN conference on Programming language design and implementa-tion. Association for Computing Machinery. doi:10.1145/1065010.1065042

- Nyman, Linus; Laakso, Mikael. "Notes on the History of Fork and Join". IEEE Annals of the History of Computing. IEEE Computer Society. 38 (3): 84–87. doi:10.1109/MAHC.2016.34. Retrieved 09, August 2020

6

Parallel Computing

The process of breaking down larger problems into smaller parts that can be executed simultaneously by multiple processors and the results of which are combined upon completion is known as parallel computing. There are four types of parallelism; Bit-level parallelism, Instruction-level parallelism, Task parallelism and Superword level parallelism. This chapter has been carefully written to provide an easy understanding of the varied facets of parallel computing.

Parallel computing is a type of computation in which many calculations or the execution of processes are carried out simultaneously. Large problems can often be divided into smaller ones, which can then be solved at the same time. There are several different forms of parallel computing: bit-level, instruction-level, data, and task parallelism. Parallelism has been employed for many years, mainly in high-performance computing, but interest in it has grown lately due to the physical constraints preventing frequency scaling. As power consumption (and consequently heat generation) by computers has become a concern in recent years, parallel computing has become the dominant paradigm in computer architecture, mainly in the form of multi-core processors.

IBM's Blue Gene/P massively parallel supercomputer.

Parallel computing is closely related to concurrent computing—they are frequently used together, and often conflated, though the two are distinct: it is possible to have parallelism without concurrency (such as bit-level parallelism), and concurrency without parallelism (such as multitasking by time-sharing on a single-core CPU). In parallel computing, a computational task is typically broken down in several, often many, very similar subtasks that can be processed independently and whose results are combined afterwards, upon completion. In contrast, in concurrent computing, the various processes often do not address related tasks; when they do, as is typical in distributed computing, the separate tasks may have a varied nature and often require some inter-process communication during execution.

Parallel computers can be roughly classified according to the level at which the hardware supports parallelism, with multi-core and multi-processor computers having multiple processing elements within a single machine, while clusters, MPPs, and grids use multiple computers to work on the same task. Specialized parallel computer architectures are sometimes used alongside traditional processors, for accelerating specific tasks.

In some cases parallelism is transparent to the programmer, such as in bit-level or instruction-level parallelism, but explicitly parallel algorithms, particularly those that use concurrency, are more difficult to write than sequential ones, because concurrency introduces several new classes of potential software bugs, of which race conditions are the most common. Communication and synchronization between the different subtasks are typically some of the greatest obstacles to getting good parallel program performance.

A theoretical upper bound on the speed-up of a single program as a result of parallelization is given by Amdahl's law.

Background

Traditionally, computer software has been written for serial computation. To solve a problem, an algorithm is constructed and implemented as a serial stream of instructions. These instructions are executed on a central processing unit on one computer. Only one instruction may execute at a time—after that instruction is finished, the next one is executed.

Parallel computing, on the other hand, uses multiple processing elements simultaneously to solve a problem. This is accomplished by breaking the problem into independent parts so that each processing element can execute its part of the algorithm simultaneously with the others. The processing elements can be diverse and include resources such as a single computer with multiple processors, several networked computers, specialized hardware, or any combination of the above.

Frequency scaling was the dominant reason for improvements in computer performance from the mid-1980s until 2004. The runtime of a program is equal to the number of instructions multiplied by the average time per instruction. Maintaining everything else constant, increasing the clock frequency decreases the average time it takes to execute an instruction. An increase in frequency thus decreases runtime for all compute-bound programs.

However, power consumption P by a chip is given by the equation $P = C \times V^2 \times F$, where C is the capacitance being switched per clock cycle (proportional to the number of transistors whose inputs change), V is voltage, and F is the processor frequency (cycles per second). Increases in frequency increase the amount of power used in a processor. Increasing processor power consumption led ultimately to Intel's May 8, 2004 cancellation of its Tejas and Jayhawk processors, which is generally cited as the end of frequency scaling as the dominant computer architecture paradigm.

Moore's law is the empirical observation that the number of transistors in a microprocessor doubles every 18 to 24 months. Despite power consumption issues, and repeated predictions of its end, Moore's law is still in effect. With the end of frequency scaling, these additional transistors (which are no longer used for frequency scaling) can be used to add extra hardware for parallel computing.

Amdahl's Law and Gustafson's Law

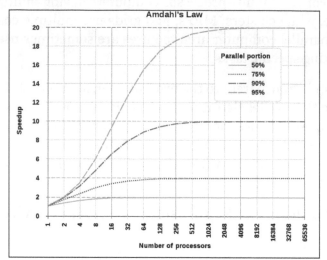

A graphical representation of Amdahl's law. The speedup of a program from parallelization is limited by how much of the program can be parallelized. For example, if 90% of the program can be parallelized, the theoretical maximum speedup using parallel computing would be 10 times no matter how many prozcessors are used.

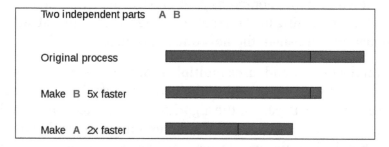

Assume that a task has two independent parts, *A* and *B*. Part *B* takes roughly 25% of the time of the whole computation. By working very hard, one may be able to make this part 5 times faster, but this only reduces the time for the whole computation by a little. In contrast, one may need to perform less work to make part *A* be twice as fast. This will make the computation much faster than by optimizing part *B*, even though part *B*'s speedup is greater by ratio, (5 times versus 2 times).

Optimally, the speedup from parallelization would be linear—doubling the number of processing elements should halve the runtime, and doubling it a second time should again halve the runtime. However, very few parallel algorithms achieve optimal speedup. Most of them have a near-linear speedup for small numbers of processing elements, which flattens out into a constant value for large numbers of processing elements.

The potential speedup of an algorithm on a parallel computing platform is given by Amdahl's law

$$S_{latency}(s) = \frac{1}{1 - p + \dfrac{p}{s}},$$

where,

S_{latency} is the potential speedup in latency of the execution of the whole task;

s is the speedup in latency of the execution of the parallelizable part of the task;

p is the percentage of the execution time of the whole task concerning the parallelizable part of the task *before parallelization.*

Since $S_{\text{latency}} < 1/(1 - p)$, it shows that a small part of the program which cannot be parallelized will limit the overall speedup available from parallelization. A program solving a large mathematical or engineering problem will typically consist of several parallelizable parts and several non-parallelizable (serial) parts. If the non-parallelizable part of a program accounts for 10% of the runtime ($p = 0.9$), we can get no more than a 10 times speedup, regardless of how many processors are added. This puts an upper limit on the usefulness of adding more parallel execution units. "When a task cannot be partitioned because of sequential constraints, the application of more effort has no effect on the schedule. The bearing of a child takes nine months, no matter how many women are assigned."

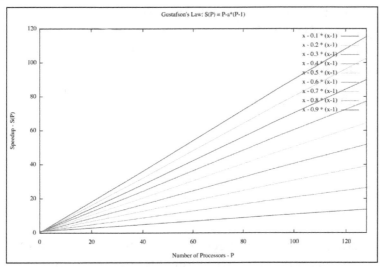

A graphical representation of Gustafson's law.

Amdahl's law only applies to cases where the problem size is fixed. In practice, as more computing resources become available, they tend to get used on larger problems (larger datasets), and the time spent in the parallelizable part often grows much faster than the inherently serial work. In this case, Gustafson's law gives a less pessimistic and more realistic assessment of parallel performance:

$$S_{latency}(s) = 1 - p + sp.$$

Both Amdahl's law and Gustafson's law assume that the running time of the serial part of the program is independent of the number of processors. Amdahl's law assumes that the entire problem is of fixed size so that the total amount of work to be done in parallel is also *independent of the number of processors*, whereas Gustafson's law assumes that the total amount of work to be done in parallel *varies linearly with the number of processors*.

Dependencies

Understanding data dependencies is fundamental in implementing parallel algorithms. No program can run more quickly than the longest chain of dependent calculations (known as the critical path), since calculations that depend upon prior calculations in the chain must be executed in order. However, most algorithms do not consist of just a long chain of dependent calculations; there are usually opportunities to execute independent calculations in parallel.

Let P_i and P_j be two program segments. Bernstein's conditions describe when the two are independent and can be executed in parallel. For P_i, let I_i be all of the input variables and O_i the output variables, and likewise for P_j. P_i and P_j are independent if they satisfy,

$$I_j \cap O_i = \varnothing,$$
$$I_i \cap O_j = \varnothing,$$
$$O_i \cap O_j = \varnothing.$$

Violation of the first condition introduces a flow dependency, corresponding to the first segment producing a result used by the second segment. The second condition represents an anti-dependency, when the second segment produces a variable needed by the first segment. The third and final condition represents an output dependency: when two segments write to the same location, the result comes from the logically last executed segment.

Consider the following functions, which demonstrate several kinds of dependencies:

1: function Dep(a, b)

2: c := a * b

3: d := 3 * c

4: end function

In this example, instruction 3 cannot be executed before (or even in parallel with) instruction 2, because instruction 3 uses a result from instruction 2. It violates condition 1, and thus introduces a flow dependency.

1: function NoDep(a, b)

2: c := a * b

3: d := 3 * b

4: e := a + b

5: end function

In this example, there are no dependencies between the instructions, so they can all be run in parallel.

Bernstein's conditions do not allow memory to be shared between different processes. For that, some means of enforcing an ordering between accesses is necessary, such as semaphores, barriers or some other synchronization method.

Race Conditions, Mutual Exclusion, Synchronization, and Parallel Slowdown

Subtasks in a parallel program are often called threads. Some parallel computer architectures use smaller, lightweight versions of threads known as fibers, while others use bigger versions known as processes. However, "threads" is generally accepted as a generic term for subtasks. Threads will often need to update some variable that is shared between them. The instructions between the two programs may be interleaved in any order. For example, consider the following program:

Thread A	Thread B
1A: Read variable V	1B: Read variable V
2A: Add 1 to variable V	2B: Add 1 to variable V
3A: Write back to variable V	3B: Write back to variable V

If instruction 1B is executed between 1A and 3A, or if instruction 1A is executed between 1B and 3B, the program will produce incorrect data. This is known as a race condition. The programmer must use a lock to provide mutual exclusion. A lock is a programming language construct that allows one thread to take control of a variable and prevent other threads from reading or writing it, until that variable is unlocked. The thread holding the lock is free to execute its critical section (the section of a program that requires exclusive access to some variable), and to unlock the data when it is finished. Therefore, to guarantee correct program execution, the above program can be rewritten to use locks:

Thread A	Thread B
1A: Lock variable V	1B: Lock variable V
2A: Read variable V	2B: Read variable V
3A: Add 1 to variable V	3B: Add 1 to variable V
4A: Write back to variable V	4B: Write back to variable V
5A: Unlock variable V	5B: Unlock variable V

One thread will successfully lock variable V, while the other thread will be locked out—unable to proceed until V is unlocked again. This guarantees correct execution of the program. Locks, while necessary to ensure correct program execution, can greatly slow a program.

Locking multiple variables using non-atomic locks introduces the possibility of program deadlock. An atomic lock locks multiple variables all at once. If it cannot lock all of them, it does not lock any of them. If two threads each need to lock the same two variables using non-atomic locks, it is possible that one thread will lock one of them and the second thread will lock the second variable. In such a case, neither thread can complete, and deadlock results.

Many parallel programs require that their subtasks act in synchrony. This requires the use of a barrier. Barriers are typically implemented using a software lock. One class of algorithms, known as lock-free and wait-free algorithms, altogether avoids the use of locks and barriers. However, this approach is generally difficult to implement and requires correctly designed data structures.

Not all parallelization results in speed-up. Generally, as a task is split up into more and more threads, those threads spend an ever-increasing portion of their time communicating with each other. Eventually, the overhead from communication dominates the time spent solving the problem, and further parallelization (that is, splitting the workload over even more threads) increases rather than decreases the amount of time required to finish. This is known as parallel slowdown.

Fine-grained, Coarse-grained, and Embarrassing Parallelism

Applications are often classified according to how often their subtasks need to synchronize or communicate with each other. An application exhibits fine-grained parallelism if its subtasks must communicate many times per second; it exhibits coarse-grained parallelism if they do not communicate many times per second, and it exhibits embarrassing parallelism if they rarely or never have to communicate. Embarrassingly parallel applications are considered the easiest to parallelize.

Consistency Models

Parallel programming languages and parallel computers must have a consistency model (also known as a memory model). The consistency model defines rules for how operations on computer memory occur and how results are produced.

One of the first consistency models was Leslie Lamport's sequential consistency model. Sequential consistency is the property of a parallel program that its parallel execution produces the same results as a sequential program. Specifically, a program is sequentially consistent if "... the results of any execution is the same as if the operations of all the processors were executed in some sequential order, and the operations of each individual processor appear in this sequence in the order specified by its program".

Software transactional memory is a common type of consistency model. Software transactional memory borrows from database theory the concept of atomic transactions and applies them to memory accesses.

Mathematically, these models can be represented in several ways. Petri nets, which were introduced in Carl Adam Petri's 1962 doctoral thesis, were an early attempt to codify the rules of consistency models. Dataflow theory later built upon these, and Dataflow architectures were created to physically implement the ideas of dataflow theory. Beginning in the late 1970s, process calculi such as Calculus of Communicating Systems and Communicating Sequential Processes were developed to permit algebraic reasoning about systems composed of interacting components. More recent additions to the process calculus family, such as the π-calculus, have added the capability for reasoning about dynamic topologies. Logics such as Lamport's TLA+, and mathematical models such as traces and Actor event diagrams, have also been developed to describe the behavior of concurrent systems.

Flynn's Taxonomy

Michael J. Flynn created one of the earliest classification systems for parallel (and sequential) computers and programs, now known as Flynn's taxonomy. Flynn classified programs and computers by whether they were operating using a single set or multiple sets of instructions, and whether or not those instructions were using a single set or multiple sets of data.

The single-instruction-single-data (SISD) classification is equivalent to an entirely sequential program. The single-instruction-multiple-data (SIMD) classification is analogous to doing the same operation repeatedly over a large data set. This is commonly done in signal processing applications. Multiple-instruction-single-data (MISD) is a rarely used classification. While computer architectures to deal with this were devised (such as systolic arrays), few applications that fit this class materialized. Multiple-instruction-multiple-data (MIMD) programs are by far the most common type of parallel programs.

According to David A. Patterson and John L. Hennessy, "Some machines are hybrids of these categories, of course, but this classic model has survived because it is simple, easy to understand, and gives a good first approximation. It is also—perhaps because of its understandability—the most widely used scheme."

Types of Parallelism

Bit-level Parallelism

From the advent of very-large-scale integration (VLSI) computer-chip fabrication technology in the 1970s until about 1986, speed-up in computer architecture was driven by doubling computer word size—the amount of information the processor can manipulate per cycle. Increasing the word size reduces the number of instructions the processor must execute to perform an operation on variables whose sizes are greater than the length of the word. For example, where an 8-bit processor must add two 16-bit integers, the processor must first add the 8 lower-order bits from each integer using the standard addition instruction, then add the 8 higher-order bits using an add-with-carry instruction and the carry bit from the lower order addition; thus, an 8-bit processor requires two instructions to complete a single operation, where a 16-bit processor would be able to complete the operation with a single instruction.

Historically, 4-bit microprocessors were replaced with 8-bit, then 16-bit, then 32-bit microprocessors. This trend generally came to an end with the introduction of 32-bit processors, which has been a standard in general-purpose computing for two decades. Not until the early twothousands, with the advent of x86-64 architectures, did 64-bit processors become commonplace.

Instruction-level Parallelism

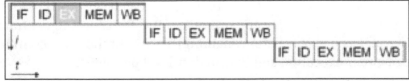

A canonical processor without pipeline. It takes five clock cycles to complete one instruction and thus the processor can issue subscalar performance (IPC = 0.2 < 1).

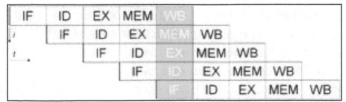

A canonical five-stage pipelined processor. In the best case scenario, it takes one clock cycle to complete one instruction and thus the processor can issue scalar performance (IPC = 1).

A computer program is, in essence, a stream of instructions executed by a processor. Without instruction-level parallelism, a processor can only issue less than one instruction per clock cycle (IPC < 1). These processors are known as *subscalar* processors. These instructions can be re-ordered and combined into groups which are then executed in parallel without changing the result of the program. This is known as instruction-level parallelism. Advances in instruction-level parallelism dominated computer architecture from the mid-1980s until the mid-1990s.

All modern processors have multi-stage instruction pipelines. Each stage in the pipeline corresponds to a different action the processor performs on that instruction in that stage; a processor with an N-stage pipeline can have up to N different instructions at different stages of completion and thus can issue one instruction per clock cycle (IPC = 1). These processors are known as *scalar* processors. The canonical example of a pipelined processor is a RISC processor, with five stages: instruction fetch (IF), instruction decode (ID), execute (EX), memory access (MEM), and register write back (WB). The Pentium 4 processor had a 35-stage pipeline.

A canonical five-stage pipelined superscalar processor. In the best case scenario, it takes one clock cycle to complete two instructions and thus the processor can issue superscalar performance (IPC = 2 > 1).

Most modern processors also have multiple execution units. They usually combine this feature with pipelining and thus can issue more than one instruction per clock cycle (IPC > 1). These processors are known as *superscalar* processors. Instructions can be grouped together only if there is no data dependency between them. Scoreboarding and the Tomasulo algorithm (which is similar to scoreboarding but makes use of register renaming) are two of the most common techniques for implementing out-of-order execution and instruction-level parallelism.

Task Parallelism

Task parallelisms is the characteristic of a parallel program that "entirely different calculations can be performed on either the same or different sets of data". This contrasts with data parallelism, where the same calculation is performed on the same or different sets of data. Task parallelism involves the decomposition of a task into sub-tasks and then allocating each sub-task to a processor for execution. The processors would then execute these sub-tasks simultaneously and often cooperatively. Task parallelism does not usually scale with the size of a problem.

Hardware

Memory and Communication

Main memory in a parallel computer is either shared memory (shared between all processing elements in a single address space), or distributed memory (in which each processing element has its own local address space). Distributed memory refers to the fact that the memory is logically distributed, but often implies that it is physically distributed as well. Distributed shared memory and memory virtualization combine the two approaches, where the processing element has its own local memory and access to the memory on non-local processors. Accesses to local memory are typically faster than accesses to non-local memory.

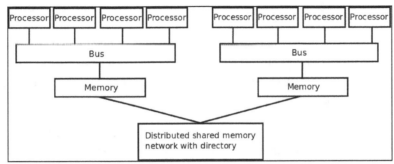

A logical view of a non-uniform memory access (NUMA) architecture. Processors in one directory can access that directory's memory with less latency than they can access memory in the other directory's memory.

Computer architectures in which each element of main memory can be accessed with equal latency and bandwidth are known as uniform memory access (UMA) systems. Typically, that can be achieved only by a shared memory system, in which the memory is not physically distributed. A system that does not have this property is known as a non-uniform memory access (NUMA) architecture. Distributed memory systems have non-uniform memory access.

Computer systems make use of caches—small and fast memories located close to the processor which store temporary copies of memory values (nearby in both the physical and logical sense). Parallel computer systems have difficulties with caches that may store the same value in more than one location, with the possibility of incorrect program execution. These computers require a cache coherency system, which keeps track of cached values and strategically purges them, thus ensuring correct program execution. Bus snooping is one of the most common methods for keeping track of which values are being accessed (and thus should be purged). Designing large, high-performance cache coherence systems is a very difficult problem in computer architecture. As a result, shared memory computer architectures do not scale as well as distributed memory systems do.

Processor–processor and processor–memory communication can be implemented in hardware in several ways, including via shared (either multiported or multiplexed) memory, a crossbar switch, a shared bus or an interconnect network of a myriad of topologies including star, ring, tree, hypercube, fat hypercube (a hypercube with more than one processor at a node), or n-dimensional mesh.

Parallel computers based on interconnected networks need to have some kind of routing to enable the passing of messages between nodes that are not directly connected. The medium used for communication between the processors is likely to be hierarchical in large multiprocessor machines.

Classes of Parallel Computers

Parallel computers can be roughly classified according to the level at which the hardware supports parallelism. This classification is broadly analogous to the distance between basic computing nodes. These are not mutually exclusive; for example, clusters of symmetric multiprocessors are relatively common.

Multi-core Computing

A multi-core processor is a processor that includes multiple processing units (called "cores") on the same chip. This processor differs from a superscalar processor, which includes multiple execution units and can issue multiple instructions per clock cycle from one instruction stream (thread); in contrast, a multi-core processor can issue multiple instructions per clock cycle from multiple instruction streams. IBM's Cell microprocessor, designed for use in the Sony PlayStation 3, is a prominent multi-core processor. Each core in a multi-core processor can potentially be superscalar as well—that is, on every clock cycle, each core can issue multiple instructions from one thread.

Simultaneous multithreading (of which Intel's Hyper-Threading is the best known) was an early form of pseudo-multi-coreism. A processor capable of simultaneous multithreading includes multiple execution units in the same processing unit—that is it has a superscalar architecture—and can issue multiple instructions per clock cycle from *multiple* threads. Temporal multithreading on the other hand includes a single execution unit in the same processing unit and can issue one instruction at a time from *multiple* threads.

Symmetric Multiprocessing

A symmetric multiprocessor (SMP) is a computer system with multiple identical processors that share memory and connect via a bus. Bus contention prevents bus architectures from scaling. As a result, SMPs generally do not comprise more than 32 processors. Because of the small size of the processors and the significant reduction in the requirements for bus bandwidth achieved by large caches, such symmetric multiprocessors are extremely cost-effective, provided that a sufficient amount of memory bandwidth exists.

Distributed Computing

A distributed computer (also known as a distributed memory multiprocessor) is a distributed memory computer system in which the processing elements are connected by a network. Distributed computers are highly scalable.

Cluster Computing

A cluster is a group of loosely coupled computers that work together closely, so that in some respects they can be regarded as a single computer. Clusters are composed of multiple standalone machines connected by a network. While machines in a cluster do not have to be symmetric, load balancing is more difficult if they are not. The most common type of cluster is the Beowulf cluster, which is a cluster implemented on multiple identical commercial off-the-shelf computers connected with a TCP/IP Ethernet local area network. Beowulf technology was originally developed by Thomas Sterling and Donald Becker. The vast majority of the TOP500 supercomputers are clusters.

A Beowulf cluster.

Because grid computing systems (described below) can easily handle embarrassingly parallel problems, modern clusters are typically designed to handle more difficult problems—problems that require nodes to share intermediate results with each other more often. This requires a high bandwidth and, more importantly, a low-latency interconnection network. Many historic and current supercomputers use customized high-performance network hardware specifically designed for cluster computing, such as the Cray Gemini network. As of 2014, most current supercomputers use some off-the-shelf standard network hardware, often Myrinet, InfiniBand, or Gigabit Ethernet.

Massively Parallel Computing

A cabinet from IBM's Blue Gene/L massively parallel supercomputer.

A massively parallel processor (MPP) is a single computer with many networked processors. MPPs have many of the same characteristics as clusters, but MPPs have specialized interconnect networks (whereas clusters use commodity hardware for networking). MPPs also tend to be larger than clusters, typically having "far more" than 100 processors. In an MPP, "each CPU contains its own memory and copy of the operating system and application. Each subsystem communicates with the others via a high-speed interconnect."

IBM's Blue Gene/L, the fifth fastest supercomputer in the world according to the June 2009 TOP500 ranking, is an MPP.

Grid Computing

Grid computing is the most distributed form of parallel computing. It makes use of computers communicating over the Internet to work on a given problem. Because of the low bandwidth and extremely high latency available on the Internet, distributed computing typically deals only with embarrassingly parallel problems. Many distributed computing applications have been created, of which SETI@home and Folding@home are the best-known examples.

Most grid computing applications use middleware (software that sits between the operating system and the application to manage network resources and standardize the software interface). The most common distributed computing middleware is the Berkeley Open Infrastructure for Network Computing (BOINC). Often, distributed computing software makes use of "spare cycles", performing computations at times when a computer is idling.

Specialized Parallel Computers

Within parallel computing, there are specialized parallel devices that remain niche areas of interest. While not domain-specific, they tend to be applicable to only a few classes of parallel problems.

Reconfigurable Computing with Field-programmable Gate Arrays

Reconfigurable computing is the use of a field-programmable gate array (FPGA) as a co-processor to a general-purpose computer. An FPGA is, in essence, a computer chip that can rewire itself for a given task.

FPGAs can be programmed with hardware description languages such as VHDL or Verilog. However, programming in these languages can be tedious. Several vendors have created C to HDL languages that attempt to emulate the syntax and semantics of the C programming language, with which most programmers are familiar. The best known C to HDL languages are Mitrion-C, Impulse C, DIME-C, and Handel-C. Specific subsets of SystemC based on C++ can also be used for this purpose.

AMD's decision to open its HyperTransport technology to third-party vendors has become the enabling technology for high-performance reconfigurable computing. According to Michael R. D'Amour, Chief Operating Officer of DRC Computer Corporation, "when we first walked into AMD, they called us 'the socket stealers.' Now they call us their partners."

General-purpose Computing on Graphics Processing Units (GPGPU)

General-purpose computing on graphics processing units (GPGPU) is a fairly recent trend in computer engineering research. GPUs are co-processors that have been heavily optimized for computer graphics processing. Computer graphics processing is a field dominated by data parallel operations—particularly linear algebra matrix operations.

Nvidia's Tesla GPGPU card.

In the early days, GPGPU programs used the normal graphics APIs for executing programs. However, several new programming languages and platforms have been built to do general purpose computation on GPUs with both Nvidia and AMD releasing programming environments with CUDA and Stream SDK respectively. Other GPU programming languages include BrookGPU, PeakStream, and RapidMind. Nvidia has also released specific products for computation in their Tesla series. The technology consortium Khronos Group has released the OpenCL specification, which is a framework for writing programs that execute across platforms consisting of CPUs and GPUs. AMD, Apple, Intel, Nvidia and others are supporting OpenCL.

Application-specific Integrated Circuits

Several application-specific integrated circuit (ASIC) approaches have been devised for dealing with parallel applications.

Because an ASIC is (by definition) specific to a given application, it can be fully optimized for that application. As a result, for a given application, an ASIC tends to outperform a general-purpose computer. However, ASICs are created by UV photolithography. This process requires a mask set, which can be extremely expensive. A mask set can cost over a million US dollars. (The smaller the transistors required for the chip, the more expensive the mask will be.) Meanwhile, performance increases in general-purpose computing over time (as described by Moore's law) tend to wipe out these gains in only one or two chip generations. High initial cost, and the tendency to be overtaken by Moore's-law-driven general-purpose computing, has rendered ASICs unfeasible for most parallel computing applications. However, some have been built. One example is the PFLOPS RIKEN MDGRAPE-3 machine which uses custom ASICs for molecular dynamics simulation.

Vector Processors

The Cray-1 is a vector processor.

A vector processor is a CPU or computer system that can execute the same instruction on large sets of data. Vector processors have high-level operations that work on linear arrays of numbers or vectors. An example vector operation is $A = B \times C$, where A, B, and C are each 64-element vectors of 64-bit floating-point numbers. They are closely related to Flynn's SIMD classification.

Cray computers became famous for their vector-processing computers in the 1970s and 1980s. However, vector processors—both as CPUs and as full computer systems—have generally disappeared. Modern processor instruction sets do include some vector processing instructions, such as with Freescale Semiconductor's AltiVec and Intel's Streaming SIMD Extensions (SSE).

Software

Parallel Programming Languages

Concurrent programming languages, libraries, APIs, and parallel programming models (such as algorithmic skeletons) have been created for programming parallel computers. These can generally be divided into classes based on the assumptions they make about the underlying memory architecture—shared memory, distributed memory, or shared distributed memory. Shared memory programming languages communicate by manipulating shared memory variables. Distributed memory uses message passing. POSIX Threads and OpenMP are two of the most widely used shared memory APIs, whereas Message Passing Interface (MPI) is the most widely used message-passing system API. One concept used in programming parallel programs is the future concept, where one part of a program promises to deliver a required datum to another part of a program at some future time.

CAPS entreprise and Pathscale are also coordinating their effort to make hybrid multi-core parallel programming (HMPP) directives an open standard called OpenHMPP. The OpenHMPP directive-based programming model offers a syntax to efficiently offload computations on hardware accelerators and to optimize data movement to/from the hardware memory. OpenHMPP directives describe remote procedure call (RPC) on an accelerator device (e.g. GPU) or more generally a set of cores. The directives annotate C or Fortran codes to describe two sets of functionalities: the offloading of procedures (denoted codelets) onto a remote device and the optimization of data transfers between the CPU main memory and the accelerator memory.

The rise of consumer GPUs has led to support for compute kernels, either in graphics APIs (referred to as compute shaders), in dedicated APIs (such as OpenCL), or in other language extensions.

Automatic Parallelization

Automatic parallelization of a sequential program by a compiler is the holy grail of parallel computing. Despite decades of work by compiler researchers, automatic parallelization has had only limited success.

Mainstream parallel programming languages remain either explicitly parallel or (at best) partially implicit, in which a programmer gives the compiler directives for parallelization. A few fully implicit parallel programming languages exist—SISAL, Parallel Haskell, SequenceL, System C (for FPGAs), Mitrion-C, VHDL, and Verilog.

Application Checkpointing

As a computer system grows in complexity, the mean time between failures usually decreases. Application checkpointing is a technique whereby the computer system takes a "snapshot" of the application—a record of all current resource allocations and variable states, akin to a core dump—; this information can be used to restore the program if the computer should fail. Application checkpointing means that the program has to restart from only its last checkpoint rather than the beginning. While checkpointing provides benefits in a variety of situations, it is especially useful in highly parallel systems with a large number of processors used in high performance computing.

Algorithmic Methods

As parallel computers become larger and faster, it becomes feasible to solve problems that previously took too long to run. Parallel computing is used in a wide range of fields, from bioinformatics (protein folding and sequence analysis) to economics (mathematical finance). Common types of problems found in parallel computing applications are:

- dense linear algebra;

- sparse linear algebra;

- spectral methods (such as Cooley–Tukey fast Fourier transform);

- N-body problems (such as Barnes–Hut simulation);

- structured grid problems (such as Lattice Boltzmann methods);

- unstructured grid problems (such as found in finite element analysis);

- Monte Carlo method;

- combinational logic (such as brute-force cryptographic techniques);

- graph traversal (such as sorting algorithms);

- dynamic programming;

- branch and bound methods;

- graphical models (such as detecting hidden Markov models and constructing Bayesian networks);

- finite-state machine simulation.

Fault-tolerance

Parallel computing can also be applied to the design of fault-tolerant computer systems, particularly via lockstep systems performing the same operation in parallel. This provides redundancy in case one component should fail, and also allows automatic error detection and error correction if the results differ. These methods can be used to help prevent single event upsets caused by transient errors. Although additional measures may be required in embedded or specialized systems, this method can provide a cost effective approach to achieve n-modular redundancy in commercial off-the-shelf systems.

History

ILLIAC IV, "the most infamous of supercomputers".

The origins of true (MIMD) parallelism go back to Luigi Federico Menabrea and his *Sketch of the Analytic Engine Invented by Charles Babbage.*

In April 1958, S. Gill (Ferranti) discussed parallel programming and the need for branching and waiting. Also in 1958, IBM researchers John Cocke and Daniel Slotnick discussed the use of parallelism in numerical calculations for the first time. Burroughs Corporation introduced the D825 in 1962, a four-processor computer that accessed up to 16 memory modules through a crossbar switch. In 1967, Amdahl and Slotnick published a debate about the feasibility of parallel processing at American Federation of Information Processing Societies Conference. It was during this debate that Amdahl's law was coined to define the limit of speed-up due to parallelism.

In 1969, company Honeywell introduced its first Multics system, a symmetric multiprocessor system capable of running up to eight processors in parallel. C.mmp, a 1970s multi-processor project at Carnegie Mellon University, was among the first multiprocessors with more than a few processors. The first bus-connected multiprocessor with snooping caches was the Synapse N+1 in 1984."

SIMD parallel computers can be traced back to the 1970s. The motivation behind early SIMD computers was to amortize the gate delay of the processor's control unit over multiple instructions. In 1964, Slotnick had proposed building a massively parallel computer for the Lawrence Livermore National Laboratory. His design was funded by the US Air Force, which was the earliest SIMD parallel-computing effort, ILLIAC IV. The key to its design was a fairly high parallelism, with up to 256 processors, which allowed the machine to work on large datasets in what would later be known as vector processing. However, ILLIAC IV was called "the most infamous of supercomputers", because the project was only one fourth completed, but took 11 years and cost almost four times the original estimate. When it was finally ready to run its first real application in 1976, it was outperformed by existing commercial supercomputers such as the Cray-1.

Consistency Model

In computer science, Consistency models are used in distributed systems like distributed shared memory systems or distributed data stores (such as a filesystems, databases, optimistic replication systems or Web caching). The system is said to support a given model if operations on memory follow specific rules. The data consistency model specifies a contract between programmer and system, wherein the system guarantees that if the programmer follows the rules, memory will be consistent and the results of memory operations will be predictable. This is different from Cache coherence, an issue that occurs in systems that are cached or cache-less is consistency of data with respect to all processors. This is not handled by Coherence as coherence deals with maintaining a global order in which writes only to a single location or a single variable are seen by all processors. Consistency deals with the ordering of operations to multiple locations with respect to all processors.

High level languages, such as C++ and Java, partially maintain the contract by translating memory operations into low-level operations in a way that preserves memory semantics. To hold to the contract, compilers may reorder some memory instructions, and library calls such as pthread_mutex_lock() encapsulate required synchronization.

Verifying sequential consistency through model checking is undecidable in general, even for finite-state cache-coherence protocols.

Consistency models define rules for the apparent order and visibility of updates, and it is a continuum with tradeoffs.

Example

Assume that the following case occurs:

- The row X is replicated on nodes M and N

- The client A writes row X to node N

- After a period of time t, client B reads row X from node M

The consistency model has to determine whether client B sees the write from client A or not.

Types

There are two methods to define and categorize consistency models; issue and view.

Issue: Issue method describes the restrictions that define how a process can issue operations.

View: View method which defines the order of operations visible to processes.

For example, a consistency model can define that a process is not allowed to issue an operation until all previously issued operations are completed. Different consistency models enforce different conditions. One consistency model can be considered stronger than another if it requires all conditions of that model and more. In other words, a model with fewer constraints is considered a weaker consistency model.

These models define how the hardware needs to be laid out and at high-level, how the programmer must code. The chosen model also affects how the compiler can re-order instructions. Generally, if control dependencies between instructions and if writes to same location are ordered, then the compiler can reorder as required. However, with the models described below, some may allow Writes before Loads to be reordered while some may not.

Strict Consistency

Strict consistency is the strongest consistency model. Under this model, a write to a variable by any processor needs to be seen instantaneously by all processors. The Strict model diagram and non-Strict model diagrams describe the time constraint – instantaneous. It can be better understood as though a global clock is present in which every write should be reflected in all processor caches by the end of that clock period. The next operation must happen only in the next clock period.

P_1: $W(x)1$	P_1: $W(x)1$
P_2: $R(x)1$	P_2: $R(x)0$ $R(x)1$
Strict Model	Non-strict Model

This is the most rigid model and is impossible to implement without forgoing performance. In this model, the programmer's expected result will be received every time. It is deterministic. A distributed system with many nodes will take some time to copy information written to one node to all the other nodes responsible for replicating that information. That time can't be zero because it takes time for information to propagate through space, and there is a limit to how fast information can travel through space: the speed of light. Therefore, strict consistency is impossible. The best one can do is design a system where the time-to-replicate approaches the theoretical minimum.

Sequential Consistency

The sequential consistency model is a weaker memory model than strict consistency. A write to a variable does not have to be seen instantaneously, however, writes to variables by different processors have to be seen in the same order by all processors. As defined by Lamport(1979), Sequential Consistency is met if "the result of any execution is the same as if the operations of all the processors were executed in some sequential order, and the operations of each individual processor appear in this sequence in the order specified by its program."

Program order within each processor and sequential ordering of operations between processors should be maintained. In order to preserve sequential order of execution between processors, all operations must appear to execute instantaneously or atomically with respect to every other processor. These operations need only "appear" to be completed because it is physically impossible to send information instantaneously. For instance, once a bus line is posted with information, It is guaranteed that all processors will see the information at the same instant. Thus, passing the information to the bus line completes the execution with respect to all processors and has appeared to have been executed. Cache-less architectures or cached architectures with interconnect networks that are not instantaneous can contain a slow path between processors and memories. These slow paths can result in sequential inconsistency, because some memories receive the broadcast data faster than others.

Sequential consistency can produce non-deterministic results. This is because the sequence of sequential operations between processors can be different during different runs of the program. All memory operations need to happen in the program order.

Linearizability (also known as atomic consistency) can be defined as sequential consistency with the real-time constraint.

Causal Consistency

Causal consistency is a weakening model of sequential consistency by categorizing events into those causally related and those that are not. It defines that only write operations that are causally related need to be seen in the same order by all processes.

This model relaxes Sequential consistency on concurrent writes by a processor and on writes that are not causally related. Two writes can become causally related if one write to a variable is dependent on a previous write to any variable if the processor doing the second write has just read the first write. The two writes could have been done by the same processor or by different processors.

As in sequential consistency, reads do not need to reflect changes instantaneously, however, they need to reflect all changes to a variable sequentially.

$$P_1: W_1(x)3$$
$$P_2: W_2(x)5\ R_1(x)3$$

W_1 is not causally related to W_2. R1 would be Sequentially Inconsistent but is Causally consistent.

P_1:W(x)1		W(x)3	
P_2:R(x)1	W(x)2		
P_3:R(x)1		R(x)3	R(x)2
P_4:R(x)1		R(x)2	R(x)3

W(x)1 and W(x) 2 are causally related due to the read made by P2 to x before W(x)2.

Processor Consistency

In order for consistency in data to be maintained and to attain scalable processor systems where every processor has its own memory, the Processor consistency model was derived. All processors need to be consistent in the order in which they see writes done by one processor and in the way they see writes by different processors to the same location (coherence is maintained). However, they do not need to be consistent when the writes are by different processors to different locations.

Every write operation can be divided into several sub-writes to all memories. A read from one such memory can happen before the write to this memory completes. Therefore, the data read can be stale. Thus, a processor under PC can execute a younger load when an older store needs to be stalled. Read before Write, Read after Read and Write before Write ordering is still preserved in this model.

The processor consistency model is similar to PRAM consistency model with a stronger condition that defines all writes to the same memory location must be seen in the same sequential order by all other processes. Process consistency is weaker than sequential consistency but stronger than PRAM consistency model.

The Stanford DASH multiprocessor system implements a variation of processor consistency which is incomparable (neither weaker nor stronger) to Goodmans definitions. All processors need to be consistent in the order in which they see writes by one processor and in the way they see writes by different processors to the same location. However, they do not need to be consistent when the writes are by different processors to different locations.

PRAM Consistency (Also known as FIFO Consistency)

PRAM consistency (Pipelined RAM) was presented by Lipton and Sandberg in 1988 as one of the first described consistency models. Due to its informal definition, there are in fact at least two subtle different implementations, one by Ahamad et al. and one by Mosberger.

In PRAM consistency, all processes view the operations of a single process in the same order that they were issued by that process, while operations issued by different processes can be viewed in different order from different processes. PRAM consistency is weaker than processor consistency. PRAM relaxes the need to maintain coherence to a location across all its processors. Here, reads to any variable can be executed before writes in a processor. Read before Write, Read after Read and Write before Write ordering is still preserved in this model.

P1:	W(x)1				
P2:		R(x)1	W(x)2		
P3:				R(x)1	R(x)2
P4:				R(x)2	R(x)1

Cache Consistency

Cache consistency requires that all write operations to the same memory location are performed in some sequential order. Cache consistency is weaker than process consistency and incomparable with PRAM consistency.

Slow Consistency

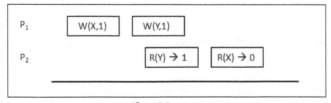

Slow Memory.

In slow consistency, if a process reads a value previously written to a memory location, it cannot subsequently read any earlier value from that location. Writes performed by a process are immediately visible to that process. Slow consistency is a weaker model than PRAM and cache consistency.

Example: Slow memory diagram depicts a slow consistency example. The first process writes 1 to the memory location X and then it writes 1 to the memory location Y. The second process reads 1 from Y and it then reads 0 from X even though X was written before Y.

Hutto, Phillip W., and Mustaque Ahamad (1990) illustrate that by appropriate programming, slow memory (consistency) can be expressive and efficient. They mention that slow memory has two valuable properties; locality and supporting reduction from atomic memory. They propose two algorithms to present the expressiveness of slow memory.

The following models require specific synchronization by programmers.

Weak Ordering

Program order and atomicity is maintained only on a group of operations and not on all reads and writes. This was derived from the understanding that certain memory operations – such as those conducted in a critical section - need not be seen by all processors – until after all operations in the critical section are completed for instance. It also exploits the fact that programs written to be executed on a multi-processor system contain the required synchronization to make sure that data races do not occur and SC outcomes are produced always. Thus, in weak ordering, operations other than synchronization operations can be classified as *data* operations.

P1	P2
X = 1;	*fence*
fence	while(!xready) {};
xready = 1;	*fence*
	y = 2;

Synchronization operations signal the processor to make sure it has completed and seen all previous operations done by all processors. In order to maintain Weak ordering, write operations prior to a synchronization operation must be globally performed before the synchronization operation. Operations present in after a synchronization operation should also be performed only after the synchronization operation completes. Therefore, accesses to synchronization variables is sequentially consistent and any read or write should be performed only after previous synchronization operations have completed. Coherence is not relaxed in this model. Once these requirements are met, all other "data" operations can be reordered.

There is high reliance on explicit synchronization in the program. For weak ordering models, the programmer must use atomic locking instructions such as test-and-set, fetch-and-op, store conditional, load linked or must label synchronization variables or use fences.

Release Consistency

This model relaxes the Weak consistency model by distinguishing the entrance synchronization operation from the exit synchronization operation. Under weak ordering, when a synchronization operation is to be seen, all operations in all processors need to be visible before the Synchronization operation is done and the processor proceeds. However, under Release consistency model, during the entry to a critical section, termed as "acquire", all operations with respect to the local memory variables need to be completed. During the exit, termed as "release", all changes made by the local processor should be propagated to all other processors. Coherence is still maintained.

The acquire operation is a load/read that is performed to access the critical section. A release operation is a store/write performed to allow other processors use the shared variables.

Among synchronization variables, sequential consistency or processor consistency can be maintained. Using SC, all competing synchronization variables should be processed in order. However, with PC, a pair of competing variables need to only follow this order. Younger Acquires can be allowed to happen before older Releases.

Entry Consistency

This is a variant of the Release Consistency model. It also requires the use of Acquire and Release instructions to explicitly state an entry or exit to a critical section. However, under Entry Consistency, every shared variable is assigned a synchronization variable specific to it. This way, only when the Acquire is to variable x, all operations related to x need to be completed with respect to that processor. This allows concurrent operations of different critical sections of different shared variables to occur. Concurrency cannot be seen for critical operations on the same shared variable. Such a consistency model will be useful when different matrix elements can be processed at the same time.

General Consistency

In general consistency, all the copies of a memory location are eventually identical after all processes' writes are completed.

Local Consistency

In local consistency, each process performs its own operations in the order defined by its program. There is no constraint on the ordering in which the write operations of other processes appear to be performed. Local consistency is the weakest consistency model in shared memory systems.

Some other consistency models are as follows:

- Causal+ Consistency
- Delta consistency
- Eventual consistency
- Fork consistency
- One-copy serializability
- Serializability
- Vector-field consistency
- Weak consistency
- Strong consistency

Several other consistency models have been conceived to express restrictions with respect to ordering or visibility of operations, or to deal with specific fault assumptions.

Relaxed Memory Consistency Models

Some different consistency models can be defined by relaxing one or more requirements in sequential consistency called relaxed consistency models. These consistency models do not provide memory consistency at the hardware level. In fact, the programmers are responsible for implementing the memory consistency by applying synchronization techniques. The above models are classified based on four criteria and are detailed further.

There are four comparisons to define the relaxed consistency:

- Relaxation: One way to categorize the relaxed consistency is to define which sequential consistency requirements are relaxed. We can have less strict models by relaxing either program order or write atomicity requirements defined by Adve and Gharachorloo, 1996. Program order guarantees that each process issues a memory request ordered by its program and write atomicity defines that memory requests are serviced based on the order of a single FIFO queue. In relaxing program order, any or all the ordering of operation pairs, write-after-write, read-after-write, or read/write-after-read, can be relaxed. In the relaxed write atomicity model, a process can view its own writes before any other processors.

- Synchronizing vs. Non-Synchronizing: A synchronizing model can be defined by dividing the memory accesses into two groups and assigning different consistency restrictions to each group considering that one group can have a weak consistency model while the other one needs a more restrictive consistency model. In contrast, a non-synchronizing Model assigns the same consistency model to the memory access types.

- Issue vs. View-Based: Issue method provides sequential consistency simulation by defining the restrictions for processes to issue memory operations. Whereas, view method describes the visibility restrictions on the events order for processes.

- Relative Model Strength: Some consistency models are more restrictive than others. In other words, strict consistency models enforce more constraints as consistency requirements. The strength of a model can be defined by the program order or atomicity relaxations and the strength of models can also be compared. Some models are directly related if they apply same relaxations or more. On the other hand, the models that relax different requirements are not directly related.

Sequential consistency has two requirements, program order and write atomicity. Different relaxed consistency models can be obtained by relaxing these requirements. This is done so that, along with relaxed constraints, the performance increases, but the programmer is responsible for implementing the memory consistency by applying synchronisation techniques and must have a good understanding of the hardware.

Potential relaxations:

- Write to Read program order

- Write to Write program order

- Read to Read and Read to Write program orders

Relaxation Models

The following models are some models of relaxed consistency:

Relaxed Write to Read

An approach to improving the performance at the hardware level is by relaxing the PO of a write followed by a read which effectively hides the latency of write operations. The optimisation this type of relaxation relies on is that it allows the subsequent reads to be in a relaxed order with respect to the previous writes from he processor. Because of this relaxation some programs like XXX may fail to give SC results because of this relaxation. Whereas, programs like YYY are still expected to give consistent results because of the enforcement of the remaining program order constraints.

Three models fall under this category. IBM 370 model is the strictest model. A Read can be complete before an earlier write to a different address, but it is prohibited from returning the value of the write unless all the processors have seen the write. The SPARC V8 total store ordering model (TSO) model partially relaxes the IBM 370 Model, it allows a read to return the value of its own processor's write with respect to other writes to the same location i.e. it returns the value of its own write before others see it. Similar to the previous model, this cannot return the value of write unless all the processors have seen the write. The processor consistency model (PC) is the most relaxed of the three models and relaxes both the constraints such that a read can complete before an earlier write even before it is made visible to other processors.

In Example A, the result is possible only in IBM 370 because Read(A) is not issued until the write(A) in that processor is completed. On the other hand, this result is possible in TSO and PC because they allow the reads of the flags before the writes of the flags in a single processor.

In Example B the result is possible only with PC as it allows P2 to return the value of a write even before it is visible to P3. This won't be possible in the other two models.

To ensure sequential consistency in the above models, safety nets or fences are used to manually enforce the constraint. The IBM370 model has some specialised *serialisation instructions* which are manually placed between operations. These instructions can consist of memory instructions such or non-memory instructions such as branches. On the other hand, the TSO and PC models do not provide safety nets, but the programmers can still use read-modify-write operations to make it appear like the program order is still maintained between a write and a following read. In case of TSO, PO appears to be maintained if the R or W which is already a part of a R-modify-W is replaced by a R-modify-W, this requires the W in the R-modify-W is a 'dummy' that returns the read value. Similarly for PC, PO seems to be maintained if the read is replaced by a write or is already a part of R-modify-W.

However, compiler optimisations cannot be done after exercising this relaxation alone. Compiler optimisations require the full flexibility of reordering any two operations in the PO, so the ability to reorder a write with respect to a read is not sufficiently helpful in this case.

```
Example A.

Initially, A=flag1=flag2=0

P1                      P2

flag1=1                 flag2=1

A=1                     A=2

reg1=A                   reg3=A

reg2=flag2               reg4=flag1


Result: reg1=1 ; reg3=2, reg2=reg4=0
```

```
Example B. Initially, A=B=0

P1              P2              P3

A=1

                if(A==1)

                B=1                     if(B==1)

                                        reg1=A


Result: B=1, reg1=0
```

Relaxed Write to Read and Write to Write

Some models relax the program order even further by relaxing even the ordering constraints between writes to different locations. The SPARC V8 Partial Store Ordering model (PSO) is the only example of such a model. The ability to pipeline and overlap writes to different locations from the same processor is the key hardware optimisation enabled by PSO. PSO is similar to TSO in terms of atomicity requirements, in that, it allows a processor to read the value of its own write and preventing other processors from reading another processor's write before the write is visible to all other processors. Program order between two writes is maintained by PSO using an explicit STBAR instruction. The STBAR is inserted in a write buffer in implementations with FIFO write buffers. A counter is used to determine when all the writes before the STBAR instruction have been completed, which triggers a write to the memory system to increment the counter. A write acknowledgement decrements the counter, and when the counter becomes 0, it signifies that all the previous writes are completed.

In the examples A and B, PSO allows both these non-sequentially consistent results. The safety net that PSO provides is similar to TSO's, it imposes program order from a write to a read and enforces write atomicity.

Similar to the previous models, the relaxations allowed by PSO are not sufficiently flexible to be useful for compiler optimisation, which requires a much more flexible optimisation.

Relaxing Read and Read to Write Program Orders

In some models, all operations to different locations are relaxed. A read or write may be reordered with respect a different read or write in a different location. The *weak ordering* may be classified under this category and two types of Release consistency models (RCsc and RCpc) also come under this model. Three commercial architectures are also proposed under this category of relaxation: the Digital Alpha, SPARC V9 relaxed memory order (RMO), and IBM PowerPC models. All these models allow reordering of reads to the same location, except the Digital Alpha. These models violate sequential in examples A and B. An additional relaxation allowed in these models that is absent ninth previous models is that memory operations following a read operation can be overlapped and reordered with respect to the read. All these models, expect the RCpc and PowerPC allow a read to return the value of another processor's early write. From a programmer's perspective all these models must maintain the illusion of write atomicity even though they allow the processor to read its own write early.

These models can be classified into two categories based on the type of safety net provided. Here, the necessity for carefully written programs is seen. The nature of the synchronization helps to categorize between Weak Ordering, RCsc and RCpc models. Where as, The Alpha, RMO and PowerPC models provide fence instructions so that program order can be imposed between different memory operations.

Weak Ordering

An example of a model that relaxes most of the above constraints (except reading others' write early) is Weak Ordering. It classifies memory operations into two categories: *Data operations* and *Synchronization operations*. To enforce program order, a programmer needs to find at least one synchronisation operation in a program. The assumption under which this works is that, reordering memory operations to data regions between synchronisation operations does not affect the outcome of the program. They just act as the safety net for enforcing program order. The way this works is that a counter tracks the number of data operations and until this counter becomes zero, the synchronisation operation isn't issued. Furthermore, no more data operations are issued unless all the previous synchronisation's are completed. Memory operations in between two synchronisation variables can be overlapped and reordered without affecting the correctness of the program. This model ensures that write atomicity is always maintained, therefore no additional safety net is required for Weak Ordering.

Release Consistency (RCsc/RCpc)

More classification is made to memory operations depending on when they occur. Operations are divided into ordinary and special. Special operations are further divided into sync or sync operations. Syncs correspond to synchronisation operations and syncs correspond to data operations or other special operations that aren't used for synchronisation. Sync operations are further divided into acquire or release operations. An acquire is effectively a read memory operation used to obtain access to a certain set of shared locations. Release, on the other hand, is a write operation that is performed for granting permission to access the shared locations.

There are two types of Release consistency, RCsc (Release consistency with Sequential consistency) and RCpc (Release consistency with processor consistency). The first type, RCsc maintains SC among special operations, while RCpc maintains PC among such operations.

For RCsc the constraints are: Acquire->All, All->Release,Special->Special.

For RCpc the write to read program order is relaxed: Acquire->All, All->Release, Special->Special(expect when special write is followed by special read).

NOTE: the above notation A->B, implies that if the operation A precedes B in the program order, then program order is enforced.

Alpha, RMO, and PowerPC

These three commercial architectures exhibit explicit fence instructions as their safety nets. The Alpha model provides two types of fence instructions, Memory barrier(MB) and Write memory barrier(WMB). The MB operation can be used to maintain program order of any memory operation before the MB with a memory operation after the barrier. Similarly, the WMB maintains program order only among writes. The SPARC V9 RMO model provides a MEMBAR instruction which can be customised to order previous reads and writes with respect to future read and write operations. There is no need for using read-modify-writes to achieve this order because the MEMBAR instruction can be used to order a write with respect to a succeeding read. The PowerPC model uses a single fence instruction called the SYNC instruction. It is similar to the MB instruction, but with a little exception that reads can occur out of program order even if a SYNC is placed between two reads to the same location. This model also differs from Alpha and RMO in terms of Atomicity. It allows write to be seen earlier than a read's completion. A combination of read modify write operations may be required to make an illusion of write atomicity.

Transactional Memory Models

Transactional Memory model is the combination of cache coherency and memory consistency models as a communication model for shared memory systems supported by software or hardware; a transactional memory model provides both memory consistency and cache coherency. A transaction is a sequence of operations executed by a process that transforms data from one consistent state to another. A transaction either commits when there is no conflict or aborts. In commits, all changes are visible to all other processes when a transaction is completed, while aborts discard all changes. Compared to relaxed consistency models, a transactional model is easier to use and can provide the higher performance than a sequential consistency model.

Consistency and Replication

Tanenbaum et al., 2007 defines two main reasons for replicating; reliability and performance. Reliability can be achieved in a replicated file system by switching to another replica in the case of the current replica failure. The replication also protects data from being corrupted by providing multiple copies of data on different replicas. It also improves the performance by dividing the work. While replication can improve performance and reliability, it can cause consistency problems between multiple copies of data. The multiple copies are consistent if a read operation returns the same value from all copies and a write operation as a single atomic operation (transaction) updates all copies before any other operation takes place. Tanenbaum, Andrew, & Maarten

Van Steen, 2007 refer to this type of consistency as tight consistency provided by synchronous replication. However, applying global synchronizations to keep all copies consistent is costly. One way to decrease the cost of global synchronization and improve the performance can be weakening the consistency restrictions.

Data-centric Consistency Models

Tanenbaum et al., 2007 defines the consistency model as a contract between the software (processes) and memory implementation (data store). This model guarantees that if the software follows certain rules, the memory works correctly. Since, in a system without a global clock, defining the last operation writes is difficult, some restrictions can be applied on the values that can be returned by a read operation.

Consistent Ordering of Operations

Some consistency models such as sequential and also causal consistency models deal with the order of operations on shared replicated data in order to provide consistency. In this models, all replicas must agree on a consistent global ordering of updates.

Sequential Consistency

The goal of data-centric consistency models is to provide a consistent view on a data store where processes may carry out concurrent updates. One important data-centric consistency model is sequential consistency defined by Lamport (1979). Tanenbaum et al., 2007 defines sequential consistency under following condition:

"The result of any execution is the same as if the (read and write) operations by all processes on the data store were executed in some sequential order and the operations of each individual process appear in this sequence in the order specified by its program."

Adve and Gharachorloo, 1996 define two requirements to implement the sequential consistency; program order and write atomicity.

- Program order: Program order guarantees that each process issues a memory request ordered by its program.

- Write atomicity: Write atomicity defines that memory requests are serviced based on the order of a single FIFO queue.

In sequential consistency, there is no notion of time or most recent write operations. There are some operations interleaving that is same for all processes. A process can see the write operations of all processes but it can just see its own read operations.

Linearizability (Atomic memory) can be defined as a sequential consistency with real time constraint by considering a begin time and end time for each operation. An execution is linearizable if each operation taking place in linearizable order by placing a point between its begin time and its end time and guarantees sequential consistency.

Causal Consistency

The causal consistency defined by Hutto and Ahamad, 1990 is a weaker consistency model than sequential consistency by making the distinction between causally related operations and those that are not related. For example, if an event b takes effect from an earlier event a, the causal consistency guarantees that all processes see event b after event a.

Tanenbaum et al., 2007 defines that a data store is considered causal consistent under the following condition:

"Writes that are potentially causally related must be seen by all processes in the same order. Concurrent writes may be seen in a different order on different machines."

Grouping Operations

In grouping operation, accesses to the synchronization variables are sequentially consistent. A process is allowed to access a synchronization variable that all previous writes have been completed. In other words, accesses to synchronization variables are not permitted until all operations on the synchronization variables are completely performed.

Continuous Consistency

The continuous consistency is defined later in the consistency protocol section.

Client-centric Consistency Models

In distributed systems, maintaining sequential consistency in order to control the concurrent operations is essential. In some special data stores without simultaneous updates, client-centric consistency models can deal with inconsistencies in a less costly way. The following models are some client-centric consistency models:

Eventual Consistency

An eventual consistency is a weak consistency model in the system with the lack of simultaneous updates. It defines that if no update takes a very long time, all replicas eventually become consistent.

Monotonic Read Consistency

Tanenbaum et al., 2007 defines monotonic read consistency as follows:

"If a process reads the value of a data item x, any successive read operation on x by that process will always return that same value or a more recent value."

Monotonic read consistency guarantees that after a process reads a value of data item x at time t, it will never see the older value of that data item.

Monotonic Write Consistency

Monotonic write consistency condition is defined by Tanenbaum et al., 2007 as follows:

"A write operation by a process on a data item X is completed before any successive write operation on X by the same process."

Read-your-writes Consistency

A value written by a process on a data item X will be always available to a successive read operation performed by the same process on data item X.

Writes-follows-reads Consistency

In Writes-follow-reads consistency, updates are propagated after performing the previous read operations. Tanenbaum et al., 2007 defines the following condition for Writes-follow-reads consistency:

"A write operation by a process on a data item x following a previous read operation on x by the same process is guaranteed to take place on the same or a more recent value of x that was read."

Consistency Protocols

The implementation of a consistency model is defined by a consistency protocol. Tanenbaum et al., 2007 illustrates some consistency protocols for data-centric models.

Continuous Consistency

Continuous consistency introduced by Yu and Vahdat (2000). In this model, consistency semantic of an application is described by using conits in the application. Since the consistency requirements can differ based on application semantics, Yu and Vahdat (2000) believe that a predefined uniform consistency model may not be an appropriate approach. The application should specify the consistency requirements that satisfy the application semantic. In this model, an application specifies each consistency requirements as a conits (abbreviation of consistency units). A conit can be a physical or logical consistency and is used to measure the consistency. Tanenbaum et al., 2007 describes the notion of a conit by giving an example. There are three inconsistencies that can be tolerated by applications.

- Deviation in numerical values Numerical deviation bounds the difference between the conit value and relative value of last update. A weight can be assigned to the writes which defines the importance of the writes in a specific application. The total weights of unseen writes for a conit can be defined as a numerical deviation in an application. There are two different types of numerical deviation; absolute and relative numerical deviation.

- Deviation in ordering Ordering deviation is the discrepancy between the local order of writes in a replica and their relative ordering in the eventual final image.

- Deviation in staleness between replicas Staleness deviation defines the validity of the oldest write by bounding the difference between the current time and the time of oldest write on a conit not seen locally. Each server has a local queue of uncertain write that is required an actual order to be determined and applied on a conit. The maximal length of uncertain writes queue is the bound of ordering deviation. When the number of writes exceeds the limit, instead of accepting new submitted write, the server will attempt to commit uncertain writes by communicating with other servers based on the order that writes should be executed.

If all three deviation bounds set to zero, the continuous consistency model is the strong consistency.

Primary-based Protocols

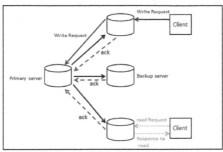

Primary backup protocol.

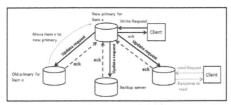

Primary-backup protocol (local-write).

Primary-based protocols can be considered as a class of consistency protocols that are simpler to implement. For instance, sequential ordering is a popular consistency model when consistent ordering of operations is considered. The sequential ordering can be determined as primary-based protocol. In these protocols, there is an associated primary for each data item in a data store to coordinate write operations on that data item.

Remote-write Protocols

In the simplest primary-based protocol that supports replication, also known as primary-backup protocol, write operations are forwarded to a single server and read operations can be performed locally.

> Example: Tanenbaum et al., 2007 gives an example of a primary-backup protocol. The diagram of primary-backup protocol shows an example of this protocol. When a client requests a write, the write request is forwarded to a primary server. The primary server sends request to backups to perform the update. The server then receives the update acknowledgement from all backups and sends the acknowledgement of completion of writes to the client. Any client can read the last available update locally. The trade-off of this protocol is that a client who sends the update request might have to wait so long to get the acknowledgement in order to continue. This problem can be solved by performing the updates locally, and then ask other backups perform their updates. The non-blocking primary-backup protocol does not guarantee the consistency of update on all backup servers. However, it improves the performance. In the primary-backup protocol, all processes will see the same order of write operations since this protocol orders all incoming writes based on a globally unique time. Blocking protocols guarantee that processes view the result of the last write operation.

Local-write Protocols

In primary-based local-write protocols, primary copy moves between processes willing to perform an update. To update a data item, a process first moves it to its location. As a result, in this approach, successive write operations can be performed locally while each process can read their local copy of data items. After the primary finishes its update, the update is forwarded to other replicas and all perform the update locally. This non-blocking approach can lead to an improvement. The diagram of the local-write protocol depicts the local-write approach in primary-based protocols. A process requests a write operation in a data item x. The current server is considered as the new primary for a data item x. The write operation is performed and when the request is finished, the primary sends an update request to other backup servers. Each backup sends an acknowledgment to the primary after finishing the update operation.

Replicated-write Protocols

In Replicated-write protocols, unlike the primary-based protocol, all updates are carried out to all replicas.

Active Replication

In active replication, there is a process associated to each replica to perform the write operation. In other words, updates are sent to each replica in the form of an operation in order to be executed. All updates need to be performed in the same order in all replicas. As a result, a totally-ordered multicast mechanism is required. There is a scalability issue in implementing such a multicasting mechanism in large distributed systems. There is another approach in which each operation is sent to a central coordinator (sequencer). The coordinator first assigns a sequence number to each operation and then forwards the operation to all replicas. Second approach cannot also solve the scalability problem.

Quorum-based Protocols

Voting can be another approach in replicated-write protocols. In this approach, a client requests and receives permission from multiple servers in order to read and write a replicated data. As an example, suppose in a distributed file system, a file is replicated on N servers. To update a file, a client must send a request to at least N/2+1 in order to make their agreement to perform an update. After the agreement, changes are applied on the file and a new version number is assigned to the updated file. Similarly, for reading replicated file, a client sends a request to N/2+1 servers in order to receive the associated version number from those servers. Read operation is completed if all received version numbers are the most recent version.

Cache-coherence Protocols

In a replicated file system, a cache-coherence protocol provides the cache consistency while caches are generally controlled by clients. In many approaches, cache consistency is provided by the underlying hardware. Some other approaches in middleware-based distributed systems apply software-based solutions to provide the cache consistency. Cache consistency models can differ in their coherence detection strategies that define when inconsistencies occur. There are two approaches to detect the inconsistency; static and dynamic solutions. In the static solution, a compiler determines which variables can cause the cache inconsistency. So, the compiler enforces an instruction in order to avoid the inconsistency problem. In the dynamic solution, the server checks for inconsistencies at run time to control the consistency of the cached data that has changed after it was cached. The coherence enforcement strategy is another cache-coherence protocol. It defines that *how* to provide the consistency in caches by using the copies located on the server. One way to keep the data consistent is to never cache the shared data. A server can keep the data and apply some consistency protocol such as primary-based protocols to ensure the consistency of shared data. In this solution, only private data can be cached by clients. In the case that shared data are cached, there are two approaches in order to enforce the cache coherence. In first approach, when a shared data is updated, the server forwards invalidation to all caches. In second approach, an update is propagated. Most caching systems apply these two approaches or dynamically choose between them.

Ocean Current Simulation

- Regular structure, scientific computing, important for weather forecast
- Want to simulate the eddy current along the walls of ocean basin over a period of time
  - Discretize the 3-D basin into 2-D horizontal grids
  - Discretize each 2-D grid into points
  - One time step involves solving the equation of motion for each grid point
  - Enough concurrency within and across grids
  - After each time step synchronize the processors

Galaxy Simulation

- Simulate the interaction of many stars evolving over time
- Want to compute force between every pair of stars for each time step
  - Essentially $O(n^2)$ computations (massive parallelism)
- Hierarchical methods take advantage of square law
  - If a group of stars is far enough it is possible to approximate the group entirely by a single star at the center of mass
  - Essentially four subparts in each step: divide the galaxy into zones until further division does not improve accuracy, compute center of mass for each zone, compute force, update star position based on force
- Lot of concurrency across stars

Ray Tracing

- Want to render a scene using ray tracing

- Generate rays through pixels in the image plane
- The rays bounce from objects following reflection/refraction laws
  - New rays get generated: tree of rays from a root ray
- Need to correctly simulate paths of all rays
- The outcome is color and opacity of the objects in the scene: thus you render a scene
- Concurrency across ray trees and subtrees

Writing a Parallel Program

- Start from a sequential description
- Identify work that can be done in parallel
- Partition work and/or data among threads or processes
  - Decomposition and assignment
- Add necessary communication and synchronization
  - Orchestration
- Map threads to processors (Mapping)
- How good is the parallel program?
- Measure speedup = sequential execution time/parallel execution time = number of processors ideally

Some Definitions

- Task
  - Arbitrary piece of sequential work
  - Concurrency is only across tasks
  - Fine-grained task vs. coarse-grained task: controls granularity of parallelism (spectrum of grain: one instruction to the whole sequential program)
- Process/thread
  - Logical entity that performs a task
  - Communication and synchronization happen between threads
- Processors
  - Physical entity on which one or more processes execute

Decomposition of Iterative Equation Solver

- Find concurrent tasks and divide the program into tasks

  - Level or grain of concurrency needs to be decided here

  - Too many tasks: may lead to too much of overhead communicating and synchronizing between tasks

  - Too few tasks: may lead to idle processors

  - Goal: Just enough tasks to keep the processors busy

- Number of tasks may vary dynamically

  - New tasks may get created as the computation proceeds: new rays in ray tracing

  - Number of available tasks at any point in time is an upper bound on the achievable speedup

Static Assignment

- Given a decomposition it is possible to assign tasks statically

  - For example, some computation on an array of size N can be decomposed statically by assigning a range of indices to each process: for k processes P_0 operates on indices 0 to (N/k)-1, P_1 operates on N/k to (2N/k)-1,..., P_{k-1} operates on (k-1)N/k to N-1

  - For regular computations this works great: simple and low-overhead

- What if the nature computation depends on the index?

  - For certain index ranges you do some heavy-weight computation while for others you do something simple

  - Is there a problem?

Dynamic Assignment

- Static assignment may lead to load imbalance depending on how irregular the application is

- Dynamic decomposition/assignment solves this issue by allowing a process to dynamically choose any available task whenever it is done with its previous task

  - Normally in this case you decompose the program in such a way that the number of available tasks is larger than the number of processes

  - Same example: divide the array into portions each with 10 indices; so you have N/10 tasks

  - An idle process grabs the next available task

- - Provides better load balance since longer tasks can execute concurrently with the smaller ones

- Dynamic assignment comes with its own overhead

  - Now you need to maintain a shared count of the number of available tasks

  - The update of this variable must be protected by a lock

  - Need to be careful so that this lock contention does not outweigh the benefits of dynamic decomposition

- More complicated applications where a task may not just operate on an index range, but could manipulate a subtree or a complex data structure

  - Normally a dynamic task queue is maintained where each task is probably a pointer to the data

  - The task queue gets populated as new tasks are discovered

Decomposition Types

- Decomposition by data

  - The most commonly found decomposition technique

  - The data set is partitioned into several subsets and each subset is assigned to a process

  - The type of computation may or may not be identical on each subset

  - Very easy to program and manage

- Computational decomposition

  - Not so popular: tricky to program and manage

  - All processes operate on the same data, but probably carry out different kinds of computation

  - More common in systolic arrays, pipelined graphics processor units (GPUs) etc.

Orchestration

- Involves structuring communication and synchronization among processes, organizing data structures to improve locality, and scheduling tasks

  - This step normally depends on the programming model and the underlying architecture

- Goal is to

  - Reduce communication and synchronization costs

- o   Maximize locality of data reference

- o   Schedule tasks to maximize concurrency: do not schedule dependent tasks in parallel

- o   Reduce overhead of parallelization and concurrency management (e.g., management of the task queue, overhead of initiating a task etc.)

Mapping

- At this point you have a parallel program

  - o   Just need to decide which and how many processes go to each processor of the parallel machine

- Could be specified by the program

  - o   Pin particular processes to a particular processor for the whole life of the program; the processes cannot migrate to other processors

- Could be controlled entirely by the OS

  - o   Schedule processes on idle processors

  - o   Various scheduling algorithms are possible e.g., round robin: process#k goes to processor#k

  - o   NUMA-aware OS normally takes into account multiprocessor-specific metrics in scheduling

- How many processes per processor? Most common is one-to-one

An Example

- Iterative equation solver

  - o   Main kernel in Ocean simulation

  - o   Update each 2-D grid point via Gauss-Seidel iterations

  - o   A[i,j] = 0.2(A[i,j]+A[i,j+1]+A[i,j-1]+A[i+1,j]+A[i-1,j])

  - o   Pad the n by n grid to (n+2) by (n+2) to avoid corner problems

  - o   Update only interior n by n grid

  - o   One iteration consists of updating all n2 points in-place and accumulating the difference from the previous value at each point

  - o   If the difference is less than a threshold, the solver is said to have converged to a stable grid equilibrium

Sequential Program

```
int n;                                              begin Solve (A)
```

```
float **A, diff;                                      int i, j, done = 0;

                                                          float temp;

                                                          while (!done)

begin main()                                                 diff = 0.0;

  read (n);   /* size of grid */                      for i = 0 to n-1

  Allocate (A);                                                        for
j = 0 to n-1

  Initialize (A);                                                  temp =
A[i,j];

  Solve (A);                                                       A[i,j]
= 0.2(A[i,j]+A[i,j+1]+A[i,j-1]+A[i-

end main                                                  1,j]+A[i+1,j]);

                                                                        diff
+= fabs (A[i,j] - temp);

                                                                         end-
for

                                                                        endfor

                                                                            if
(diff/(n*n) < TOL) then done = 1;

                                                                       endwhile
                                                          end Solve
```

Decomposition of Iterative Equation Solver

- Look for concurrency in loop iterations
  - In this case iterations are really dependent
  - Iteration (i, j) depends on iterations (i, j-1) and (i-1, j)

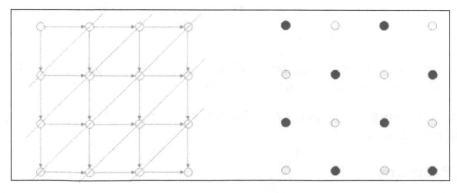

  - Each anti-diagonal can be computed in parallel

- o   Must synchronize after each anti-diagonal (or pt-to-pt)

- o   Alternative: red-black ordering (different update pattern)

- Can update all red points first, synchronize globally with a barrier and then update all black points

  - o   May converge faster or slower compared to sequential program

  - o   Converged equilibrium may also be different if there are multiple solutions

  - o   Ocean simulation uses this decomposition

- We will ignore the loop-carried dependence and go ahead with a straight-forward loop decomposition

  - o   Allow updates to all points in parallel

  - o   This is yet another different update order and may affect convergence

  - o   Update to a point may or may not see the new updates to the nearest neighbors (this parallel algorithm is non-deterministic)

```
while (!done)

    diff = 0.0;

    for_all i = 0 to n-1

        for_all j = 0 to n-1

            temp = A[i, j];

          A[i, j] = 0.2(A[i, j]+A[i, j+1]+A[i, j-1]+A[i-1, j]+A[i+1, j]);

            diff += fabs (A[i, j] - temp);

        end for_all

    end for_all

    if (diff/(n*n) < TOL) then done = 1;

end while
```

- Offers concurrency across elements: degree of concurrency is n^2

- Make the j loop sequential to have row-wise decomposition: degree n concurrency

Assignment

- Possible static assignment: block row decomposition

  - o   Process 0 gets rows 0 to (n/p)-1, process 1 gets rows n/p to (2n/p)-1 etc.

- Another static assignment: cyclic row decomposition

- o Process 0 gets rows 0, p, 2p,...; process 1 gets rows 1, p+1, 2p+1,....
- Dynamic assignment
  - o Grab next available row, work on that, grab a new row,...
- Static block row assignment minimizes nearest neighbor communication by assigning contiguous rows to the same process

Shared memory version

```
/* include files */

MAIN_ENV;

int P, n;

void Solve ();

struct gm_t {

    LOCKDEC (diff_lock);

    BARDEC (barrier);

    float **A, diff;

} *gm;

int main (char **argv, int argc)

{

    int i;

    MAIN_INITENV;

    gm = (struct gm_t*) G_MALLOC (sizeof (struct gm_t));

    LOCKINIT (gm->diff_lock);

BARINIT (gm->barrier);

    n = atoi (argv);

    P = atoi (argv);

    gm->A = (float**) G_MALLOC ((n+2)*sizeof (float*));

    for (i = 0; i < n+2; i++) {

        gm->A[i] = (float*) G_MALLOC ((n+2)*sizeof (float));

    }

    Initialize (gm->A);

    for (i = 1; i < P; i++) {  /* starts at 1 */

        CREATE (Solve);

    }

    Solve ();
```

```
   WAIT_FOR_END (P-1);

   MAIN_END;

}

void Solve (void)

{

   int i, j, pid, done = 0;

   float temp, local_diff;

   GET_PID (pid);

   while (!done) {

      local_diff = 0.0;

      if (!pid) gm->diff = 0.0;

      BARRIER (gm->barrier, P);/*why?*/

      for (i = pid*(n/P); i < (pid+1)*(n/P); i++) {

         for (j = 0; j < n; j++) {

            temp = gm->A[i] [j];

         gm->A[i] [j] = 0.2*(gm->A[i] [j] + gm->A[i] [j-1] + gm->A[i] [j+1] +
gm->A[i+1] [j] + gm->A[i-1] [j]);

local_diff += fabs (gm->A[i] [j] - temp);

         }   /* end for */

      }    /* end for */

      LOCK (gm->diff_lock);

      gm->diff += local_diff;

      UNLOCK (gm->diff_lock);

      BARRIER (gm->barrier, P);

      if (gm->diff/(n*n) < TOL) done = 1;

      BARRIER (gm->barrier, P); /* why? */

   }   /* end while */

}
```

Mutual Exclusion

- Use LOCK/UNLOCK around critical sections
  - o Updates to shared variable diff must be sequential
  - o Heavily contended locks may degrade performance

o   Try to minimize the use of critical sections: they are sequential anyway and will limit speedup

o   This is the reason for using a local_diff instead of accessing gm->diff every time

o   Also, minimize the size of critical section because the longer you hold the lock, longer will be the waiting time for other processors at lock acquire

LOCK Optimization

- Suppose each processor updates a shared variable holding a global cost value, only if its local cost is less than the global cost: found frequently in minimization problems

```
LOCK (gm->cost_lock);

if (my_cost < gm->cost) {

gm->cost = my_cost;

}

UNLOCK (gm->cost_lock);

/* May lead to heavy lock contention if everyone tries to update at the
same time */

if (my_cost < gm->cost) {

LOCK (gm->cost_lock);

if (my_cost < gm->cost)

{ /* make sure*/

gm->cost = my_cost;

}

UNLOCK (gm->cost_lock);

} /* this works because gm->cost is monotonically decreasing */
```

More Synchronization

- Global synchronization
  o   Through barriers
  o   Often used to separate computation phases
- Point-to-point synchronization
  o   A process directly notifies another about a certain event on which the latter was waiting
  o   Producer-consumer communication pattern
  o   Semaphores are used for concurrent programming on uniprocessor through P and V functions

    o Normally implemented through flags on shared memory multiprocessors (busy wait or spin)

P_0: A = 1; flag = 1;

P_1: while (!flag); use (A);

Message Passing

- What is different from shared memory?

  o No shared variable: expose communication through send/receive

  o No lock or barrier primitive

  o Must implement synchronization through send/receive

- Grid solver example

  o P_0 allocates and initializes matrix A in its local memory

  o Then it sends the block rows, n, P to each processor i.e. P_1 waits to receive rows n/P to 2n/P-1 etc. (this is one-time)

  o Within the while loop the first thing that every processor does is to send its first and last rows to the upper and the lower processors (corner cases need to be handled)

  o Then each processor waits to receive the neighboring two rows from the upper and the lower processors

- At the end of the loop each processor sends its local_diff to P_0 and P_0 sends back the done flag

Major Changes

```
/* include files */                          BARINIT (gm->barrier);
MAIN_ENV;                                     n = atoi (argv[1]);
int P, n;                                     P = atoi (argv[2]);
void Solve ();                                gm->A = (float**) G_MALLOC
struct gm_t {                                   ((n+2)*sizeof (float*));
   LOCKDEC (diff_lock);          Local       for (i = 0; i < n+2; i++) {
   BARDEC (barrier);             Alloc.         gm->A[i] = (float*) G_MALLOC
   float **A, diff;                               ((n+2)*sizeof (float));
} *gm;                                         }
                                              Initialize (gm->A);
int main (char **argv, int argc)              for (i = 1; i < P; i++) { /* starts at 1 */
{                                                CREATE (Solve);
   int i; int P, n; float **A;                }
   MAIN_INITENV;                              Solve ();
   gm = (struct gm_t*) G_MALLOC              WAIT_FOR_END (P-1);
   (sizeof (struct gm_t));                    MAIN_END;
   LOCKINIT (gm->diff_lock);                  }
```

```
void Solve (void)                              local_diff += fabs (gm->A[i] [j] –
{                                          temp);
  int i, j, pid, done = 0;                     } /* end for */
  float temp, local_diff;                    } /* end for */
  GET_PID (pid);                             LOCK (gm->diff_lock);    Send local diff
  while (!done) {      if (pid) Recv rows, n, P   gm->diff += local_diff;   to P₀
    local_diff = 0.0;         Send up/down      UNLOCK (gm->diff_lock);  Recv diff
    if (!pid) gm->diff = 0.0;   Recv up/down    BARRIER (gm->barrier, P);
    BARRIER (gm->barrier, P);/*why?*/          if (gm->diff/(n*n) < TOL) done = 1;
    for (i = pid*(n/P); i < (pid+1)*(n/P);     BARRIER (gm->barrier, P); /* why? */
    i++) {                                   } /* end while */
      for (j = 0; j < n; j++) {            }
        temp = gm->A[i] [j];
        gm->A[i] [j] = 0.2*(gm->A[i] [j] +
        gm->A[i] [j-1] + gm->A[i] [j+1] + gm-
        >A[i+1] [j] + gm->A[i-1] [j];
```

Message Passing

- This algorithm is deterministic

- May converge to a different solution compared to the shared memory version if there are multiple solutions: why?

  - There is a fixed specific point in the program (at the beginning of each iteration) when the neighboring rows are communicated

  - This is not true for shared memory

Message Passing Grid Solver

MPI-like Environment

- MPI stands for Message Passing Interface

  - A C library that provides a set of message passing primitives (e.g., send, receive, broadcast etc.) to the user

- PVM (Parallel Virtual Machine) is another well-known platform for message passing programming

- Only need to know

  - When you start an MPI program every thread runs the same main function

  - We will assume that we pin one thread to one processor just as we did in shared memory

- Instead of using the exact MPI syntax we will use some macros that call the MPI functions

```
MAIN_ENV;
```

```
/* define message tags */
 #define ROW 99
#define DIFF 98
#define DONE 97
int main(int argc, char **argv)
{
    int pid, P, done, i, j, N;
    float tempdiff, local_diff, temp, **A;
    MAIN_INITENV;
    GET_PID(pid);
    GET_NUMPROCS(P);
    N = atoi(argv);
    tempdiff = 0.0;
    done = 0;
    A = (double **) malloc ((N/P+2) * sizeof(float *));
    for (i=0; i < N/P+2; i++) {
        A[i] = (float *) malloc (sizeof(float) * (N+2));
    }
    initialize(A);
while (!done) {
    local_diff = 0.0;
    /* MPI_CHAR means raw byte format */
    if (pid) {  /* send my first row up */
        SEND(&A, N*sizeof(float), MPI_CHAR, pid-1, ROW);
    }
    if (pid != P-1) {  /* recv last row */
        RECV(&A[N/P+1], N*sizeof(float), MPI_CHAR, pid+1, ROW);
    }
    if (pid != P-1) {  /* send last row down */
        SEND(&A[N/P], N*sizeof(float), MPI_CHAR, pid+1, ROW);
```

```
    }

    if (pid) {   /* recv first row from above */

        RECV(&A, N*sizeof(float), MPI_CHAR, pid-1, ROW);

    }

    for (i=1; i <= N/P; i++) for (j=1; j <= N; j++) {

            temp = A[i][j];

            A[i][j] = 0.2 * (A[i][j] + A[i][j-1] +             A[i-1][j] + A[i]
[j+1] + A[i+1][j]);

            local_diff += fabs(A[i][j] - temp);

        }
if (pid) {   /* tell P0 my diff */

        SEND(&local_diff, sizeof(float),    MPI_CHAR, 0, DIFF);

        RECV(&done, sizeof(int), MPI_CHAR, 0, DONE);

    }

    else {   /* recv from all and add up */

        for (i=1; i < P; i++) {

            RECV(&tempdiff, sizeof(float), MPI_CHAR, MPI_ANY_SOURCE, DIFF);

            local_diff += tempdiff;

        }

        if (local_diff/(N*N) < TOL) done=1;

        for (i=1; i < P; i++) {

            /* tell all if done */

            SEND(&done, sizeof(int), MPI_CHAR, i, DONE);

        }

    }

}   /* end while */

MAIN_END;

}   /* end main */
```

- Note the matching tags in SEND and RECV

- Macros used in this program

- o GET_PID

- o GET_NUMPROCS

- o SEND

- o RECV

- These will get expanded into specific MPI library calls

- Syntax of SEND/RECV

  - o Starting address, how many elements, type of each element (we have used byte only), source/dest, message tag

Bit-level Parallelism

Bit-level parallelism is a form of parallel computing based on increasing processor word size. Increasing the word size reduces the number of instructions the processor must execute in order to perform an operation on variables whose sizes are greater than the length of the word. (For example, consider a case where an 8-bit processor must add two 16-bit integers. The processor must first add the 8 lower-order bits from each integer, then add the 8 higher-order bits, requiring two instructions to complete a single operation. A 16-bit processor would be able to complete the operation with single instruction.)

Originally, all electronic computers were serial (single-bit) computers. The first electronic computer that was not a serial computer—the first bit-parallel computer—was the 16-bit Whirlwind from 1951.

From the advent of very-large-scale integration (VLSI) computer chip fabrication technology in the 1970s until about 1986, advancements in computer architecture were done by increasing bit-level parallelism, as 4-bit microprocessors were replaced by 8-bit, then 16-bit, then 32-bit microprocessors. This trend generally came to an end with the introduction of 32-bit processors, which have been a standard in general purpose computing for two decades. Only recently, with the advent of x86-64 architectures, have 64-bit processors become commonplace.

On 32-bit processors, external data bus width continues to increase. For example, DDR1 SDRAM transfers 128 bits per clock cycle. DDR2 SDRAM transfers a minimum of 256 bits per burst.

Instruction-level Parallelism

Instruction-level parallelism (ILP) is a measure of how many of the instructions in a computer program can be executed simultaneously.

There are two approaches to instruction level parallelism:

- Hardware

- Software

Atanasoff–Berry computer, the first computer with parallel processing.

Hardware level works upon dynamic parallelism whereas, the software level works on static parallelism. Dynamic parallelism means the processor decides at run time which instructions to execute in parallel, whereas static parallelism means the compiler decides which instructions to execute in parallel. The Pentium processor works on the dynamic sequence of parallel execution but the Itanium processor works on the static level parallelism.

Consider the following program:

1. e = a + b

2. f = c + d

3. m = e * f

Operation 3 depends on the results of operations 1 and 2, so it cannot be calculated until both of them are completed. However, operations 1 and 2 do not depend on any other operation, so they can be calculated simultaneously. If we assume that each operation can be completed in one unit of time then these three instructions can be completed in a total of two units of time, giving an ILP of 3/2.

A goal of compiler and processor designers is to identify and take advantage of as much ILP as possible. Ordinary programs are typically written under a sequential execution model where instructions execute one after the other and in the order specified by the programmer. ILP allows the compiler and the processor to overlap the execution of multiple instructions or even to change the order in which instructions are executed.

How much ILP exists in programs is very application specific. In certain fields, such as graphics and scientific computing the amount can be very large. However, workloads such as cryptography may exhibit much less parallelism.

Micro-architectural techniques that are used to exploit ILP include:

- Instruction pipelining where the execution of multiple instructions can be partially over-lapped.

- Superscalar execution, VLIW, and the closely related explicitly parallel instruction computing concepts, in which multiple execution units are used to execute multiple instructions in parallel.

- Out-of-order execution where instructions execute in any order that does not violate data dependencies. Note that this technique is independent of both pipelining and superscalar. Current implementations of out-of-order execution dynamically (i.e., while the program is executing and without any help from the compiler) extract ILP from ordinary programs. An alternative is to extract this parallelism at compile time and somehow convey this information to the hardware. Due to the complexity of scaling the out-of-order execution technique, the industry has re-examined instruction sets which explicitly encode multiple independent operations per instruction.

- Register renaming which refers to a technique used to avoid unnecessary serialization of program operations imposed by the reuse of registers by those operations, used to enable out-of-order execution.

- Speculative execution which allow the execution of complete instructions or parts of instructions before being certain whether this execution should take place. A commonly used form of speculative execution is control flow speculation where instructions past a control flow instruction (e.g., a branch) are executed before the target of the control flow instruction is determined. Several other forms of speculative execution have been proposed and are in use including speculative execution driven by value prediction, memory dependence prediction and cache latency prediction.

- Branch prediction which is used to avoid stalling for control dependencies to be resolved. Branch prediction is used with speculative execution.

It is known that the ILP is exploited by both the compiler and hardware support but the compiler also provides inherit and implicit ILP in programs to hardware by compilation optimization. Some optimization techniques for extracting available ILP in programs would include scheduling, register allocation/renaming, and memory access optimization.

Dataflow architectures are another class of architectures where ILP is explicitly specified.

Some limits to ILP are compiler sophistication and hardware sophistication. To overcome these limits, new and different hardware techniques may be able to overcome limitations. However, unlikely such advances when coupled with realistic hardware will overcome these limits in the near future.

In recent years, ILP techniques have been used to provide performance improvements in spite of the growing disparity between processor operating frequencies and memory access times (early ILP designs such as the IBM System/360 Model 91 used ILP techniques to overcome the limitations imposed by a relatively small register file). Presently, a cache miss penalty to main memory costs several hundreds of CPU cycles. While in principle it is possible to use ILP to tolerate even such memory latencies the associated resource and power dissipation costs are disproportionate. Moreover, the complexity and often the latency of the underlying hardware structures results in reduced operating frequency further reducing any benefits. Hence, the aforementioned techniques prove inadequate to keep the CPU from stalling for the off-chip data. Instead, the industry is heading towards exploiting higher levels of parallelism that can be exploited through techniques such as multiprocessing and multithreading.

Task Parallelism

Task parallelism (also known as function parallelism and control parallelism) is a form of parallelization of computer code across multiple processors in parallel computing environments. Task parallelism focuses on distributing tasks—concurrently performed by processes or threads—across different processors. In contrast to data parallelism which involves running the same task on different components of data, task parallelism is distinguished by running many different tasks at the same time on the same data. A common type of task parallelism is pipelining which consists of moving a single set of data through a series of separate tasks where each task can execute independently of the others.

Description

In a multiprocessor system, task parallelism is achieved when each processor executes a different thread (or process) on the same or different data. The threads may execute the same or different code. In the general case, different execution threads communicate with one another as they work, but is not a requirement. Communication usually takes place by passing data from one thread to the next as part of a workflow.

As a simple example, if a system is running code on a 2-processor system (CPUs "a" & "b") in a parallel environment and we wish to do tasks "A" and "B", it is possible to tell CPU "a" to do task "A" and CPU "b" to do task "B" simultaneously, thereby reducing the run time of the execution. The tasks can be assigned using conditional statements as described below.

Task parallelism emphasizes the distributed (parallelized) nature of the processing (i.e. threads), as opposed to the data (data parallelism). Most real programs fall somewhere on a continuum between task parallelism and data parallelism.

Thread-level parallelism (TLP) is the parallelism inherent in an application that runs multiple threads at once. This type of parallelism is found largely in applications written for commercial servers such as databases. By running many threads at once, these applications are able to tolerate the high amounts of I/O and memory system latency their workloads can incur - while one thread is delayed waiting for a memory or disk access, other threads can do useful work.

The exploitation of thread-level parallelism has also begun to make inroads into the desktop market with the advent of multi-core microprocessors. This has occurred because, for various reasons, it has become increasingly impractical to increase either the clock speed or instructions per clock of a single core. If this trend continues, new applications will have to be designed to utilize multiple threads in order to benefit from the increase in potential computing power. This contrasts with previous microprocessor innovations in which existing code was automatically sped up by running it on a newer/faster computer.

Example

The pseudocode below illustrates task parallelism:

```
program:

...

if CPU-"a" then

    do task "A"

else if CPU="b" then

    do task "B"

end if

...

end program
```

The goal of the program is to do some net total task ("A+B"). If we write the code as above and launch it on a 2-processor system, then the runtime environment will execute it as follows.

- In an SPMD system, both CPUs will execute the code.

- In a parallel environment, both will have access to the same data.

- The "if" clause differentiates between the CPUs. CPU "a" will read true on the "if" and CPU "b" will read true on the "else if", thus having their own task.

- Now, both CPU's execute separate code blocks simultaneously, performing different tasks simultaneously.

Code executed by CPU "a":

```
program:

...

do task "A"

...

end program
```

Code executed by CPU "b":

```
program:
```

```
...

do task "B"

...

end program
```

This concept can now be generalized to any number of processors.

Language Support

Task parallelism can be supported in general-purposes languages either built-in facilities or libraries. Notable examples include:

- C++ (Intel): Threading Building Blocks

- C++ (Open Source/Apache 2.0): RaftLib

- C, C++, Objective-C (Apple): Grand Central Dispatch

- D: tasks and fibers

- Go: goroutines

- Java: Java concurrency

- .NET: Task Parallel Library

Examples of fine-grained task-parallel languages can be found in the realm of Hardware Description Languages like Verilog and VHDL.

References

- Hutto, Phillip W.; Mustaque Ahamad (1990). "Slow memory: Weakening consistency to enhance concurrency in distributed shared memories.". IEEE: 302–309. doi:10.1109/ICDCS.1990.89297

- Steinke, Robert C.; Gary J. Nutt (2004). "A unified theory of shared memory consistency.". Journal of the ACM (JACM). 51 (5): 800–849. doi:10.1145/1017460.1017464

- Hicks, Michael. "Concurrency Basics" (PDF). University of Maryland: Department of Com-puter Science. Retrieved 08, May 2020

- David E. Culler, Jaswinder Pal Singh, Anoop Gupta. Parallel Computer Architecture - A Hardware Software Approach. Morgan Kaufmann Publishers, 1999. ISBN 1-55860-343-3, pg 15

- Paolo Viotti; Marko Vukolic (2016). "Consistency in Non-Transactional Distributed Stor-age Systems". ACM Computer Surveys. 49 (1): 19:1––19:34. doi:10.1145/2926965

- Lamport, Leslie (Sep 1979). "How to make a multiprocessor computer that correctly executes multiprocess programs.". Computers, IEEE Transactions. C–28 (9): 690–691. doi:10.1109/TC.1979.1675439

- Sarita V. Adve; Kourosh Gharachorloo (December 1996). "Shared Memory Consistency Models: A Tutorial" (PDF). IEEE Computer. 29 (12): 66–76. doi:10.1109/2.546611. Re-trieved 28, May 2020

- Quinn, Michael J. (2007). Parallel programming in C with MPI and openMP (Tata McGraw-Hill ed. ed.). New Delhi: Tata McGraw-Hill Pub. ISBN 0070582017

Permissions

Index